Having the
Mind of
Christ

Having the
Mind of
Christ

Paul E. Miller &
Phyllis Cole-Dai

Abingdon Press
Nashville

HAVING THE MIND OF CHRIST

Copyright © 1996 by Abingdon Press

This book is printed on acid-free paper.

ISBN 0-687-109418
Cataloging-in-Publication Data available from the Library of Congress.

All Scripture quotations are from the New Revised Standard Version Bible, copyright © 1989, by the Division of Christian Education of the National Council of the Churches of Christ in the United States of America.

MANUFACTURED IN THE UNITED STATES OF AMERICA

To Pat,
my companion on the journey
of spiritual growth

—PM

To Jihong,
for being a messenger of God
in my life

—PCD

Acknowledgments

$\mathcal{T}$he creation of this book has been a brief but meaningful part of our spiritual journey. Along the way we have been deeply grateful for the support and advice received from our fellow travelers. From among these people we would like especially to acknowledge the following:

Karen, Jimmy, and the rest of the community at the Barnes & Noble Bookstore, who regularly served us coffee, smiles, bad jokes, and words of encouragement as we worked at the "Miller table";

Nancy Watson, Nancy Munn, and Mary Munn, who so capably and joyfully filled Phyllis's shoes when she took vacation from work in order to write;

Ruth Wood, Betty English, Steve Grimm, Wendy Field, Joyce Craig, and Roderick Stewart, who graciously read portions of the manuscript and offered suggestions toward its improvement;

Anne Stevens, whose expert fingers typed hundreds of scripture texts and main ideas on index cards;

And, most of all, our spouses, Pat Miller and Jihong Cole-Dai. Without their willingness to brainstorm, feed us stir-fry, make coffee, give us honest feedback, and provide comic relief and moral support, we would still be on the way to where we are now. We love you both.

To these people, and to so many others who must remain nameless, we express our heartfelt thanks. You have truly blessed our path.

Introduction

Let the same mind be in you that was in Christ Jesus.

—Philippians 2:5

Do not be conformed to this world, but be transformed by the renewing of your minds.

—Romans 12:2

*O*n your journey of faith, are you standing still? Do you feel the desire to become a more faithful disciple but lack a way by which to move ahead? Or are you standing at a crossroads, waiting for a guide to point you in the right direction? Spread before you are various paths. Which of them would Christ have you follow?

To answer this, you must become aware of the mind of Christ that is already within you. Having the mind of Christ is being aware that the Holy Spirit is at work within you, as it was within Jesus. It is relying on the Spirit to guide you, teach you, comfort you, and rejoice with you. It is allowing the Spirit to create through you; it is participating in the healing of the world.

In this book we lead you on a year's journey during which you will come to know and trust the mind of Christ within you. You will become more attuned to its promptings, and you will be renewed, and *changed*, under its guidance. As Paul writes in his letter to the Romans, those who know Christ are to "be transformed." So, as the mind of Christ grows within you, your perspectives on the world will shift. Your priorities will be reordered. Your commitment to the things of the Spirit will deepen.

Your abilities to offer forgiveness, to provide healing, and to make peace will be enhanced. Wherever you are on the path right now, as you walk through the pages of this book you will gain deeper insight into the relevance of spiritual truth to your everyday life.

How to Use This Book

We hope that as you read this book, you will be not only inspired but also transformed. In other words, you will undergo a gradual and continual process of spiritual growth. You will deliberately set out on a journey of faith, trusting it to unfold as it will, and, as much as possible, you will allow yourself to learn from it, to be renewed and changed by it.

We have deliberately arranged the daily readings to take you on a journey through thirteen themes:

The Journey of Transformation

The Need for Awareness

The Unity of Creation

The Intrusion of Fear

The Nature of Conflict

The Gift of Forgiveness

The Power of Compassion

The Growth of Community

The Indwelling of the Spirit

The Work of Healing

The Experience of the Divine

The Presence of Peace

The Welcoming of Miracles

You will spend seven days on one theme before moving on to the next, and you will revisit each theme four times during the year. At the end of the book, we will encourage you to return to the beginning and start again. We have not designed *Having the Mind of Christ* to be used and shelved. We have designed it to be used and used again. Each journey you take through the book will be different from the last.

Each day begins with the statement of a main idea to focus your mind. Then comes a passage of scripture that relates to the main idea. After the scripture there is a brief meditation, which includes a unique feature of the book: an exercise meant to help you apply the main idea during the day. Finally, the main idea is restated, both to bless you and to challenge you to action.

As you move through the book, revisiting its thirteen themes, more will gradually be asked of you; your understanding and experience of the Christian faith will be stretched. We strongly recommend that you do no more than one reading per day. Sometimes you might do one over several days. Set your own pace. There is no need for you to hurry. There is only a need for you to "be mindful." You will see this phrase often, especially early in the book when you may need more frequent reminders to think with the mind of Christ, to allow the Holy Spirit to lead you. You will sometimes receive the same reminder in other phrases, such as "be aware," "be open to the Spirit," "be intentional," or "center yourself."

Just as you may set your own pace, you may also adapt the daily exercises to suit your special interests or life circumstances. Sometimes you will be tempted not to do an exercise for various reasons. Challenge yourself to try it anyway, or create an alternative. The important thing is that you *practice the main idea in the midst of everyday life*. In this way, you will be nurturing the mind of Christ within you.

We have included many kinds of exercises. Among them are object lessons, experiences in nature, personal inventories, social tasks, and different forms of prayer. One form of prayer we frequently suggest is "meditative prayer." This is directed prayer, in which we invite you to close your eyes, relax, and visualize a particular scene in your mind. Here you are asked to await a communication from the Spirit or to experience the presence of God in some way. In meditative prayer, you do very little talking to God. Instead, you listen and watch for messages *from* God. As you practice meditative prayer, you will have to determine the best way to pray while also being guided by the text. For example, you might want to read through all of the text first, getting the imagery firmly in mind, and then lay the book aside and enter into prayer. Or you might have a partner slowly read the text to you while you are in prayer. Or you might record the text on a cassette and play it back when you are ready to begin. However you proceed, feel free to adapt the text of the meditative prayer any way that you wish.

Certain exercises will ask you to make lists, write responses to questions, draw time-lines, and so on. For this reason, we encourage you to use a notebook or journal as a companion to *Having the Mind of Christ*. In addition to providing a place for you to complete the exercises, this notebook can become a chronicle of your spiritual journey as you record any insights, prayers, special memories, plans, and hopes that the Spirit might inspire.

The choice to take up the journey of faith is an individual one. *You* decide. But once you begin, you can share your journey with fellow travelers united by the mind of Christ. You might want to invite some of those fellow travelers to work through this book with you. For example, you might use *Having the Mind of Christ* in a sharing group or Sunday school class. We have structured the book to help you do this. Since a new theme is explored every seven days, you can easily use the book in a group that gathers on a weekly basis for discussion and support. And, since all the themes are visited every thirteen weeks, you can conveniently use the book in a group that meets throughout a quarter. (You would complete the book in four quarters.) Whether you choose to make use of this book as an individual or as a group, your commitment will lead you to a profound awareness of the Spirit's guidance in your life, each and every day.

Now you are ready to begin your journey through these pages. Wherever your path takes you, be patient and gentle with yourself. Allow the way to unfold before you. Let the mind of Christ guide you when the way is unclear. Let the mind of Christ strengthen you when the way is difficult. And let the mind of Christ forgive you when you go astray. On such a journey, there are no mistakes. There are only lessons to be learned.

We wish you well on your journey of transformation.

Day 1   **I am on a journey.**

Let the same mind be in you that was in Christ Jesus.

—Philippians 2:5

*T*he life of faith is a spiritual journey. Each day you walk a little further along the path, and though you may be unsure of what lies ahead, you trust God to guide you through it. With each step you take, God offers you the opportunity to grow wiser, more compassionate, more trusting. You become increasingly aware of God's presence all around you. You become increasingly sensitive to the Spirit's voice within you, celebrating life with you.

Then one day you notice that the tangled forests on your path seem somehow less dark than they used to be. The rugged mountains seem less steep. The wastelands seem less barren. The raging rivers seem less deep. But make no mistake. The world around you hasn't changed at all. *You* have. The mind of Christ has grown stronger within you.

So, where are you on your journey? Are you moving along at a fast pace? Too fast, perhaps? Are you at a resting place, waiting for further direction? Or are you simply stuck, haunted by the past and uncertain of the future? How does it feel to be where you are *right now?*

Today, take up your journey with a renewed commitment. Choose to see life with the mind of Christ. Let go of your past. Be open to the future. Be prepared to move forward as the Spirit leads. Be ready each moment to love.

On an index card or small piece of paper, draw a picture that somehow represents your spiritual journey. Or if you prefer, attach a photo clipped from a magazine. Your picture might be a map, a suitcase, a road stretching into the distance, or a pair of shoes. Carry this visual reminder with you during the day. Glance at it often and affirm today's central idea:

I am on a journey.

Day 2   **I am guided on my journey.**

Let me hear of your steadfast love in the morning, for in you I put my trust. Teach me the way I should go, for to you I lift up my soul.

—Psalm 143:8

*T*hink of a time when you were confused, puzzled by the choices you had to make. Remember how guidance came to you. Perhaps it was through a biblical passage that especially spoke to you. Perhaps it was through a friend who really listened and helped you clarify your thoughts and feelings. Perhaps it was through a still small voice within you, an inner sense of knowing. Or perhaps it was through prayer that the answer came.

All of these different types of guidance have but one source. They all come from God. All of them are reminders that your spiritual journey is not day after day of aimless wandering. All of them are promises that if you remain open to God's presence, you will always find the direction you need.

Yesterday you carried a visual affirmation of the fact that you are on a spiritual journey. Now add a second picture to that card to symbolize the guiding presence of God on your path. For example, you might draw a cross, or attach a magazine photo of a mountain sunrise. Keep this reminder card with you throughout the day, and rejoice in your awareness that God's guidance is always available.

I am guided on my journey.

Day 3   **I am moving toward God.**

Then you will understand righteousness and justice and equity, every good path; for wisdom will come into your heart, and knowledge will be pleasant to your soul.

—Proverbs 2:9-10

*H*ave you ever gone to visit someone you wanted very much to see, only to find the person not at home? Such disappointment! The anticipation that you had felt, the time together that you had imagined—all of it came to nothing in that moment when you knocked on the door and no one answered. There was nothing you could do but turn and walk away.

Your intended destination supplies hope and joy for your journey. It also provides a sense of direction. The more certain you are of your destination, the more abundant your hope, the more radiant your joy, and the more confident your way. The good news is that, on your spiritual journey, your destination is very clear. You are going to God's house, and God is always at home.

Journey into your soul, and God will not disappoint you but will greet you with spiritual gifts. God will give to your mind an understanding of every good path; to your heart, an abundance of wisdom.

Today, extend God's hospitality to every person you encounter. Be mindful. Whenever possible, look each person in the eye, smile, and silently bless him or her, saying, "May you be at home with God." With every act of blessing, you yourself will be blessed with the knowledge:

I am moving toward God.

Day 4   I move one step at a time.

Do not be conformed to this world, but be transformed by the renewing of your minds, so that you may discern what is the will of God—what is good and acceptable and perfect.

—Romans 12:2

*A*re you a planner? Do you select a destination and then determine the quickest and surest route by which to reach it?

Or do you like to keep your options open? Do you set off on a trip without consulting the map and wander to whatever place your whims may lead you?

Whichever way you travel through life, *be mindful.* Even the best-laid plans will ultimately be thwarted if they conform to the world's demands rather than the promptings of the Spirit. And even an array of possible destinations will finally prove disappointing if the Spirit does not bless your way. So, with each step you take, open your mind to God. Walk the life path that is to be yours with full awareness and intention, and your feet will fall on firm ground.

At some point today, take a walk. Before you actually begin, stand with eyes closed and quiet your mind. Silence any distracting thoughts. Do not worry about all the other things you should be doing instead. Set your intention to walk in awareness of the Spirit. Finally, when you are ready, open your eyes. Step out with one foot, very slowly and deliberately, feeling the movement of your body. Pause a moment, then step out with the other foot. Sense the Spirit of God moving through you. Take another step, and then another, thinking of nothing else. Keep your stride deliberate. If you lose mindfulness, stop where you are, refocus your intention, and step out once again. Continue in this manner for at least ten minutes. Let your walking be a parable of your life, a reminder of how to move ahead on your journey with faithful mind, soul, and heart.

Throughout the day, remind yourself:

I move one step at a time.

Day 5   **Each step I take has purpose.**

The Lord is my shepherd, I shall not want. He makes me lie down in green pastures; he leads me beside still waters; he restores my soul. He leads me in right paths for his name's sake.

—Psalm 23:1-3

The words of this psalm often provide comfort and reassurance in the face of death. Receive them today as comfort and reassurance in the midst of life. Know that the place where you are is a holy place, because God has made it so. Know that this moment you are in is a holy moment, because God has made it so. And know that the footsteps that have brought you here are holy, because God has made them so. No step that you have ever taken has been wasted. No step you ever take will be empty. Each step you take belongs to God.

With holy steps you are brought by God into life's abundance, evidenced not by material wealth but by prosperity of the soul. You are ushered into *green* pastures, you are led beside *still* waters, you are shown *right* paths provided by the Spirit. With each step your sense of personal wholeness is restored and strengthened, that you might fulfill the purposes that God reveals for you.

With pencil and paper at hand, quiet your mind. Close your eyes, relax, and visualize the following scene. The Spirit of God has led you into the land of promises. You wander through the trees, across a meadow filled with colorful wildflowers. Not far away is a shimmering lake. You go and sit down beside it. You relax into the warmth of the sunshine, the sound of the lapping water. After a time, something on top of the hill across the lake catches your eye. You can't quite tell what it is, but you instantly know that God has sent it to you. It will bring you a message about something specific that God wants you to do. You await its full revelation with great expectancy. Before long, you are able to see it clearly. What is it?

When your vision fades, reflect on its meaning for a few minutes. Then, in one or two sentences, write down the message that God has given you. Be specific. What step is God asking you to take? For what purpose? If a clear message didn't come to you during this period of meditative prayer, be patient. Don't force anything. A message *will* come, in its own time. Perhaps it will come today, perhaps tomorrow. Be attentive. Whenever you receive the revelation, hold fast to it and prepare to do as God has prompted.

Each step I take has purpose.

Day 6   **I am always safe.**

For you have delivered my soul from death, and my feet from falling, so that I may walk before God in the light of life.

—Psalm 56:13

Safety. Security. Sanctuary. We want them. We seek them. But often we seek them where they are not to be found.

Your protection does not lie outside you but within, in the Spirit that can make you strong and keep you from falling. Open yourself to it. Let the power of God shine up and through you. Walk in the light, and you will inspire others also to accept the Source of refuge and strength, a very present help in trouble.

Take out a number of small slips of paper and a pencil. Light a candle in recognition of the light in which you walk. Calm your mind. Now ask your heart to name persons or things that worry, frighten, or intimidate you. Be specific. Write each one on a separate slip of paper. When you are done, do the following ritual for each fear: Hold it in the palm of your hand for a few moments, acknowledging the power it has exercised over you. Now lay it beside the candle and offer a prayer to God that its power might be broken. For example, you might say, "O God, my financial problems worry me. Take away my fear. Help me to know that in your presence, I am always safe." When you have laid aside all your fears, find a way of burning them. Realize that the power of all of them together is nothing when compared to the power of God, which is your protection.

Today, whenever you feel anxious, afraid, or defensive, remember that God is your strength and your deliverance. Remind yourself:

I am always safe.

Day 7   **I am not alone on the path.**

But if we walk in the light as he himself is in the light, we have fellowship with one another.

—*1 John 1:7*

*Y*ou are not alone on your journey of transformation. All
around you are fellow travelers who also walk in the light, seeking growth in spiritual understanding. You and they may be at
quite different places on your journeys. Indeed, your life paths
may appear to have little or nothing in common. But it is your
awareness of being on a journey, not the specifics of the journeys
themselves, that unites all of you; that makes you teachers of one
another; that makes all of you sisters and brothers.

What will your diverse companions teach you today? The
lessons will be too many to count. So you must focus. Ask your
soul which question your companions will answer for you today,
and await a reply. The reply may be very distinct; you may
instantly realize, for example, that you want to know how best to
help a friend who is sick. Or the reply may come less obviously,
as in the form of a feeling. Say that you suddenly feel lonely.
Your question, then, may be, "How do I overcome this sense of
isolation?", or "Whom might I connect with today?"

Whatever question your soul presents, set it firmly in your
mind, and be certain that God will answer it. Throughout the
day, closely observe the people around you. What are they teaching you? Their instruction may come through what they do. It
may come through what they do *not* do. Watch, listen, feel; inter-
nalize the messages you receive from them, however subtle.

If by some circumstance you are completely removed from
other people today, pay close attention to phone conversations.
And, if you feel moved to call someone, act on the impulse. God
will appoint messengers, and the answers to your questions will
come, often in unexpected ways. Be alert. Maintain your mindfulness by repeating, throughout the day:

I am not alone on the path.

Day 8   **I am growing in awareness.**

"Do not judge by appearances, but judge with right judgment."

—*John 7:24*

$\mathcal{J}$esus once stood in the temple with his followers and asked them to carefully observe the giving patterns of persons contributing to the treasury. As they did so, he shared his perceptions of the motives behind the giving. Those who were contributing the largest sums of money, he said, were giving conspicuously, in order to be honored. But the widow who put in the last coins she had, expecting nothing in return, was giving from pure devotion (see Mark 12:41-44).

That day the followers of Jesus learned, among other things, that they needed to grow in awareness. They needed to begin looking past surface appearances to deeper, more significant truths. We are called to do the same. How often we glance at objects or situations and immediately assume that we have taken in their meaning! Yet, as we are so fond of saying and even fonder of forgetting, "There is much more to life than meets the eye."

Seeing more than the obvious requires practice and patience. Select an object of beauty near you, such as a painting, a plant, the sky, a sculpture, or the photograph of someone you love. Describe what you see on first glancing at the object. Then look at it again, this time focusing your attention on its color(s), noticing even subtle variations in shading. And look yet again, observing different lines and shapes. Contrast the parts of the object to the whole. Think about how the various parts interrelate. Finally, glance at the object of beauty one last time, and understand that it is a gift to you from the Creator. What purpose is there in such a gift? What truth about God does it reveal?

As you go about your activities today, give careful attention to the objects in your environment. Look at them twice, first noting their surface appearance, and then really *seeing* them, perhaps as you never have before.

I am growing in awareness.

$\mathcal{D}ay$ *9*   **I search for God.**

When you search for me, you will find me.

—Jeremiah 29:13a

$\mathcal{W}$hen you lose an object of value, you search diligently until you find it. You may spend hours looking, even days, and may even ask friends to help you hunt. No amount of time or effort is too much to give to the cause if you really value what you have lost. Finally, if you are lucky, the search ends in success. What you had lost is found. There is a moment of celebration, and then, life goes on.

A relationship with God is worth more than anything else in life. So we seek God, longing deeply to know the One who created us. But our search for God is different from our search for a lost valuable in at least one significant respect. When we find God, our search does not end. It only begins. We set off on a life-long journey, during which our relationship with God is strengthened and our understanding of God is increased.

Take a few moments to reflect upon the magnificence of God's creation. List the features of the natural world that you most enjoy, that bring you into a sense of the divine and remind you of the Creator. Next, jot down three to five descriptive words for each part of creation that you have listed ("powerful," "bright," "peaceful," and so on). Now review your descriptive words and circle those that can also serve to describe God. Do you see how you can come to know God better by becoming more observant of creation? Conclude your reflections by writing a brief description of God.

As you move through the day, pause occasionally to remember that your life is a search for God. May you be exhilarated in your search.

I search for God.

Day 10   # I am becoming aware of God.

The fear of the LORD is the beginning of wisdom, and the knowledge of the Holy One is insight.

—Proverbs 9:10

$\mathcal{L}$et's say that you have always wanted to play the piano. So you buy recordings of Chopin's *Complete Works* and memorize every lovely phrase of his music. You read book after book on keyboard technique. You attend the concerts of famous pianists and the recitals of your daughter, whose halting but brave performance of "Mary Had a Little Lamb" fills you with admiration. You do all of these things, but until you actually sit down on a bench and begin to tickle the ivories, you cannot really say that you know the piano.

Knowing about the piano is very different from *knowing* the piano. In the same way, *knowing about* God is not the same as *knowing* God. Today's scripture text declares that "knowledge of the Holy One is insight." What kind of knowledge is this? It is more than just intellectual knowledge; the author of James tells us that even demons can have that (2:19). No, this knowledge of God is experiential; it is found in the heart as well as in the mind. Our goal is not only to *know about* God, but also to *know* God, up close and personally.

Take time today for this meditative prayer: Sit comfortably in a chair that is away from distractions. Breathe deeply. Allow each muscle of your body to relax. Release any tension that you may feel. Now, picture yourself on a sunny beach. Bask in the sunshine. Let it warm every fiber of your body. As you do so, begin to think of the sun as a symbol for God, and to think of your body as being warmed by God's presence. Experience the joy of knowing God as a gentle presence that comes to you and fills you with love. Know God as someone who is as close to you as the sun's rays every moment of your life. Whenever the worries and struggles of life leave you feeling cold and lonely, return in your mind to this scene on the beach. Let the loving presence of God flow into you once again and warm every part of your being.

I am becoming aware of God.

Day 11 God gives me wisdom when I ask for it.

If any of you is lacking in wisdom, ask God, who gives to all generously and ungrudgingly, and it will be given you.

—*James 1:5*

$\mathcal{D}$o you remember when you were a child and you thought that adults had all the answers? You couldn't wait to grow up so that you, too, could "know it all." But when you yourself finally became an adult, you discovered that life presents a great many questions for which there are no clear-cut answers. And now you may be wondering if you will ever know enough to be called "wise."

God has promised that when we seek wisdom, we will receive it. God wants us to grow in understanding, to know truth, so that we can make the wisest and best decisions possible. All we have to do is remember to ask daily for the wisdom we need.

Today, ask a friend or family member how he or she once gained insight into a difficult situation. For instance, perhaps she had once felt torn between wanting to keep her career on a financial fast-track and needing to have greater job satisfaction. Or, maybe he had been forced to decide whether or not his elderly father should move into a nursing home. Whatever the case, how did the person finally determine the best course of action? Did the person consult with others? Pray? Receive an answer in a dream? And, did the person realize at the time that God was giving the necessary wisdom, or did that realization come only in hindsight?

Let your friend's experience inspire you to become more intentional in seeking wisdom and to recognize it more quickly when it comes. Remember:

God gives me wisdom when I ask for it.

Day 12   **Wisdom opens me to new ways of seeing.**

He said to [his disciples], "But who do you say that I am?"

—Matthew 16:15

*J*esus had been traveling about the countryside, astonishing crowds with his teaching, healing lepers and paralytics, helping Roman soldiers, calming storms, walking on water, casting out demons, raising the dead. . . . People could not agree on what kind of man he was. Some thought he was a prophet; others, a miracle worker or healer. Still others called him "Rabbi," teacher. But now Jesus wanted to know how he was perceived by those who knew him best. Jesus was testing his followers, yes, but at the same time he may have been checking on the effectiveness of his own ministry. His gospel was a message from God, and for any message to be effectively communicated, there must be a congruency—a consistency—between the content of the message and the way in which it is delivered. Without congruency, the result is a mixed message, and mixed messages can cause problems. Was Jesus' message clear enough? And were his disciples wise enough to see who he really was?

Let's leave the disciples for a moment and consider the case of a little boy who came running into the house after school one afternoon. He was very excited about his day and tried to tell his mother all about it as she shuffled back and forth between folding laundry, scrubbing the bathtub, and preparing dinner. Finally he said in exasperation, "Oh, all right. If you don't want to listen, I won't talk." Even though his mother had been participating in the conversation with her "uh-huh's" and "mmmmm's" and "that's wonderful's," the youngster had picked up all the visual signals which said that she was really too busy to listen, that her household tasks had her full attention. His declaration so startled her that she immediately stopped what she was doing, sat down with him, and listened intently.

As your spiritual awareness grows, you will become better at perceiving the messages that come to you. If a message is mixed, you will recognize a feeling of uneasiness, which may intensify as the conversation continues. In such moments, pause to ask yourself how well what you are seeing matches what you are hearing. Interestingly, when the two do not match, we put more faith in what we see. If the two *do* match, however, we really believe the message. So it is that the disciples believed that Jesus was the Christ. What they saw him do perfectly corresponded to what they heard him say.

Throughout the day, observe the messages you receive. Look for congruency, and be alert to signs of incongruency.

Wisdom opens me to new ways of seeing.

Day 13   **Wisdom opens me to new ways of hearing.**

"But blessed are your eyes, for they see, and your ears, for they hear."

—*Matthew 13:16*

*J*esus often taught using parables. These were stories that had at least two levels of understanding. On the surface, they were stories about everyday life. Beneath the surface, however, they carried deep truths that not everyone was ready to hear. So Jesus had to be a patient storyteller, realizing that many people in the crowds who gathered to hear him teach would understand the meaning of his parables only later. Perhaps much later. The difference in what people heard was a matter of wisdom. The more wisdom they grew to have, the more truth they came to understand.

The same is often true of the stories we tell, especially those stories that we tell over and over again. For example, there was a woman named Fern who retired after working for twenty years in the same shoe store in her hometown. After her retirement, Fern began to tell everyone about how she had trained herself to remember every customer's shoe size. "I never had to measure the same foot twice," she would always say with pride. It wasn't long before people grew tired of hearing the story repeated. But gradually they began to understand the "story beneath the story." They came to realize that Fern was missing the days when she rendered special care to her customers and received personal attention in return. She longed for someone to give her such personalized care again. When her listeners began to address that issue, their communication with her began to take place at a much deeper level.

Hear in a new way today. Know that, like the parables of Jesus, the stories that others tell you will often have more than one level of meaning. Listen for themes or feelings hidden beneath the words. May God give you the wisdom to hear the truth.

Wisdom opens me to new ways of hearing.

Day 14   # Wisdom helps me sense the kingdom of God.

"The time is fulfilled, and the kingdom of God has come near."

—*Mark 1:15a*

𝓘s the kingdom of God here and now? Or will it come later? The answer is, "Both!"

The kingdom of God exists whenever and wherever the will of God is being done. The more completely that God's will is accomplished, the more fully God's kingdom is present. The kingdom is unfolding in our midst, becoming more real every day. Wisdom helps us to sense it. Wisdom helps us to bring it into being.

Jesus taught his disciples to pray, "Your kingdom come. Your will be done on earth, as it is in heaven" (Matthew 6:10). Wouldn't the joy be indescribable if all the people of the world could some-how join together, decide to do only what God wants them to do, and thereby establish the kingdom of God on this earth? Unfor-tunately, such a vision is not likely to come to pass anytime soon. However, we can make God's kingdom an ever more present real-ity if each of us, in whatever humble way we can, simply takes responsibility for doing whatever God is asking us to do. Then, day by day, God will join all of our righteous acts together, and we will feel the reality of the kingdom more fully established in our midst.

As you go about your routine today, take note of people who are doing what is good and right in the sight of God. Their deeds may be large or small; the size does not matter. Celebrate them with a grateful heart. At the same time, pay no attention to those people who are are not doing what is good and right. They receive far too much notice as it is. For this day, give your mind over to seeing only what is consistent with the will of God. In doing so, you will begin to sense the nearness of God's kingdom.

Wisdom helps me sense the kingdom of God.

Day 15 God is in charge.

Lord, you have been our dwelling place in all generations. Before the mountains were brought forth, or ever you had formed the earth and the world, from everlasting to everlasting you are God.

—Psalm 90:1-2

We do not know where God's world begins. We do not know where God's world ends. But from beginning to end, it *is* God's world, and God is in control, acting in ways that we can only begin to comprehend.

Having set the world in motion, God has set you down in one itty-bitty little corner of it all. It is a thrilling, humbling, enchant-ing, puzzling, frightening, fascinating, amusing, distressing, eye-opening, heart-warming place to be. At times, you may feel over-whelmed and think, "If I could just get control of my life, everything would be all right." So you work hard. Yet, no matter how hard you try, before long you are discouraged, having failed to meet the high expectations you had set up for yourself and others; or, you are disappointed, having succeeded only to conclude that your expectations had not been high enough, that they could never be high enough to keep you above the turmoil of life.

The fact is, once you convince yourself that you are in charge, you are lost. Being in charge is not your place. From everlasting to everlasting, *God* is God.

On a sheet of paper list specific aspects of your life that you are seeking to control without God's guidance or support. List as many as you can. Consider carefully your relationships, your work, your finances, your emotions, your personal habits, your leisure activities. Now, for each item on your list, think of a word that best describes *how* you are trying to control it. For example, you might be trying to control your grief over a loved one's death by *ignoring* or *denying* it. Here is a sample list of "how-I-control" words:

contain	master	subdue	limit
conquer	restrict	rule over	dominate
suppress	obtain	use	manipulate
punish	direct	ignore	fix

Today, refuse to exercise control in the ways you have listed. If you are tempted to do so, regain perspective by reminding yourself that you are not in charge. Act only if you sense that God is leading you to act.

Throughout the day, reaffirm:

God is in charge.

Day 16   **Everything is God's.**

For the LORD is a great God, and a great King above all gods. In his hand are the depths of the earth; the heights of the mountains are his also.

—*Psalm 95:3-4*

*G*od creates. God sustains. God provides.

These are simple words. You have heard them often. But how often have you felt their power? Just imagine. In the palm of God's hands rest the smallest details of infinity, the pettiest particulars of eternity. There is nothing that is not God's. And there is nothing that is yours instead of God's. How often have you let this mind-blowing truth explode through the clichés?

Look around you. Let your eyes fall on one thing, one person at a time. A book, a cat, a scar on your leg, a clock, a picture of a friend who just died, a chair, a pencil, a child. Say to each, "You are God's." Get up and move to a window. What do you see? A tree, a homeless woman, flowers past their prime, a robin, a mail carrier, a sidewalk, a storm cloud—to each of them, "You are God's." Close your eyes. Listen. What do you hear? Violin music, sirens, a car in need of a muffler, a baby's cry, rain falling, voices arguing, birds singing—"You are God's." What do you smell? The soil of springtime, the scent of a candle, coffee brewing, cologne, the smoke of a fire—"You are God's."

Be mindful today of the world in which you walk. Remember, whenever and wherever possible:

Everything is God's.

Day 17   **Everything lives in God.**

Thus says God, the LORD, who created the heavens and stretched them out, who spread out the earth and what comes from it, who gives breath to the people upon it and spirit to those who walk in it.

—Isaiah 42:5

Whatever lies above you, whatever comes from below, whatever moves upon the face of the earth—all of it, each in its own way, has life in God. All of creation is breathing, sighing, eating, stretching, singing, dancing, trickling, dripping, flooding, raging, sprouting, growing, bursting, resting, enduring, tumbling, rolling, hovering, darting. God, being God, creates endless forms of life.

Today, behold the beauty of these forms. Begin simply. From your possessions, select three very different items to study (for instance, an orange, an aquarium, and a woven basket). Examine each of them as if it is totally new to you. Use as many of your senses as you can. Take your time. When you have studied all three forms separately, consider them as a group. Celebrate their differences. Yet, recognize that they have at least one thing in common: they owe their existence to God.

Be perceptive today. Each thing that you taste, each thing that you smell, each thing that you see and hear and touch begins and ends in God. Regard each item with respect, as you would a teacher. Regard it with compassion, as you would a companion. Regard it with care, as you would a child. Do not forget:

Everything lives in God.

Day 18   **God lives in everything.**

The God who made the world and everything in it, he who is Lord of
heaven and earth, does not live in shrines made by human hands, nor is
he served by human hands, as though he needed anything, since he himself gives to all mortals life and breath and all things.

—Acts 17:24-25

*C*reation is the temple in which God dwells. It is a living temple, a holy place without walls. There are no walls that can contain God; there are no walls that can keep God out. There is no
place where God is not; there is no thing from which God is
absent. As a seed is in the flower that sprouts from it; as a child
is in the adult that she becomes; as a spring is in the river that
flows forth from it; as food is in the body that it fuels—so too
does God the Creator reside within creation.

Sometimes you may have difficulty believing that God lives
even in hatred, in chaos, in pain, and in death. But there, especially, does God live, as a redeeming presence. God does not erad-
icate hatred, but overcomes it with love; does not eliminate chaos,
but moves it toward order; does not abolish pain, but converts it
into wholeness; does not end death, but resurrects it into life.

Identify one aspect of your life that seems hateful, chaotic,
painful, or dead. Close your eyes and focus on this for a few minutes. What colors do your feelings evoke? What shapes? Do you
see any images? Any faces? Any objects? Any places?

Now, envision God being present in the midst of your problems. For example, you might think of God as a pinpoint of light
that begins to shine more and more brightly through the darkness, or as a lush green oasis that awaits you in the desert. In
what ways does God's presence affect the situation? How does it
affect *you?*

Celebrate God as a dynamic, creating, transforming presence.
God is the Source and will not be separated from the world.
Remind yourself as often as possible:

God lives in everything.

Day 19   **I praise God.**

O LORD, our Sovereign, how majestic is your name in all the earth!

—Psalm 8:1a

$\mathcal{S}$uppose that a child you adore brings you a picture that he has enthusiastically scribbled on paper with crayons. "I made this just for you!" he says, with a bright blush on his cheeks. How would you respond? No doubt you would praise him to high heaven, even if you couldn't quite make out what the picture was meant to be. You would thank him so approvingly that he would run off at once to make you another one. And, of course, you would hang each picture he made on your already crowded refrigerator door.

If this would be your response to the creativity of a child, then what be your response to God's? Praise is the loving response of a grateful heart. It can take an infinite variety of forms. List specific ways that you praise God on a piece of paper. Think of the things you say and do. How do you share your gratitude and joy with your creator?

Now create a second list. Identify new ways in which you might praise God. Consider planting some flowers, writing a poem, sharing your joy with someone who needs cheering up, walking gratefully through a park. . . . The possibilities are endless. Make a commitment to explore praise. Offer your thanks to God in fresh, even experimental forms.

Hang your list where you will be sure to see it often. Then choose one new way to praise God today.

I praise God.

Day 20   **All creation praises God.**

And Ezra said: "You are the LORD, you alone; you have made heaven, the heaven of heavens, with all their host, the earth and all that is on it, the seas and all that is in them. To all of them you give life, and the host of heaven worships you."

—Nehemiah 9:6

$\mathcal{T}$oday the words of a mighty hymn will guide your soul in adoration and unite you in praise with all things that God has made, great and small, visible and invisible. Meditate upon each of these joyous phrases taken from Henry Van Dyke's "Joyful, Joyful, We Adore Thee." As you do, lift up specific remembrances of how the Creator has touched your life.

Joyful, joyful, we adore thee, God of glory, Lord of love;
Hearts unfold like flowers before thee, opening to the sun above.
Melt the clouds of sin and sadness; drive the dark of doubt away;
Giver of immortal gladness, fill us with the light of day!

All thy works with joy surround thee, earth and heav'n reflect thy
    rays,
Stars and angels sing around thee, center of unbroken praise;
Field and forest, vale and mountain, flowery meadow, flashing
    sea,
Chanting bird and flowing fountain, call us to rejoice in thee.

Now, on the basis of your remembrances, compose your own lines of praise to God. Recall how joy has entered your life, how sorrow and doubt have been driven away. Reflect on how beauty and power have come to you through the natural world. Whether in verse or in prose, worship God with your words, and know that your praise is but one harmonious part of creation's endless song.

Today, be united with the joy of a jubilant creation. In everything you do, and wherever you are, remember:

All creation praises God.

Day 21   Life is praise.

"You are worthy, our Lord and God, to receive glory and honor and power, for you created all things, and by your will they existed and were created."

—Revelation 4:11

*O*ne dictionary defines *praise* as "an expression of approval, esteem, or commendation." This definition was produced by the mind. The heart, on the other hand, has its own definition. To the heart, true praise is the living of life to its fullest in grateful response to the love of God. The living of life *to its fullest*.

When praising God and living life become one and the same, you experience a joy that cannot be fathomed by your mind or expressed by your tongue. Your spirit must simply surrender to it, and rejoice.

Praise-life happens when you keep yourself centered; when, no matter what is going on around you, you consistently rest in that still place within you where you can feel the indwelling presence of God, where you can hear the Word. Resting in God, you are renewed, transformed. You come to have the mind within you that was in Christ. You celebrate life. You celebrate the Giver of life. You celebrate the life-purposes you are given.

Today's exercise will require great mindfulness. Every half-hour, no matter where you find yourself, take a moment to prayerfully center yourself in today's central idea. If it will help, write the idea on a small card and keep it near you as a reminder. Sometimes you may forget. Do not worry. Let this exercise be not a burden but a blessing. Just remember the best you can, and whenever you do, celebrate the remembrance, knowing that your Creator celebrates with you.

Life is praise.

Day 22 **Praise is limited by my choices.**

[God] said, "Who told you that you were naked? Have you eaten from the tree of which I commanded you not to eat?" The man said, "The woman whom you gave to be with me, she gave me fruit from the tree, and I ate."

—*Genesis 3:11-12*

*N*othing like passing the buck, eh, Adam?

Like Adam and Eve, we do not always choose wisely. Sometimes, intentionally or not, we make the wrong choice. Other times, things happen so fast that we do not even realize that we have made a choice. We feel that life is simply happening to us without our having much to say about it.

We are *always* making choices, however. For example, even when we have no way of altering external events, we choose how we will respond to them. In every situation we decide whether we will focus on the negative or the positive, whether we will complain about the bad or affirm the good.

Think about what happens when a loved one dies. If you are like many people, your first reaction is to look at the loss, the grief, the tragedy of the death. While this is certainly understandable, you *could* choose to respond differently. You could intentionally decide to focus on the significance of the person's life, to celebrate the times you shared with the person, to rejoice over the gift of eternal life. Instead of giving your emotional energy to anger or bitterness, which helps no one, you could give your love and comfort to those needing support; you could give praise to God for being with you and for welcoming the one who has died. The bottom line is, how you respond is a choice.

The same is true of how you interact with others, especially during conflicts. In any disagreement you choose whether you will react to the other person in a negative way or respond in a more helpful way. Give yourself time to think before you choose. For example, ask yourself what might be going on in the mind of the other person that led him to do whatever offended you. Or, put yourself in his place for a moment, imagine his perspective and his feelings, and *then* respond. This would enable you to be more understanding and possibly ease the conflict.

Slow things down today. Take time to think about situations before responding to them. Consider all your options. And choose to do that which would best praise God.

Praise is limited by my choices.

Day 23   **Anxiety is a choice.**

Cast all your anxiety on him, because he cares for you.

—*1 Peter 5:7*

*B*e not afraid" is a message that we read repeatedly in the scriptures. God invites us time and again to let go of our worries and fears. In other words, God lets us know that we have a choice about whether or not we will be anxious about the things of this life.

Much of our anxiety is rooted in the mistaken assumption that we are facing life alone. We wonder how we can possibly carry all our burdens, solve all our problems, overcome all our obstacles, all by ourselves. But we are not alone, are we? And not being alone can make all the difference.

Suppose that you must move a new piano up a flight of stairs to your apartment. If it were up to you to do alone, the piano would probably stay at the bottom of the stairs, if not in the back of your truck. But if you asked some friends to help, the task, though still difficult, would become possible. So it is with most of what we worry about. Our burdens become lighter, our problems more manageable, our obstacles smaller, when we realize that we are not alone. So, the choice is ours. We can either think of ourselves as standing all alone against the troubles of the world, or we can draw strength and help from God and the people around us.

Write on a piece of paper one area of your life that is currently causing you some stress or anxiety. Now find a quiet place where you can be in meditative prayer. Settle in. Close your eyes. Relax. When you are ready, visualize yourself sitting in a comfortable chair in a very peaceful room. Sink down in the chair; feel how it is supporting you. Absorb the pleasantness of the room.

Now see Jesus entering the room. He comes and sits down in an empty chair across from you, close enough that you could reach out and touch him. You exchange no words with him, but you don't need to; you know that he understands what you are thinking and feeling. Begin to focus your mind on the problem that you named on the piece of paper. Feel the weight of carrying this burden alone. Decide to hand a little of it to Jesus. See him receive it from you, willingly. Feel your burden lighten a bit. Reach out again, giving more of your anxiety away. Again, Jesus freely takes it. Continue sharing your problem until you have let all of it go.

Now Jesus rises from his chair. Notice how easily he stands up, how effortlessly he carries your problem out of the room. When he is gone, you still have an awesome sense of his presence. Continue to draw strength and reassurance from it until you are ready to close your time of prayer.

Today, when frustrations and difficulties begin to mount, remember that Jesus is with you to help carry the load. Choose to surrender your anxiety. Give your concerns over to him.

Anxiety is a choice.

Day 24   **Anxiety is meaningless.**

"And can any of you by worrying add a single hour to your span of life?"
—*Luke 12:25*

*I*magine that you are sitting in a rocking chair. You rock back and forth, back and forth, hour after hour. And when the day ends, you are right where you began. You have exerted great effort to get nowhere.

So it is with anxiety. You can waste a great deal of time and energy stewing and worrying, but in the end all of your stewing and worrying will have gotten you nowhere.

List all the worries that you have today, whether small or large. Be thorough. Be specific. When your list is complete, go back over it, crossing out those things that you cannot change. Then spend some time reflecting on the remaining, "can-change" items. Which one of them is so important that you would be willing to take at least one positive step toward changing it? Mark it with a star. Now, what specific step can you take? It may be that the problem cannot be solved immediately or easily. All you are asked to do today is name one way in which you can move toward change. Resolve to follow through.

To worry about things that you cannot change is meaningless. To *only* worry about things that you *can* change is pointless. It gets you nowhere. Ask God for wisdom; let go of what you cannot change, and take appropriate action on what you can.

Anxiety is meaningless.

Day 25 I choose not to focus on my fear.

"Therefore I tell you, do not worry about your life, what you will eat or what you will drink, or about your body, what you will wear. Is not life more than food, and the body more than clothing?"

—*Matthew 6:25*

*P*erhaps you have heard about the faraway village which received word, early one December, that the Savior would visit around Christmastime.

"Oh my!" all the town's leaders exclaimed. "Our houses are not grand enough!"

"The harvest this year was poor," complained all the cooks. "Our food will not be fine enough!"

"There's been a cold going around," observed all the singers. "Our anthems will not be sweet enough!"

"There's not enough yard goods in our stores," whined all the tailors. "Our clothing will not be new enough!"

"The town is full of sinners," lamented all the ministers. "Our spirits will not be righteous enough!"

And so it went, the villagers growing more humbuggy by the hour.

Christmastime finally came—and went. No Savior appeared. The villagers gathered for a meeting in the town square. "We must not have been good enough," they eventually decided, after much discussion. "The Savior must have passed us by for some other town." They all turned away and walked sadly toward their homes, never noticing the beggar who was frolicking in the snow with the villagers' children, pulling their sleds with nail-scarred hands.

What we focus on grows in importance. And the more we focus on what we fear and what could go wrong, the less we can sense God's presence in our midst.

Today, try to be aware of when you are becoming nervous, worried, or frightened. Ask yourself why you are feeling that way. Then, choose to turn your attention elsewhere—to praise, for example. Begin to affirm what is good in your life. Concentrate on what you are grateful for, and you will feel your fear losing its power.

I choose not to focus on my fear.

Day 26   **I openly seek what is good.**

After these things, Joseph of Arimathea, who was a disciple of Jesus, though a secret one because of his fear of the Jews, asked Pilate to let him take away the body of Jesus. Pilate gave him permission; so he came and removed his body. Nicodemus, who had at first come to Jesus by night, also came.

—John 19:38-39

*J*oseph of Arimathea had been a *secret* disciple of Jesus. Nicodemus had come to Jesus *by night*. Focusing on their fear, both of these men had been reluctant to openly seek out and acknowledge someone whom they knew to be good. Not until *after* Jesus had been killed by those who could see only bad in him had they mustered the courage to step forth from the shadows.

Do you openly seek out and acknowledge what is good in others? Or do you more often look for the bad?

A sociologist who wanted to learn more about the behavior of toddlers placed little microphones on a group of two-year-olds. For one day, all of the children's interactions with adults were recorded. Studying the tapes, the sociologist discovered that more than 80 percent of all the comments the adults made to the children were negative. Furthermore, the sociologist noted that when the children were behaving appropriately, only rarely did anyone remark on their behavior. The moment they began to misbehave, however, someone scolded them at once. How unfortunate that the children's negative behavior received nearly all the attention!

Many of us have difficulty acknowledging what is good in others. Often this is because we are unable to acknowledge what is good in ourselves. We put ourselves down. We deflect compliments paid to us by others. "It's really nothing," we might say, and the person who has praised us walks away feeling a little deflated. Why couldn't we just have said "Thank you"?

We must be comfortable acknowledging the good in ourselves before we can begin to openly acknowledge the good in others. Take a moment to jot down some of the things that *you* do well. What are some compliments others might give you regarding these things? When you have created a list of at least ten compliments that you would like to hear, read them aloud. After each statement, practice saying "Thank you." Say nothing more. Continue doing this until you are comfortable responding to each item on the list. (If possible, have a trusted friend read the compliments to you and receive your responses.)

I openly seek what is good.

Day 27   I boldly seek what is good.

The wicked flee when no one pursues, but the righteous are as bold as a lion.

—Proverbs 28:1

*Y*esterday you listed some compliments that you would appreciate hearing from other people. Now, what keeps you from more openly acknowledging the good you see in *them*? For example, are you afraid of how they might react to unexpected praise?

We can never be certain how our acts of kindness will be received. But we must never let this fact weaken our determination to act. Let others receive the good that we do or say as they will, but let us always choose to do and say it.

Think of a friend, family member, or colleague whom you will be with today. Make a list of at least five compliments that you might share. Read this list aloud, practicing each statement until you are comfortable saying it. Do not allow yourself to worry about how the person might respond to you, but remain focused on what you appreciate about this individual.

Go forth with courage today and share at least one compliment with this person. Whether or not the compliment is one of those that you rehearsed is unimportant. The rehearsal was simply meant to prepare your spirit to more boldly seek out and acknowledge the good in others. Do so with gladness.

I boldly seek what is good.

Day 28   **I do not fear.**

God is our refuge and strength, a very present help in trouble. Therefore we will not fear, though the earth should change, though the mountains shake in the heart of the sea; though its waters roar and foam, though the mountains tremble with its tumult.

—Psalms 46:1-3

*T*he rocks line the shore, defining the shape of the lake. They have been there for generations, and will be for generations more. Gray waves pound against them, but they do not move. The approaching storm will come and go like countless others have, and tomorrow the rocks will still be there, as solid and secure as ever. Resting on the ground a little distance from the lake is a tree. At an early age it was battered and beaten until finally it lay on its side, as if held down by the weight of an unknown burden. Now, decades later, the tree is still growing, in an "L," running along the ground and then turning up to the sky. It has not been defeated by its hardships.

Think for a moment of the oldest feature of the natural world that you have been privileged to see. What did it look like? What feelings did it inspire in you? Try to imagine all the adversities it has faced through the years. And yet, it has survived, in spite of them all.

Such images of nature speak to us of enormous strength and resilience. And just think: All of creation is as nothing when compared to its Creator! Infinitely strong, God has been around forever, and will be forevermore. And this is the One who reaches out to us and counts us as friends, as children. What have we to fear?

I do not fear.

Day 29   # Fear destroys.

Now after they had left, an angel of the Lord appeared to Joseph in a dream and said, "Get up, take the child and his mother, and flee to Egypt, and remain there until I tell you; for Herod is about to search for the child, to destroy him."

— Matthew 2:13

*H*ave you ever built a house of cards? The higher you go, the more afraid you become. The more afraid you become, the more unsteady your hand. The more unsteady your hand, the more quickly the house collapses.

The house of Herod was not all that big, but it was *his* house, and he was not about to lose it. Especially not to a baby, who was rumored to be a king. Herod's hand began to tremble, then to shake. In fear he ordered the slaughter of the innocents.

The fear that caused Herod to attack and destroy was not the same fear that motivated Mary and Joseph to flee with their youngster into Egypt. Theirs was the fear that God arouses, which summons forth courage in defense of life. While Herod's fear was inspired by weakness and malice, the fear of the holy parents was inspired by strength and love.

Examine a newspaper or a magazine, such as *Time* or *Newsweek*. Or tune into a news broadcast. Regard each news story in terms of its fear factor. Do you see fear involved in the facts, and/or in the way that the news is being reported? What kind of fear is it? What kind of effect, if any, do you think the media has on the public's fears? On your own fears?

Try an experiment. For one week do not expose yourself to the news. Read no papers, watch no broadcasts. You may find the withdrawal more difficult than you think. At the end of the week, reflect on how you feel.

Fear destroys.

Day 30   # Pride divides.

For by the grace given to me I say to everyone among you not to think of yourself more highly than you ought to think, but to think with sober judgment, each according to the measure of faith that God has assigned.

—Romans 12:3

*J*ust as there are two types of fear, there are two kinds of pride. The pride inspired by God is the satisfaction and joy you feel when you are living in harmony with the divine will. This kind of pride heightens your awareness of being one with God's creation. Witness a child being born, enjoy your beloved, comfort a friend, labor hard and well at what gives you pleasure, stand silently and watch the sun going down in a palette of purples and pinks, rest at the end of a day that felt *just right*—do such things, and you will feel the pride that is produced by praise-living.

The other kind of pride heightens only your awareness of yourself. It builds you up at someone else's expense, even if that person is unaware of it, and at your own expense, even if you do not believe it. This pride is the conceit that praises itself and no other. It is the vanity that looks only at its own face in the mirror. It is the false dignity that strikes a pose for effect. It is the false modesty that puts itself down in order to get attention.

Today you will begin to close the door on the self-serving pride that separates you from your neighbor. Make a list of ways in which you indulge in vanity. Think about the clothing you wear; the titles you wish to be addressed by; the home you live in; the company you keep; the car you drive; the activities you engage in; the things you talk about; the charities you support, and so on. How much of your life is determined by your desire to "build yourself up" in the eyes of others? On the other hand, how much of your life is dedicated to praise-living—to finding satisfaction in living in harmony with God's will? What will you do to decrease your self-serving pride?

Pride divides.

Day 31

Judgment returns.

"Do not judge, so that you may not be judged. For with the judgment you make you will be judged, and the measure you give will be the measure you get."

—*Matthew 7:1-2*

*P*erhaps you remember times when, in your childhood, an adult would catch you pointing a finger of blame. "Don't point!" you were told. "When you point at someone else, three of your fingers are pointing back at you!"

Somewhere along the line, you probably stopped pointing with your finger and started pointing with your words, your thoughts, your facial expressions, or your actions. You gradually sharpened your aim. At the same time, you began to steel yourself against other people, because more and more you felt under assault. Over time your armor became thicker and heavier. You put it on each morning by habit; you never wondered why you were having to work so hard to protect yourself. So, you never understood that most of the attacks on you were just your own attacks on others, boomeranging right back.

Judgmental attacks on others rebound to become attacks on yourself. Keep this childhood lesson firmly in mind as you carry out this symbolic act. At the end of your day, stand in front of a large mirror. Imagine that the clothes you are wearing are actually a heavy suit of armor. Feel its weight. See its scratches and dents from a lifetime of blows.

Now undress slowly, deliberately taking off each burdensome piece of armor. You do not need it anymore, because you are not going to judge anymore. Now you realize that judgment is not yours to render. If it were, your judgments would be gratefully received by those you judge, instead of turning back against you. When you have removed your armor, rejoice that God's love and power will protect you in its place.

Choose to render love instead of blame, to offer understanding instead of condemnation. What you give will return to you in full measure.

Judgment returns.

Day 32   Envy brings strife.

Those conflicts and disputes among you, where do they come from? Do they not come from your cravings that are at war within you?

—James 4:1

*L*ike judgment, envy is an attack on others that returns. Envy is seeing with desire. It is craving something that someone else has because you don't have it. Money, attractiveness, power, children, freedom, talent, leisure time, possessions, love, education, respect, success—whatever it is, when you are envious, some part of you secretly or openly resents its being possessed by others.

Envy is not a creation of the mind of Christ. It is the creation of a jealous world. It brings strife to you and your relationships. Today's exercise is meant to help you acknowledge how much this strife weighs on you and to help you cast it off. Begin by making a very honest and specific list of those you envy and why. For example, "I envy (name) because she got the promotion I wanted," "I envy (name) because he has a son and I don't," "I envy (name) because her body is graceful and mine isn't," and so on. Envy always has two parts: what someone else has or is, and what you think you don't have or aren't. Include both parts in each statement.

Now, take out a large bag. For each of your statements, put something fairly heavy into it, such as a can of food or a book. When you have loaded your bag, pick it up. Imagine carrying it with you twenty-four hours a day, no matter where you go. Realize that this symbolic burden is far lighter and less cumbersome than the one an envious spirit actually bears from day to day.

Now remove the articles from your bag, one at a time. Say aloud for each, "With God's help I will not carry this envy anymore." When you have emptied the bag, destroy your list and rejoice in your release.

Envy brings strife.

Day 33 Stubbornness brings confusion.

All we like sheep have gone astray; we have all turned to our own way, and the LORD has laid on him the iniquity of us all.

—*Isaiah 53:6*

*P*erhaps you have heard it said, "There is my way, there is your way, and there is the right way." When "my way" gets defined as the "one and only way," confusion—and often outright conflict —is the result.

This kind of stubbornness is not to be mistaken for sincere resolve. Resolve is born of a faithful spirit. It is not proud or inflexible. It remains willing to listen, to try to understand, to explore compromise, to envision new possibilities, even to admit it is wrong. Resolve works toward resolution, toward a meeting of the minds. Hardhearted, muleheaded stubbornness, on the other hand, leads only toward dissolution, toward a parting of the ways.

Write responses to the following:

(1) Identify at least one specific thing that you feel you need to be right about, right now.

41

(2) Regarding this issue, are you:
  (a) still listening?
  (b) still trying to understand?
  (c) still exploring compromise?
  (d) still envisioning new possibilities?
  (e) willing to admit you are wrong, if it begins to seem that way?
(3) On a scale of 1 to 10, how badly do you need to be right about this issue?
(4) What price, if any, might you have to pay for needing to be right? For example, might a relationship be injured? What price would you be willing to pay?
(5) Are you wanting to win or to achieve a fair resolution? If it is a resolution that you seek, what are you willing to do to help bring it about?

Use these questions to distinguish where you are being stubborn from where you are being resolute. Ask God for wisdom, that you might see your path clearly. Always remember: **Stubbornness brings confusion.**

Day 34 Simplicity brings clarity.

"Let your word be 'Yes, Yes' or 'No, No'; anything more than this comes from the evil one."

—*Matthew 5:37*

*S*even-year-old Jimmy came running into the house from the backyard where he had been playing with his friends. He demanded of his mother to know where he had come from. Having prepared herself for this inevitable question, she marched him into the living room and brought out some children's books that explained the birth process. Then she launched into a lecture, explaining every detail. Before she was finished, Jimmy interrupted. "That's not what I want to know. Bobby said he came from Chicago, and I just wondered where I came from."

We would do well to slow our conversations down. Like Jimmy's mother, we need to allow ourselves time to really hear what the other person is saying. Too often we assume that we know what someone means instead of really listening. At the same time, we need to allow the other person time to really hear what *we* are saying. Too often we bombard others with too many words. And the faster and more emotional our words are, the more difficult they are to comprehend. According to research, members of an audience will walk away from a lecture remembering about 10 percent of what they heard. The other 90 percent is not retained; it cannot be recalled. Does this suggest that we could cut the number of words in our conversations by 90 percent and communicate just as effectively? Probably not, but it is an interesting question to consider. Much of what we say does not really need to be said.

Keeping speech simple and taking time to hear what is said helps to keep communication clear. Reflect on a recent conversation with a friend or family member that left you feeling dissatisfied or even troubled. Think back through the conversation to things you said which your friend might not have understood correctly. Ponder the other possible meanings for your words. Also ask yourself if you might have spoken too fast for your friend to comprehend, or with too much emotion for your friend to feel comfortable.

When you have the opportunity, talk to your friend again. Check out at least one of your perceptions about your previous conversation. Ask for feedback. What did your friend understand you to be saying? How did your friend feel about how you said it? And did you hear your friend correctly? Learn from these observations. Begin to see the value of simplicity in communication.

Simplicity brings clarity.

Day 35   **I can only serve one God.**

"No one can serve two masters; for a slave will either hate the one and love the other, or be devoted to the one and despise the other. You cannot serve God and wealth."

—Matthew 6:24

*C*onflict often results from divided loyalties. For example, you can't serve both yourself and God, for, to paraphrase Matthew, either you will hate yourself and love God, or you will love yourself and hate God. Faith cannot be split down the middle and still be faith. By its very nature, faith is whole.

Which god, then, will you choose to serve: the one of your own making, or the One who has made you? You have already answered this question, in theory, or you would not be reading this book. In daily practice, however, you must answer this question again and again.

Picture your every act of faithful service as accomplishing three things at once. Because the Creator and the creation are so intimately joined, everything you do for God is, at the same time, done for others and for yourself. Serving God is three-dimensional, dynamic:

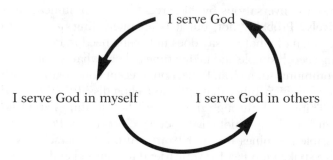

I serve God

I serve God in myself

I serve God in others

In contrast, serving yourself is one-dimensional. "I serve myself" stops dead in its tracks, right where it begins—with "I." A self-serving act has no life beyond itself. It gives God no joy and the world no good. So, you see, whom you choose to serve makes a world of difference.

Identify one way in which you will serve another person today. Clearly set your intention, then perform your service, knowing that by serving someone else, you are also serving God.

I can only serve one God.

Day 36   # God forgives.

But you are a God ready to forgive, gracious and merciful, slow to anger and abounding in steadfast love, and you did not forsake them.

—*Nehemiah 9:17c*

*A*ll relationships depend upon forgiveness. Without it, relationships wither and die. But what *is* forgiveness, exactly?

Forgiveness is placing a greater value on a relationship with someone than on a particular offense that person has committed. It looks past a behavior to focus on the bond of love. Understanding that no one and no relationship can be perfect, it has the ability to say, "Let's try again." It accepts the other "as is," complete with faults and mistakes.

We can offer forgiveness to others because we experience the forgiveness offered by God. God accepts us just as we are, even when we do not live up to our calling. Whenever we sin, God cleanses us and gives us the opportunity to begin again; God understands that having a relationship with us is infinitely more important than any single mistake that we might make.

List on paper some of the sins and mistakes that you have committed in the past several days, the big ones and the small ones. Be honest; no one will see your list except you. Now, read your list aloud, saying after each item, "God forgives me." Repeat this until it becomes natural to hear the words of forgiveness.

Remember throughout the day that forgiveness is a free gift that God offers to you. Receive it as freely as it is given.

God forgives.

Day 37   I forgive.

"Whenever you stand praying, forgive, if you have anything against anyone; so that your Father in heaven may also forgive you your trespasses."

—*Mark 11:25*

*R*emembering God's forgiveness of your own mistakes enables you to more willingly forgive the mistakes of others. You know what it feels like to be given a new start, to be invited back into right relationship. So you can more freely offer others the same possibilities that God has offered you.

An interesting thing happens when you willingly forgive another person. You are blessed as much as the one that you forgive. Not only do you restore the potential for the relationship to grow, but you also lighten your own burden of unresolved hostility.

List at least ten wrongs that others have committed against you about which you still have strong feelings. Some of these may be recent offenses; others you may have carried with you for a long time. Now, read your list aloud and, after each offense, say with assurance, "I willingly forgive." You may want to add the name of the person who has offended you to each statement of forgiveness: "I willingly forgive (name)." Repeat the process until the statement of forgiveness rings true.

Whenever one of these hurts comes back into your mind,

45

repeat the forgiveness phrase again. Think of your gift of forgiveness as a gift to yourself as well as to the other person.

I forgive.

Day 38 I am quick to forgive.

Those with good sense are slow to anger, and it is their glory to overlook an offense.

—Proverbs 19:11

*W*atching children play together can teach us much about forgiveness. They can be fighting one moment and playing together the next, as if nothing had ever happened. Sometimes we interfere in their conflicts only to discover that they do not need our help to resolve their differences. They do not hold onto resentments, and can therefore restore their broken relationships very quickly.

We adults, on the other hand, have unfortunately learned to hold on to our grievances. We carry them around with us like prized possessions, sometimes for a lifetime. The longer we carry them, the harder it is to give them up. It is much easier to forgive an offense sooner than later. The passage of time can cloud the original issue or intensify the hurt.

Learning to forgive quickly, while vitally important, is very difficult. When we are wronged, we become angry. When we become angry, our adrenalin pumps up. Our heart rate increases. Our breathing becomes rapid and shallow. This "fight or flight" response prepares the body to protect itself by either fighting or fleeing. This phenomenon happens whenever we are upset or angry, whether we want it to or not.

While you cannot prevent your body's instinctive fight or flight response, you *can* decide how you will react to it. For example, you might decide to intensify it by allowing yourself to get more and more upset. Or, you might decide to suppress it by denying your feelings, either consciously or subconsciously. Or, you might decide to let the hurt go. If you do this, you change your body's reaction because you change the message that it is receiving. In forgiveness, "fight or flight" becomes "love and have no fear."

Learn to recognize when your body is reacting in anger to the behavior of another person. Then you can quickly intercede in

your body's instinctive response pattern. You can decide to forgive when the event happens rather than waiting for an apology
that may never come or for a deeper understanding of the situation that may not be possible. Today, be aware of your bodily
sensations. Notice when you feel yourself tightening up, as if getting ready for a fight. Notice when your pulse increases. Notice
when your breathing changes. Become aware of other signals
that your body sends when you are angry.

In moments of anger, remember that while you may have no
choice about what the other person is doing, you *do* have a
choice about how you will respond. Choose to quickly forgive.

I am quick to forgive.

Day 39   God does not condemn me.

Come now, let us argue it out, says the LORD: though your sins are like
scarlet, they shall be like snow; though they are red like crimson, they
shall become like wool.

—Isaiah 1:18

*S*uppose that you are to lead a workshop. You walk into your
meeting room and discover that the chalkboard is still covered
with writing from an earlier session. The first thing that you do
is look for an eraser. Quickly wiping off the board, you are now
ready to begin.

The grace of God works in the same way. No matter what
errors have been written on the "chalkboard" of our lives, grace
can always wipe them away. God gives us the chance to surrender our guilt, to see ourselves as worthy of love, to begin again.

That God's forgiveness is free is very difficult for us to accept. We
are used to loving each other conditionally—*if* the other person
behaves the way we want, *if* she is meeting our needs, *then* we will
love her. But God's love is unconditional. It is there for us no matter what we do. When we happen to do wrong, that love forgives
us, not because we have earned it but because God wants to restore
the relationship. Once we have experienced this free gift from God,
we know how powerful receiving and giving forgiveness can be.

Find a pen, a red piece of paper, and a white piece of paper—
both approximately the same size. The white paper should be
thick enough that you cannot see through it. Place the white
paper in front of you and focus your attention on it. It represents

the way you were created to be—innocent and loved. Feel the joy of your right relationship with God. Now, list on this paper some of the hopes and dreams that you believe God has for your life. Be as specific and thorough as possible.

Next, turn your attention to the red piece of paper. This represents the hurt you feel when your relationship with God seems strained or broken. List on this paper some of your personal weaknesses, limits, and mistakes that have contributed to that hurt. What parts of yourself have sometimes caused you to feel lost from God, or guilty before God, or angry toward God? Again, be specific.

When you have finished this second list, slowly slip the red sheet of paper over the white. Pause occasionally to reflect on your feelings as you see the white paper disappearing beneath the red. When all the white paper has disappeared, offer a prayer of confession for your past mistakes.

Now, open yourself to God's free gift of forgiveness. Slip the white paper out and begin to slowly slide it over the red. This act represents God's forgiveness of you. Be aware of your feelings as you see the white returning. Celebrate the knowledge that your relationship with God is fully restored.

God does not condemn me.

Day 40   **I do not condemn others.**

"Do not judge, and you will not be judged; do not condemn, and you will not be condemned. Forgive, and you will be forgiven."

—*Luke 6:37*

*W*hen we see a toddler beginning to take his first steps, we are exhilarated. We celebrate each little bit of progress that he makes. When he falls down, we quickly lift him up and encourage him to try again. We do not yell at him that he is stupid and slow, that he will probably never be able to walk or he would have gotten it right the first time.

Isn't it interesting that we provide a child with such a patient, forgiving space in which to learn, but as the child grows older, we become very impatient and demanding?

Because we realize that a toddler is doing the best that he or she can, we do not condemn the child if his or her progress is slow. But we forget that all of us, no matter our age, are doing the best that we can. None of us deliberately chooses to progress slowly or act foolishly or decide poorly. Each of us does the best that we know how to do in any given moment. The best we can do will sometimes be wrong. Sometimes we won't have enough information to make a wise choice. Or, we won't have the emotional stamina to be more helpful. Or, we won't have the moral understanding that might lead us to do otherwise. We can do the best we can and still do wrong, for any number of reasons. Yet we are quick to condemn and slow to forgive one another.

Reflect back over the past week. Think of an incident in which someone hurt your feelings or did something that was not helpful to you. Can you imagine what she might have been thinking, what good intentions and motivations she might have had that somehow went wrong? Say aloud with confidence: "(Name) was doing the best that he/she could." Repeat the statement over and over, even if you want to argue with it. Let it become an affirmation of the goodness of the person who has injured you.

Write the following statement on a slip of paper or notecard: "We are all doing the best that we can." Place this statement where you will see it often throughout the day. Let it be a reminder that other people, just like yourself, are still in the process of learning to walk the path.

I do not condemn others.

Day 41   **I do not condemn myself.**

Therefore you have no excuse, whoever you are, when you judge others; for in passing judgment on another you condemn yourself, because you, the judge, are doing the very same things.

—*Romans 2:1*

*W*hen you focus on a mistake you give it power. You can see this happen, for example, when you are typing. You sit down at the keyboard with a positive attitude, and for awhile your typing goes fairly well. Inevitably, though, you make a mistake. As you correct it, you criticize yourself for your clumsiness. Then, when you begin to type again, your mistakes begin to multiply. "My fingers just aren't working today," you remark to yourself, and your words quickly become a self-fulfilling prophecy. Your frustration mounts with every error, until you are making so many of them that you must quit and distract your mind with another task for a few minutes. When you return, you find that you can once again type without errors. Somehow your mind has been cleared!

Whenever you condemn yourself for mistakes, you inhibit your spiritual growth. Your spirit cannot flourish in an environment of frustration, anger, embarrassment, and guilt. What if, instead, you accepted your mistakes as opportunities to learn? What if you forgave yourself, and worked to foster for yourself an environment of hope, encouragement, patience, and self-respect? Your spirit would then not only grow, but thrive.

On a piece of paper, create a time line, marking every five years of your life. Then jot down the talents, skills, and abilities that you acquired at different ages. Here is a brief example:

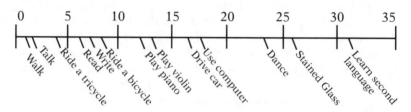

Now reflect on your timeline. Do you notice periods of greater and lesser growth in terms of your talents and abilities? Do you see any connection between your growth and the kind of "environment" in which your talents were trying to take root? Did negative feelings, such as frustration or fear of failure, ever prevent further development of an ability? Did positive feelings, such as encouragement or patience, ever promote further development? Are you now in a period of greater or lesser growth?

Realize that you are still in the process of becoming. Celebrate the progress you have made in the past, and create for yourself a more forgiving environment in which your spirit can flourish in the future.

I do not condemn myself.

Day 42   **Forgiveness returns.**

"For if you forgive others their trespasses, your heavenly Father will also forgive you."

—*Matthew 6:14*

*B*ob had a large garden in his backyard. Being something of an organic gardener, he always dumped his kitchen scraps onto the plot and then hoed them under to add nutrients to the soil.

One day, when he was in a great hurry, he ran outside with a pan full of potato peelings. Not wanting to take time to turn the peelings under the soil, he simply tossed them into the air. Unfortunately, he had forgotten to check the wind direction. He wore a good number of those peelings back into the house!

Judging others is like throwing potato peelings into the wind. It comes back on you. And forgiving others is no different, except that what comes back is more appealing, if you will pardon the pun.

The positive power of forgiveness returns to you in many ways. First, by forgiving someone else you are able to more fully appreciate God's forgiveness of *you*. Second, you experience the release of resentments and disappointments that otherwise could build up and cause damage to your spirit and even to your body. Third, you help to create a more forgiving environment in which you and others may thrive. Finally, you are able to get in touch with the truth about your anger; for example, you may discover that your extreme frustration with someone else's behavior is rooted in a secret frustration with a similar behavior of your own.

A simple yet helpful technique for getting in touch with your feelings around anger and forgiveness is called "writing through to the truth." When you are feeling annoyed with someone, sit down and write a clear statement of what is upsetting you. Then continue to write whatever comes to your mind about that particular situation. Do not stop writing, even when you think that you have nothing more to say. Forcing yourself to write on, you will notice a gradual shift in content. Your focus will change from the other person's frustrating behavior to your own feelings about the situation, and then to your deepest reasons for being upset. At this point, you may realize that you are disappointed in how you handled the situation or reacted to the person. In this moment, allow the forgiveness that God so freely offers to enter your heart and then to pass through you to the other person. Feel the joy of forgiveness.

Forgiveness returns.

Day 43   **God fills me with love.**

And may the Lord make you increase and abound in love for one another and for all, just as we abound in love for you.

—*1 Thessalonians 3:12*

51

In the English language "love" is a catchall word. It is used to express anything from admiration of a star athlete to appreciation for chocolate, from enjoyment of a favorite TV show to adoration of a beloved. This overuse seems to cheapen the word.

The Greek language of the New Testament is richer in its words for love. Today we are concerned with only two of them, *agape* (ah-gah'-pay) and *adikia* (ad-ik-ee'-ah). You may have heard of *agape*. It is that unconditional, no-strings-attached, always-here-when-you-need-it kind of love that is given perfectly and completely by God. We humans give it to each other less perfectly and less completely, but it is nevertheless our divinely-appointed mission to lovingly meet the legitimate needs of others without regard for our own desires.

The problem is, you probably have received less *agape* in your life than you have *adikia*. *Adikia* tries to meet the needs of others only in order to get its own needs met. It likes to play games. It pulls strings and attaches strings. Sometimes it even masquerades as *agape* in order to get what it wants. Telling the difference between *agape* and *adikia* requires great wisdom. The more you receive *adikia*, the more you give it, not because you are a bad person, but because you believe the world operates that way. You may not even realize that another kind of love exists. But it does. *Agape*—God's love—is yours if you open yourself to it. The more you receive *agape*, the more *agape* you will give.

Deliberately offer *agape* to someone who especially needs it today. Offer it anonymously. Send a note or a flower; cook a favorite dish and leave it at the door; do a quiet, unexpected favor—the possibilities are endless. As you expose the recipient to *agape*, know that both of you are being opened to a source of love that can never be exhausted.

God fills me with love.

Day 44   **Love is powerful.**

And now faith, hope, and love abide, these three; and the greatest of these is love.

—*1 Corinthians 13:13*

When you begin to see yourself as God sees you, you begin to be what God intends you to be. When you begin to see others as

God sees them, you help them to do the same. This is the transforming power of *agape*. It resides in you. It flows through you.

Your gaze is one way that *agape* flows through you. Your eyes are very revealing. By looking into them, people can sense whether or not to trust you, can be attracted to you or put off by you, can detect compassion or ill will within you. And when people look into your eyes and see *agape*, they can catch a glimpse of God.

Today's exercise will help you to experience the power of love's gaze. If convenient, enlist the help of a family member or close friend. Sit across from each other, knees almost touching. Close your eyes and quiet your mind. When you are ready, open your eyes again, and look into the eyes of your companion. Both of you should try to communicate the love of God through your gaze. Be open to its power. Let your mind think "love." Let your gaze *be* love. Do not stare, but see, deeply. Be still, and remain with each other like this for at least five minutes. End your time by expressing gratitude to one another.

If you have no friend to help you, sit before a mirror and look into your own eyes. See there the transforming love of God, which is always within you. Recognize it. Celebrate it. This is the powerful love that fills you. This is the powerful love that flows through you.

Remain open to *agape* throughout the day. Offer it to others. You cannot exhaust its Source.

Love is powerful.

Day 45 — **My love shows mercy.**

For judgment will be without mercy to anyone who has shown no mercy; mercy triumphs over judgment.

—James 2:13

Mercy is a very powerful concept. When we are merciful, we are ready to assist and do kindness to one another. We are prepared to show *agape* and reach out without hesitation. We are willing to offer forgiveness and take the initiative to repair relationships. Mercy is first rendered by God to us. Then, in gratitude, we render mercy to one another:

> Brightly beams our Father's mercy
> From his lighthouse evermore;
> But to us he gives the keeping

Of the lights along the shore.
Let the lower lights be burning!
Send a gleam across the wave!
Some poor fainting, struggling seaman
You may rescue, you may save.

—Philip B. Bliss

Read James 2:13 and the preceding lyrics from the hymn "Brightly Beams Our Father's Mercy" aloud. Then respond in writing to the following questions:

(1) How would *you* define mercy? How is it related to judgment? To *agape*?
(2) Have you ever been treated mercifully by another person? Describe how it feels.
(3) Do you consider yourself "merciful"? Why or why not? (Be specific.)
(4) Do you know a "fainting, struggling seaman," someone who is troubled, depressed, battered, tired, or isolated? How might you "send a gleam across the wave"?
(5) If *you* are that struggling sailor, what "lights along the shore" are being kept for you? Who might help you? Are you willing to seek that person out?

As you give mercy, so, too, shall you receive it. As you receive mercy, so, too, shall you give it. In God, the circle of mercy is unbroken.

My love shows mercy.

Day 46   **My love listens.**

If you close your ear to the cry of the poor, you will cry out and not be heard.

—Proverbs 21:13

*I*nsofar as you listen, you, too, shall be heard. Insofar as you are heard, you, too, shall listen. In God, once again, the circle is unbroken.

And just as God is aware of the cries of all and not just those of a favored few, so shall you be.

Listening with love requires you to be mindful. It is an active process in which you are fully present to the speaker. You maintain constant eye contact and also take note of nonverbals (facial expressions, gestures, tone of voice, and so on). You tune in not only to the words but to the emotions behind the words, and you feel sympathy with the person speaking. You give feedback by rephrasing what the person has said. You ask questions only in order to clarify what you have heard. Finally, and perhaps most important, *you do not give advice* unless directly asked to do so. Even then, you speak with caution.

To become more natural, these active listening skills must be practiced. So invite someone to have a "practice conversation" with you. Arrange a convenient time and place to meet so that you can both be relaxed.

When you meet, ask your friend to open the conversation by speaking about herself or himself for twenty minutes. Your friend will probably be surprised by your request, and perhaps a bit reluctant. Many people think they have nothing important to say about themselves; still others are uncomfortable being the center of attention. Simply reassure your friend that you *are* interested, that you really want to *listen*.

As your friend talks, practice your active listening skills: maintain eye contact, take note of nonverbals, be aware of unspoken emotions, rephrase what is said so that you are clear in your understanding, ask appropriate questions, and give no advice. When the twenty minutes are up, ask your companion to give you feedback on how well you listened. Then, of course, you may continue the conversation (don't, however, discontinue your active listening). When you and your friend finally go your separate ways, spend some time reflecting on the experience.

Make active listening a natural part of your interactions. Remember, insofar as you listen, you, too, will be heard.

My love listens.

Day 47 **My love sympathizes.**

Do not rejoice when your enemies fall, and do not let your heart be glad when they stumble.

—*Proverbs 24:17*

*T*o sympathize: to feel what another person is feeling. To feel within yourself the anger, the pain, the happiness, the embarrassment, the frustration, the fear, the hope, the confusion, the despair, the concern, the love that belongs to another. To comingle your heart with that of another, which multiplies the joys and diminishes the woes.

To *not* sympathize: to refuse to feel what another person is feeling. This is an attack on creation. It is an attempt to break the circle of *agape*. Sometimes you may feel justified in withholding your sympathy; especially in the case of your adversaries and rivals, it may seem the wisest, most natural thing to do. But doing so is contrary to the love of God.

Today's exercise, like all the others, requires great honesty. Search your heart for the face of someone whose feelings you have chosen to dismiss, deny, mock, or ignore. Now lift up your heart in prayer for this person. Acknowledge the existence of his or her feelings, and ask for a sympathetic spirit. Struggle to feel what he or she feels (or felt). *Understand*, not just with your head, but also with your heart. Now, from this depth of feeling, can you identify something this person needs? If so, reach out and try to meet this need in the best way that you can.

My love sympathizes.

Day 48   **My love returns.**

Whoever is kind to the poor lends to the LORD, and will be repaid in full.

—Proverbs 19:17

*T*ina and her grandmother had always been very close. When Tina was in high school, her grandmother offered to teach her to crochet. Tina learned slowly but steadily; and when she finally completed an afghan, she gave it to her grandmother. Her grandmother was so proud that she would use the afghan only on special occasions.

Many years later, Tina's grandmother died, and all of her possessions were sold or given away. Then, on Tina's birthday, she was presented with a gift by some friends. When she opened the box, she was stunned. "Where did you get this?" she stammered. "At the church bazaar," her friends replied, adding, "It looked like the perfect gift for you." Inside the box was the afghan she had made for her grandmother.

The love we give to others returns to us. This is a fact of our loving, though not the motivation for it. Its return may come from a different direction or in a different form from the one in which we sent it forth. However, it does come back, in full measure.

With a pencil and paper beside you, enter into a time of meditative prayer. Close your eyes; calm your thoughts. Gradually relax your entire body. When you feel ready, picture yourself sitting on a beautiful beach. Feel the gentle sun on your face. Taste the salty breeze. Hear the ocean waves spilling onto the shore. Watch the blue-green water swelling and sinking, swelling and sinking, as far as your eyes can see.

You know that somewhere, far out on the water, there is someone you love very much. Who is it? Allow his or her face to come into your mind. When you know who it is, ask yourself what message that person needs to hear from you right now. Write that message on your paper. When you are finished writing, close your eyes again and relax. You are still on the beach. Picture yourself putting the message you have written into a bottle. Seal the bottle. Now, with all the might of the love in your heart, toss the bottle out over the sea. Be amazed at how far it flies before it splashes down. Imagine it bobbing, bobbing, bobbing toward the person you want to receive it.

Wait patiently for a reply. When it comes, it does not come in a bottle. How do you receive it as you are sitting there on the beach? What does the message say? Open your eyes and write the message on your sheet of paper.

If you don't receive an answer during your period of meditation, trust that it will come in its own time, in its own way. Prayer is an act of love, and love does not return empty. Be patient, be mindful, and rejoice when it arrives.

Carry the paper with its message of love with you today, or put it where you will see it often. Let it be a powerful reminder that as love flows forth from you, so too will it return.

My love returns.

Day 49 My love overcomes evil.

Do not be overcome by evil, but overcome evil with good.

—*Romans 12:21*

*I*t is one thing to *think* that the love of God, working through you, always overcomes evil. It is quite another thing to *believe* it. Confronted by tragedy and senseless suffering, with atrocities filling our TV screens and our streets, many of us can be riddled by doubt. Does good *really* overcome evil, or is that just our naïve hope?

Today's exercise will allow you to acknowledge your doubt and to declare your faith, that your belief might be strengthened. Take out a sheet of paper and a pencil. Reflect for a few moments on certain times in your life when you have felt confronted by evil or the power of sin. Remember your reactions. Remember the outcomes. Now, draw upon this wealth of life experience as you write a few lines or a paragraph in response to each of these statements (be very specific):

To me, "overcome evil with good" means . . .
Sometimes I have doubted that love overcomes evil because . . .
Sometimes I have been sure that love overcomes evil because . . .
When I encounter evil in the future, I will . . .

Rather than destroying your faith, doubt can be a catalyst that helps your faith to grow. Accept the existence of your doubt. Examine it. Offer it your love, and you will gradually overcome it. As your faith increases, *agape* will flow more freely through you. And with your every act of *agape*, the power of evil will be subdued.

My love overcomes evil.

Day 50   **I choose community.**

But Ruth said, "Do not press me to leave you or to turn back from following you! Where you go, I will go; where you lodge, I will lodge; your people shall be my people, and your God my God."

—*Ruth 1:16*

*T*o be in community is to be deeply aware of two very important things. First, you are aware that there are people in your life who care about you and who are willing to share in your journey. Second, you are aware that there are people in your life about whom you care and in whose journeys you are willing to share. Being in community is not a necessary choice; some of us find that our spiritual journeys lead to places of joyous solitude where our relationship with God takes root and flourishes. But if you choose to commit to a group of people, you will experience the dynamic synergy of community.

"Synergy" means that 1 + 1 = more than 2. It is a process in which the individual parts of something combine to yield a result that is greater than just the sum of those parts. As an example, say that you have the seed of a flower, some soil, sunshine, and water. Each of these is important and good alone. But when you bring them together under the right conditions, the seed grows into a plant and eventually yields a beautiful blossom. This flower is much more than the sum of the parts that went into its making. Its growth was synergetic.

Several years ago, a woman named Winifred was worried about her grandson, Jason. Jason, who was in high school, was experiencing a deep crisis of faith. In an effort to provide him with support and encouragement, Winifred invited half a dozen persons of various ages and backgrounds to meet with him in her home. She trusted all of these persons to talk freely with Jason about their own faith journeys. More than that, she trusted that they would listen to him, understand his struggle, reassure him that he was not alone, and share any insights they might have. That meeting at Winifred's was soon followed by a second, and then a third; and today the group still meets every six weeks or so. The original group of six people has now grown to twenty. The group's original purpose has been met; Jason's crisis has long since passed. But members of the group, ranging in age from sixteen to eighty-five, still gather at Winifred's to celebrate the joys and challenges of being on the journey. The group has done far more and has become far greater than anyone ever intended. This is synergy: 1 + 1 = more than 2.

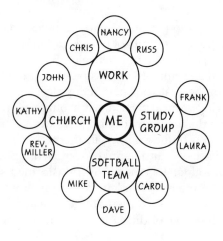

In the center of a sheet of paper, draw a small circle and label it "me." Now, in larger circles connected to "me," name some of the communities to which you belong (see page 59). Finally, in small circles connected to the "community" circles, name a few of the individuals in these groups whom you know well.

Reflect on your diagram. Which of these communities do you belong to *by choice?* To what extent are you *choosing community?* Do you see how synergy is at work in any of these communities? When you choose community, you open yourself to a bigger world than you might experience alone. You open yourself to 1 + 1 = more than 2. Synergy becomes an obvious dynamic of your life.

Renew your sense of belonging. Water the plant. Participate in the group. Share the journey.

I choose community.

Day 51   **Community lightens the load.**

A friend loves at all times, and kinsfolk are born to share adversity.

—Proverbs 17:17

*O*ften when children are playing together, a problem will arise, such as how to climb over a fence. At first, the problem seems insurmountable. The fence is just too high, or they are just too short. Before long, though, they will solve their dilemma. They may give each other a boost over the top, or locate a sturdy box to step up on, or hunt for a ladder—whatever strategy they decide on, they will quickly lend each other a helping hand to accomplish their goal.

How easy it is to forget that we do not have to face the difficulties of life alone! A community of friends can help us meet our challenges and make it through our struggles. Being in community can often transform a seemingly impossible task into a relatively easy one. Perhaps in the past you spent many sleepless nights and restless days stewing over a particularly troubling problem—a relationship was on the rocks, or your finances were in bad shape. Suddenly, though, you found yourself in the presence of friends, and you began to discuss your dilemma. Your friends offered a number of ideas and insights. Together you brainstormed solutions until, finally, "a light came on." You left their company wondering why you had not thought to seek their advice sooner.

Think of a challenge or difficulty that you are facing right now.

Who are the people that might give you support or help you find a wise solution? From whom might you seek assistance and counsel? Go to them as soon as possible, ready to ask their help, knowing that this is what a community is for.

Community lightens the load.

Day 52 I offer myself to the community.

Live in harmony with one another; do not be haughty, but associate with the lowly; do not claim to be wiser than you are.

—Romans 12:16

An interesting passage of scripture tells how Jesus, ready to teach, came down from a hillside and stood on a level place with the gathered crowd (Luke 6:17). If we assume that this little detail was not added by the gospel writer just to make the story longer, what significance might it have? What might it say about Jesus? That he wanted to be on the same level as the people he was teaching? That he did not want to appear superior, and so he voluntarily came down to be with them? If so, Jesus was in good company. Most of the great spiritual teachers of the world have preferred that their students not hold them in awe. They have not wanted to be regarded as experts who, having reached their journeys' end, now know all the answers. They have wanted to be viewed as fellow learners who are still on the way.

When we look at another person as our superior, we create a barrier to a meaningful relationship. Certainly it is appropriate to respect another person's wisdom and position, but if we think of someone as being "above" us, we will have a difficult time relating to that person. The same is true when we think of someone as being "beneath" us. We may feel sorry for the person, we may even wish him or her the best, but unless we see the individual as being "on the level" with us, we will not be able to relate to that person in any significant way. Whenever we view others as either "above" or "beneath" us, our relationship with them cannot be truly harmonious.

With paper and pencil beside you, think about a community to which you belong. Now, list those persons in the community whom you regard as being "above" you. Then list those whom you regard as being "beneath" you. Finally, list those whom you regard as being on the same level as you.

61

Now go back and reflect on your lists. Identify feelings that you experience when relating to the people you regard as "above" you. For example, do you feel somehow intimidated, awkward, or embarrassed in their presence? How do your feelings influence your behavior around them?

Next, identify feelings that you experience when relating to those whom you regard as "beneath" you. Do you feel, for instance, judgmental, impatient, or condescending? How do these feelings affect your behavior in their presence?

Finally, identify feelings that you have when relating to people whom you regard as your equals. Perhaps you feel trust, joy, or confidence; perhaps you feel the excitement of learning together, of sharing knowledge and insights with one another. How do these feelings influence your behavior?

When we offer ourselves to the community, we must do so in a spirit of mutual respect. We must regard one another as being "on one level." Among the children of God, there is none who is greater or lesser. There is only the harmony of full relationship.

I offer myself to the community.

Day 53   **I build community.**

Love one another with mutual affection; outdo one another in showing honor.

—*Romans 12:10*

*J*esus once suggested to his disciples that when they attended a wedding banquet, they should not opt to sit in the positions of honor at the table for fear that the host might come and ask them to move (Luke 14:7-11). But if each person were always to defer to the next, who would finally be seated in the place of honor? Six centuries later, according to legend, King Arthur solved this problem by seating his knights at the Round Table. A round table has no place of honor. Or rather, it should be said that a round table has nothing but places of honor.

How should we properly address those who sit with us at the Round Table of God? For example, is the person sitting next to us "Reverend" or "Pastor" or simply "Elizabeth?" Is she "Doctor" or "Ms." or simply "Jean"? Is he "Judge" or "Your Honor" or simply "David"? Of course, the form of address we choose to use may not indicate the true depth of our respect. What we actually say is less important than how we feel. When we deeply regard others as children of God, we honor them with our hearts and minds. And by honoring others, we build community. Affirming others' God-given gifts and graces, we encourage their active involvement in the Round Table. We can offer no higher position of honor in all of creation.

Today, whenever you encounter another person, think of that person as a child of God. Notice the individual's specific contributions to your community. Share a word of appreciation for who he or she is and what he or she does. By honoring someone, you will strengthen the person's spirit, and he or she, in turn, will honor another.

I build community.

Day 54   **Building community brings wholeness.**

Let us then pursue what makes for peace and for mutual upbuilding.

—Romans 14:19

*S*it for a minute and try not to think of a pink elephant!

Now it is hard not to, isn't it?

This old challenge points to the fact that when you try to push something out of your mind, it keeps popping back up like a jack-in-the-box.

In his book *Make Your Life Worthwhile*, Emmet Fox talks about the law of substitution, which suggests that instead of trying to rid your mind of a particular thought, you would do better to substitute another thought in its place. As quickly as the unwanted thought pops up in your mind, you substitute the desired one. For example, if you don't want to think of a pink elephant, think of a blue rhino instead. Such substitution can easily be done.

This law of substitution is what Paul suggests in Philippians 4:8. He challenges us to fill our minds only with those things that are true, honorable, just, and pure. These substitute for the things in our minds that are untrue, dishonorable, unjust, and impure. By setting our minds on the good, we allow very little room for the bad. This is what makes for peace.

In community, we always have a choice about the thoughts that we will entertain about one another. On the one hand, we can be critical; it is not difficult to find something to complain about, even in the greatest of persons. On the other hand, we can be affirming; it is not difficult to find something to honor, even in the most disagreeable of persons. So which shall fill our minds—thoughts of the good or the bad? We cannot really entertain both at once. We must choose.

The mind of Christ chooses to be filled with thoughts of the good that can be seen in others. This lays the foundation for peace within the community. It builds positive connections between individuals that strengthen the entire group.

Think about a particular person with whom you have an ongoing relationship. On a piece of paper, list everything about this person that annoys you—all the big and little things that bug you. Now, on a second sheet of paper, list everything about this person that you find worthy of praise—the good qualities and the potential you may see. Be imaginative! Place these two sheets of paper at opposite ends of the room. Now, look at both of them at the same time. You can't, can you? You must choose to look at either the negative or the positive comments. So it is with our minds. We must decide with what we will fill them. Filling them with thoughts of what we appreciate about one another helps to bring wholeness to our community.

Building community brings wholeness.

Day 55   In community I celebrate life.

How very good and pleasant it is when kindred live together in unity!

—Psalm 133:1

*L*iving together in unity with one another does not mean that all of us must agree on everything. It does not mean that all of us must have the same interests. The unity of community is not all of us singing the same note at the same time. That is melody. And it might become monotony, if we sing that same note for too long. No, to be united in community is to sing in *harmony*, with all of our individual notes blending into one beautiful chorus. We promote harmony in our community by sharing our unique gifts and graces at just the right moment and in just the right way.

A harmonious community gives great cause for joy. For what one of us lacks can now be found in another. What one of us possesses is now needed by another. When in community we open ourselves to sharing with one another in the spirit of humility and *agape*, we truly have cause to celebrate.

Find a recipe for a cake, a pie, or a batch of cookies. (If you don't want to make sweets, substitute another kind of recipe.) Get out all of the ingredients and utensils that you will need. Measure out the items that the recipe calls for, putting each in a separate bowl. Survey what you have. In front of you is everything you need. But you cannot celebrate the cake just yet! It does not exist. Now, combine all the ingredients according to the directions. Look again at what you have. This, too, is good, but it is still not what you want. Finally, bake the cake. When at last you pull it out of the oven, you do, indeed, have cause for celebration!

What was separate has come together. What was good alone is now wonderful together. And what had great potential has come to fulfillment. This is what we celebrate in harmonious community.

In community I celebrate life.

Day 56 **Community lives in me.**

I am reminded of your sincere faith, a faith that lived first in your grandmother Lois and your mother Eunice and now, I am sure, lives in you.

—2 Timothy 1:5

*T*hink about the color of your eyes, the texture of your hair, the build of your body. You have inherited much of your appearance—as well as your personality, health tendencies, and so on—from your ancestors. But have you ever pondered over your spiritual inheritance?

Much of your faith may have been influenced in one way or another by those who came before you. Reflect for awhile on the spiritual journeys of your parents and grandparents. How did they affect your own journey? Which of their personal values, faith understandings, and religious practices did they try to pass on to you? While you may have rejected some of what they held to be important, your ancestors still contributed in diverse ways to your journey.

Identify at least one important value that you hold that has also been important to other members of your family. Trace this value back as far as you can through the generations. Feel free to talk with other relatives as you try to examine how this value influenced your parents, grandparents, even great-grandparents, or others. Finally, ask yourself whether this value has influenced your life in the same ways that it influenced theirs.

As an example, perhaps you value "keeping your word." How did you come to value this? Think back. Maybe you remember how your mother was trusted by so many people in the community because "she could always be counted on to do what she said." Maybe you recall how your father once kept an important promise he had made to you. Maybe you grew up hearing your grandparents say, "A man is as good as his word." Or maybe you saw how this value was reflected in your relatives' long marriages, or in other major commitments they made. When you have gained a clear idea of your value's influence on your ancestors, ask yourself how it has been expressed in your own life decisions, relationships, and so on.

Now list the values that you would like to pass on to members of the next generation of your family or community. What are your most cherished beliefs and principles? Know that just as your ancestors live in you, enriching your spiritual journey, you will also live in others. Joyfully share your faith.

Community lives in me.

Day 57   **God's Spirit lives in me.**

Do you not know that you are God's temple and that God's Spirit dwells in you?

—1 Corinthians 3:16

*I*t is all too easy to look at our bodies with scorn. We are surrounded by a multitude of voices that command us to be thinner, bigger, faster, stronger, more attractive, more youthful. . . . And when we look in the mirror and see something else, we may regard our bodies with contempt. We may lament them with *if onlys*. We may put them through repeated diets and obsessive exercise, or cover them with expensive cosmetics, wrinkle creams, and hair dyes. As they age, we may make the mistake of equating them with our ageless souls.

Your body is the sanctuary of God's Spirit. It is the site of holy communication between your soul and your Source. It is not to be abused, but cared for. So, where your body has weakness, seek to strengthen it; where it has need, provide for it; where it has ability, celebrate it; where it has potential, nurture it; where it has sickness, tend it. Do all of these things with gentleness and, above all, with respect. Esteem your body properly, as a beautiful creation of God.

Do at least one thing today to show respect for your body. Soak in a hot bath. Take a long walk. Eat a nutritious meal. Dance. Sit in the sunshine. Rest. Look in the mirror and be grateful for what you see. Rejoice that your body has been created to house your soul.

God's Spirit lives in me.

Day 58   I do not quench the Spirit.

Do not quench the Spirit.

—1 Thessalonians 5:19

The Spirit burns like a holy fire within the body, the temple of God. It can never be extinguished. But it can be dampened and left to smolder like the charred remains of a burned-out building.

How do we quench the Spirit? The Spirit speaks to us, and, for whatever reason, we choose not to listen. The Spirit directs us, and we choose not to go. The Spirit sends us, and we choose to walk away. The Spirit rises up within us, and we choose to force it down. The Spirit prompts us, and we choose to put it off. With every such choice, we throw another pail of water on the sacred fire.

Today you are asked to choose differently. Enter into a time of prayerful reflection. Acknowledge ways that you may have been dousing the sacred fire. You might want to look particularly at an unsatisfactory area of your life. Where have you felt the guidance of the Spirit but been unwilling to act? Where have you refused to go? What have you walked away from? Forced down? Put off?

Act today on one of the promptings that you have not followed in the past. As you make this choice, know that, instead of quenching the Spirit, you are learning to fan its flame. Feel its warmth as it burns hotter. See its light as it burns brighter. Let yourself be perfected in the love and wisdom of its blaze.

I do not quench the Spirit.

Day 59   The Spirit helps me understand.

But truly it is the spirit in a mortal, the breath of the Almighty, that makes for understanding.

—Job 32:8

$\mathcal{T}$he poet Robert Frost once wrote, "We dance round in a ring and suppose, But the Secret sits in the middle and knows."

Work to know stillness within your soul, despite the commotion of your world. Choose to sit in your "secret" center, while others "dance round in a ring and suppose." From your center, where the Spirit dwells, comes forth understanding. There you experience having the mind of Christ. There you experience your profound connection to the Creator and all of creation.

Living from your center means living one sacred moment at a time. And it means sustaining a stillness of spirit, even in the midst of chaos. Especially in the midst of chaos. If in the midst of chaos you can listen from your center, with understanding, before too long all the discordant noises around you will have blended into a symphony.

The next time you are in a very noisy place that is making you tense, allow the Spirit to transform your understanding. Sit or stand quietly in the midst of the commotion. Then, from your center, feel the pulse of the noise. Feel its rising and falling. Sense its pockets of rest. Forget yourself. Forget exactly where you are. Just relax into the sounds. Gradually, without your knowing how, the noise of the place will become a music all its own.

The Spirit helps me understand.

$\mathcal{D}ay$ 60 The Spirit strengthens me.

I pray that, according to the riches of his glory, he may grant that you may be strengthened in your inner being with power through his Spirit.

—*Ephesians 3:16*

$\mathcal{A}$ desperate father lifts a wrecked car off his injured daughter's body. A man with AIDS runs a marathon. A rape victim confronts her assailant from the witness stand. A man with terminal prostate cancer sees his cancer gradually disappear. An elderly woman drags her unconscious husband from their burning house. A crack addict kicks her habit. A man loses his job and his home, and somehow allows it to be the best thing that has ever happened to him.

Each of these persons exhibited remarkable spiritual strength. Drawing upon their inner resources, they performed difficult, even heroic, feats. The Spirit's strength was manifested through their bodies, their minds, their hearts. And just as it was available to them, so it is available to us all, always, and in all ways.

In what ways are you weak? Focus your thoughts. Where, specifically, are you in need of strength? Endurance? Bravery? Assurance? Trust? Compassion? Determination? Renewal?

Take time now to be in meditative prayer. Imagine that you are standing in front of massive wooden doors. You want to open them, but you are too weak. So you knock, and at once the doors begin to swing open, slowly. A brilliant light falls upon you. When your eyes have begun to adjust, you venture over the threshold. Once inside, you are amazed by what you see. The room is absolutely radiant, and so huge that the ceiling and walls are literally out of sight. And the room is *full*. Everywhere are shelves stocked high, cupboards ready to burst, trunks filled to overflowing. The stockpiled goods are not *things*, exactly. You pass a box labeled "Courage for Children Having Nightmares," a chest marked "Wisdom for Divorce Proceedings," a file cabinet that reads "Inspiration for Painters Only." On and on it goes. Suddenly you realize where you are. No wonder there is no end to it! You are standing in the storehouse of God, and God's cupboards are never bare.

Wander through God's storehouse until you discover the specific strength you need. Take it gladly, and feel your weakness passing away. When finally you are ready to leave, rejoice that the massive wooden doors are never locked. Whenever you knock, they will always swing open. Whenever you ask, you will be welcomed in. Whenever you seek, you will find your treasure.

The Spirit strengthens me.

Day 61   **The Spirit blesses me.**

Now we have received not the spirit of the world, but the Spirit that is from God, so that we may understand the gifts bestowed on us by God.

—1 Corinthians 2:12

We are often told to count our blessings. But how often do we count the blessings of our blessings?

Once bestowed by the Spirit, a blessing grows beyond what it originally was. Like a baby bird that has pecked through its shell, it is nurtured by the Spirit until it can leave its nest and soar toward heaven. The blessing soars higher and higher, and its flight-path is radiant with the light of God.

On a sheet of paper, do the following exercise (as illustrated below). Draw a small circle. Write inside it one way that your life has been blessed by the Spirit. Next, draw a second, interlocking circle, and write in it how that first blessing led to another. Continue in this way for a third blessing, and a fourth, and so on. This series of interlocking circles represents the flight-path of your original blessing.

All blessings have flight-paths; each of them grows and soars beyond what it originally was. Celebrate this dynamic power of the Spirit, witnessed at work in and through your life.

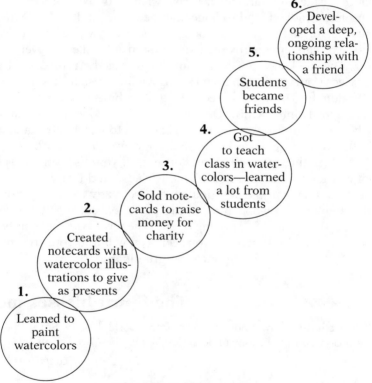

6. Developed a deep, ongoing relationship with a friend

5. Students became friends

4. Got to teach class in watercolors—learned a lot from students

3. Sold notecards to raise money for charity

2. Created notecards with watercolor illustrations to give as presents

1. Learned to paint watercolors

The Spirit blesses me.

Day 62   **I abide in the Spirit.**

So we have known and believe the love that God has for us. God is love, and those who abide in love abide in God, and God abides in them.

—1 John 4:16

*A*biding in the Spirit = Expressing *agape*.

This is the simple equation that this passage of scripture sets forth. However, as you well know, translating this equation into real-life terms is not quite so simple. Nevertheless, this is our daily task—and, ultimately, our only task—on the journey of faith.

There are many impediments to expressing *agape*. One of them is our own self-righteousness. When we are self-righteous, we criticize and even punish others for not living up to the rules (often unspoken) that we have established for them. These rules may take the form of expectations, of *wills* and *won'ts*; for example, "My husband *will* be happy when I tell him about my promotion," or "My friend *won't* say no when I ask her for help." Or, the rules may take the form of demands, of *shoulds* and *shouldn'ts*: "He *should* listen to me instead of watching television," or "She *shouldn't* talk to me that way."

When our expectations are disappointed or our demands are not met, we often seek to punish the offender. We roll our eyes, scold, shout, accuse, give the silent treatment, slam the phone down, run out of the house, quit, plot revenge. All of these punishments are forms of attack, and they usually lead to some form of counterattack. Then a vicious cycle begins.

According to Christ, there is only one rule: the rule of *agape*. Beginning today, work to discern where you are not allowing *agape* to govern your relationships. Take out a piece of paper and pencil. Describe in detail a recent quarrel, confrontation, or conflict. Next, jot down what you were thinking and feeling while the incident was happening. Be honest, and as thorough as possible. Now, analyze your thoughts and feelings. Did you have any unspoken expectations of the other person? Were any *wills*, *won'ts*, *shoulds*, or *shouldn'ts* operating? Realize that, even with the best of intentions, you might have allowed your judgment of what *ought to be* to cloud your understanding of what *was*. What might have happened if you had been able to step back, recognize what was going on in your head, and focus on *agape* instead of anger?

Whenever you feel angry, guilty, misunderstood, unappreciated, or *under attack in any way*, choose to abide in the Spirit. Step back from the situation. Carefully examine your thoughts and feelings. Determine if unspoken expectations are in operation. Ask if any demands are being made. Gain a fresh perspective on the situation—the perspective of *agape*.

I abide in the Spirit.

Day 63   **I am full of joy.**

"You have made known to me the ways of life; you will make me full of gladness with your presence."

*T*oday, feel the joy of God's presence. Sit in a comfortable position. Close your eyes. Release the tensions from your body and the worries from your mind. Relax your jaw, so that your mouth opens slightly. Feel your breath entering you, passing from you. Let your breathing be deep and easy.

Now sink into a deep awareness of God's presence within you. Feel its tender warmth. Feel its lightness, its fullness. Be glad in it. Then, when you are ready, begin to smile, not with your lips, necessarily, but with your soul. With your mind's eye imagine a radiant smile at your core, spreading out from your center. Let the joy of that smile saturate your entire being. Let no part of you escape it. Rest in it, until you are ready to proceed with your day.

This reservoir of joy is always within you. It is a tremendous gift of the Spirit. Be mindful of it. Draw upon it, anytime, anyplace. Whenever you feel the absence of joy, grow quiet and return to the radiant smile within you. God is never absent from your soul.

I am full of joy.

Day 64   **My joy in the Lord heals me.**

Heal me, O LORD, and I shall be healed; save me, and I shall be saved; for you are my praise.

—Jeremiah 17:14

*D*oes it take more of your energy to smile or to frown?

Frowning requires more muscles. Holding a frown for very long is tiring. It even feels unnatural. We were obviously meant to smile.

We were also meant to laugh. It is one of the most healing things we can do. Researchers in psychoneuroimmunology have discovered that when we laugh, our bodies produce and release large quantities of endorphins. These are natural painkillers, and they enhance our bodies' ability to fight disease.

If smiling and laughing are so good for us, then it is natural to assume that our spiritual journey should be filled with joy and celebration. So why do so many of us seem to think that faith requires one to be gloomy and serious? Perhaps we allow our religion to focus too much on the negative.

Try this little exercise. Intertwine your fingers and squeeze your hands together tightly, thinking of all the "thou shalt not's" that you have ever heard. Still clasping your hands, draw your elbows into your sides. Press them in hard as you remember all the negatives that you may have experienced in your religious life. At the same time, pull your chin down on your chest. Now scowl. Tighten up all of your facial muscles as you think of all the "must do's" of many people's faith.

Hold this position and try to shout, "Joy, Joy, Joy!" It is nearly impossible to do. Yet this is how many of us approach our spiritual journey. It is as though we expect the journey to be quite unpleasant, if not painful.

Now, begin to relax. Remember once again that you are not alone on your journey. God walks with you each step of the way, and God wants the very best for you, every moment of your life. Lift up your head. Smile! Unclasp your hands and hold them out in front of you with your palms upturned. Stand tall. Try that "Joy, Joy, Joy!" again. This time it will ring true. This time it will feel good. This is the feeling of wholeness that each of us longs for. This is the joy of healing.

My joy in the Lord heals me.

Day 65　　　　　# I am promised healing.

For I will restore health to you, and your wounds I will heal, says the LORD.

—Jeremiah 30:17a

*P*eg suffered from the extreme pain of arthritis. Many nights the pain was so intense that she couldn't sleep. She began to use those sleepless hours to create breathtaking pieces of liturgical art. All who saw her liturgical hangings on display in churches and galleries were inspired by their beautiful expressions of faith. Peg never found relief from her arthritis, but by accepting her disease she was able to transform her pain into gifts for others.

God promises that we will always find healing. Its form may be different from the one we want or expect. Like Peg, for example, we may not be relieved of the physical condition that afflicts us; instead, we may experience a sense of spiritual wholeness that comes with accepting our illness. Healing does not require the perfection of our bodies, but the perfection of our Christ-minds. In fact, we may experience our most important healing as our bodies die. When we understand that our physical journey is almost over and that we can peacefully release ourselves from our imperfect bodies, our sense of wholeness is complete.

Spend some time quietly reflecting on the hurts of the past and how you have grown because of them. Think of a specific time when you were able to find a sense of wholeness in the midst of pain. Rejoice in the healing that you have experienced— sometimes in surprising ways.

I am promised healing.

Day 66   **Healing is mine.**

Then they cried to the LORD in their trouble, and he saved them from their distress; he sent out his word and healed them, and delivered them from destruction.

—Psalm 107:19-20

*S*uppose that a young child comes to you and asks for your help. If you say, "Wait a minute," and then go on with what you are doing, the child will become impatient, even if the wait is only a short time. Why?

To an adult, a minute is a very insignificant amount of time. But a child who has spent only a couple of years on this earth will perceive it differently. A child's understanding of time is more immediate. Parents tend to forget this. "Don't be impatient," they may say, "it's just a few months until Christmas." But this statement makes little sense to a young child. A few months may represent a tenth of the child's life.

As a child's understanding of time is not the same as an adult's, so ours is not the same as God's. The psalmist tells us that a thousand years in our sight is like a day in God's (90:4). We must keep these different views of time in mind when we consider the healing process. When we ask for healing and it doesn't seem to be happening, we may be caught in our own limited perspective.

God has promised to make us whole—but healing may not happen exactly when we want it to. Learning to be patient and accepting the time-frame that God has in mind is not always easy. As we wait, it helps if we try to remember how God has brought healing to our lives in the past. Where we are today is just another place on our life's journey toward wholeness.

Locate several photographs of you taken at different ages, going back as far in your life as you can. Lay them out in order, from the earliest to the most recent. Review your physical growth. Think also about how your understandings and abilities have changed over the years, even during the most difficult times. How have you grown stronger spiritually? Give thanks to God that your life is always moving toward wholeness.

Healing is mine.

Day 67   **My healing brings peace.**

Peace, peace, to the far and the near, says the LORD; and I will heal them.
—*Isaiah 57:19*

*A*ccording to the germ theory, sickness is caused by small particles, invisible to the naked eye, which can pass from one person to another. We spread illness by sharing these contagious germs with one another.

Could it be that healing, too, can be contagious? Could it be that when one person experiences healing of some sort, other people also benefit?

None of us is separate and unto ourselves. So, when one of us is restored to wholeness, the potential for all of us to heal is increased, and peace results. Truly, then, there is "peace, peace, to the far and near." Healing begins with us, and the peace created by our healing can reach far, far beyond us.

Suppose that you have a big argument with your spouse at breakfast. Once you are at work, you can't keep your mind on what you are doing. You snap at your co-workers, who are soon either snapping back at you or staying out of your way. You make one mistake after another. Finally, ready to explode, you pull a friend aside and ask if you can talk about your troubles. Your friend listens to you vent your frustration without interrupting or passing judgment. Soon you are feeling better. You let go of your anger and hurt. You return to your work with a clear head. The atmosphere around you improves dramatically. The work gets done in good shape. And when you go home at the end of the day, you and your spouse are able to resolve your dispute calmly. So, the healing of your emotional pain, which required only a few minutes with a wise friend, "infected" those who came in touch with you with peace, just as your "sickness" had "infected" them with discord.

Today's exercise requires great mindfulness. Throughout the day, wherever you go and whatever you do, sense when you are becoming tense or upset. See these as signs that you need some form of healing. Take time for healing. Take time to release your thoughts and feelings about whatever has wounded or infected you with "dis-ease." Release them appropriately, in such a way that peace will result. You might talk to a friend. You might close your eyes, breathe slowly and deeply, and relax your body. You might take a long walk. Whatever strategies you use, open yourself to healing, and feel the peace that comes to the near and far!

My healing brings peace.

Day 68   **I remember my healing.**

Yet it was I who taught Ephraim to walk, I took them up in my arms; but they did not know that I healed them.

—Hosea 11:3

*C*an you remember learning to ride a bicycle? Do you remember how difficult it was to balance yourself, steer, and pedal at the same time? Once you caught on, though, riding that bike was great fun. And today, while you may not have ridden a bicycle for years, you would still know how to ride one. What a wonderful gift is the gift of memory!

The gift of memory is one of God's greatest gifts. As the years pass, we gather many kinds of knowledge that we need for daily living. Without the gift of memory, we would have to spend our days relearning the lessons that we had learned the day before. With it, however, we are able to go on to a lifetime of new learnings.

This gift can reassure and empower us. When we remember difficult times in the past and how we found the strength to face them, we realize that we will also be able to face the challenges of today. God's healing power, always so generously provided to us in times of trial, will continue to be available. If the words of a favorite hymn once got us through a crisis, repeating them today will strengthen us. If a certain place was a favorite haven during moments of deep distress, going there today will soothe us. Even if we cannot physically go back, we can return there in our minds and discover that its well still has healing waters. Such is the powerful gift of memory.

Do an inventory of your life's healing moments—those times when the strength that you needed was given to you. Jot down what the situation was and how healing came. Rejoice in your remembrances, and know the God that heals you!

I remember my healing.

Day 69   My healing strengthens me.

Therefore lift your drooping hands and strengthen your weak knees, and make straight paths for your feet, so that what is lame may not be put out of joint, but rather be healed.

—*Hebrews 12:12-13*

*N*o one in the congregation noticed what the minister did just before he stood up to preach the sermon. He touched the ring on his little finger, just like he did every Sunday, at just this point in the service. Touching the ring was a gesture he repeated whenever he felt uncertain or insecure. The ring had been a gift from his mentor in the ministry. It had great sentimental value, but, more than that, it had great spiritual value. Each time he touched it, he felt a strong sense of power rise up within him. It was as though that gesture called forth all the God-given strength and wisdom he had ever received from his mentor.

Decide on a gesture of your own which you can easily repeat without other people noticing. The gesture may be as simple as touching a ring, placing your hand over your heart, or stroking your hair. Do it a couple of times. Now, remember a difficult time when God gave you the spiritual power and wisdom that you needed. Reliving that experience of success, allow your positive feelings to grow. When they are especially strong, very deliberately do the gesture that you have selected. In this way you connect the gesture with the feelings inside you. Now, think of another time when you felt capable of handling a difficult situation. Once again, get in touch with your feelings of strength and repeat your gesture. Remember additional times when God "lifted your drooping hands and strengthened your weak knees," repeating your gesture each time your feelings swell. After some practice, your gesture will instantly connect you—through the gift of memory—to God's power within you.

God is faithful. The same God who has given you strength in the past is with you today. God will never leave your side nor forsake you in a moment of need. This is a promise that God has made. You can count on it. When you feel discouraged or weak, when you are uncertain that you can continue in the struggle, repeat your gesture of power. Allow it to remind you of all the times that God has given you a sense of wholeness by supplying all that you needed.

My healing strengthens me.

Day 70   I flourish.

The LORD will guide you continually, and satisfy your needs in parched places, and make your bones strong; and you shall be like a watered garden, like a spring of water, whose waters never fail.

—Isaiah 58:11

Have you ever stood at the top of Niagara Falls—or any waterfall—and watched the endless tumbling of the water? What a magnificent display of the strength of the Creator! Have you ever wondered where all that water comes from? Or how it can continue to flow day after day, month after month, and year after year? There is no end to it.

So it is with the gift of God's healing in our lives. God always gives us what we need in abundance. If we allow ourselves to really think about this, we will be astounded. So few things in life are unlimited that we have a difficult time imagining God's unlimited power to heal. But we don't have to imagine it. We can—and do—experience it. God's gift of healing makes us whole. To receive it, we only need to open ourselves to God's love. Whenever we lift our cups to the Lord, they are filled to overflowing.

Turn on a water faucet. Fully open the tap. For a few moments, just stand and watch the water flow out. Imagine that it is the love of God pouring out into your life. Since it comes from the Source of all that is good, it has no end. Now, put your hands under the water. Feel the force of it rushing over your hands. Then try to stop its flow with your hands. What happens?

You cannot stop the healing love that God sends you unless

you choose to turn off the tap. Choose, instead, to open your spirit and flourish.

I flourish.

Day 71   **I am visited by God.**

In the sixth month the angel Gabriel was sent by God to a town in Galilee called Nazareth, to a virgin engaged to a man whose name was Joseph, of the house of David. The virgin's name was Mary. And he came to her and said, "Greetings, favored one! The Lord is with you."

—Luke 1:26-28

In this very dramatic passage of scripture, Mary receives a message from God. Greeting her, the angel reminds her of a fact that she should already know, but which she is now going to experience in a most profound way. "The Lord," Gabriel announces, "is with you!"

Like Mary, we are constantly sent reminders that God is with us. We may know this in our minds, but sometimes we forget it in our hearts. The reminders or "visitations" that we receive may be more or less dramatic, but each can have a powerful effect if we choose to pay attention.

God's visitations take various forms. You may receive divine guidance during prayer. You may have an especially revealing dream. You may be inspired by a delightful day spent in nature, an insightful book, a meaningful encounter with a stranger, a timely phone call from a friend. You may hear a comforting voice when no one is near, or see a vision, or sense a strong, reassuring presence in the midst of despair. However the reminders come, you can trust God to get your attention in the ways and at the times that will be most helpful to you.

Make a list of visitations that you have experienced, or describe one of them in detail. If you aren't sure that an incident actually *was* a visitation, don't dismiss it. No incident can be too insignificant or too commonplace to be a reminder of the divine; there is no drama meter or rating scale that measures such occurrences. All of them are important.

Throughout your day, be mindful. How is God communicating with you? What is God trying to tell you? Remind yourself, again and again:

I am visited by God.

Day 72   I welcome God's presence.

Then there appeared to [Zechariah] an angel of the Lord, standing at the right side of the altar of incense. When Zechariah saw him, he was terrified; and fear overwhelmed him. But the angel said to him, "Do not be afraid, Zechariah, for your prayer has been heard. Your wife Elizabeth will bear you a son, and you will name him John."

—Luke 1:11-13

Zechariah's experience of the divine presence teaches us that we don't have to fear divine visitations. Rather, we can welcome them as life-affirming, life-changing, even life-giving events. They always bring us the gospel—*good news*!

God's visitations are constant. Our awareness of them, however, is not. Let us be more attentive. Even when life is most difficult, when we are tempted to curl up behind some closed door and never come out again, let us find the courage to say, "Okay, God, where are you? My life's a mess, so if you come, you should really be conspicuous!" It is precisely when we are in the pits or in a rut or feeling stuck or feeling down that we may be most receptive to God's good news.

Spend some time in quiet reflection. Where are you in need of good news right now? Identify one area of your life that you need to have affirmed, changed, or revitalized. Acknowledge your need to God, being very specific. Express your trust that God will visit you in a life-affirming, life-changing, or life-giving way. Finally, state your intention to watch continually for God's visitations until you receive the good news you need.

I welcome God's presence.

Day 73   I sense God's presence.

A spirit glided past my face; the hair of my flesh bristled. It stood still, but I could not discern its appearance. A form was before my eyes; there was silence, then I heard a voice.

—Job 4:15-16

The cliché is true: God *does* move in mysterious ways. And, if you are open to God's presence, if you truly welcome divine visitations with all your body, mind, and soul, you will begin to more profoundly experience those mysterious ways. God will come, and you will suddenly see something that is, yet is not, there. God will come, and you will suddenly hear something that can, yet cannot, be heard.

Such mysterious experiences will sometimes lead you to doubt yourself. You will doubt your senses. You will doubt your hunches. The doubt may stem from your inability to account for what happened to you. After all, we live in a society where the unexplainable is generally regarded as unbelievable. So when we experience God's presence in a particularly strange, indescribable way, we tuck the memory of it away, deep down inside, and rarely if ever bring it out into the light of day.

Yet trying to describe such experiences can be an important part of accepting them as real, and of recognizing that they are just God's way of doing things. So today, enter into a conversation with a trusted mentor, friend, or family member. Begin by sharing with each other responses to these questions:

In what different ways do you sense God's presence?
Have you experienced God in ways that you are afraid to talk about?
Why are you afraid? Or, if you aren't afraid, can you imagine why some people might be?
What does fear imply about God?
Have you ever witnessed a miracle?
Have you ever seen a spirit or an angel?
Have you ever heard the voice of God?
Do you want to sense God's presence in ever new and more mysterious ways?

As you share your experiences of the divine presence with someone you trust, you will create a "safe place" where together you may celebrate the mysteries of God's movement in your lives. Let this be only a beginning.

I sense God's presence.

Day 74 I stand at the gate of heaven.

Then Jacob woke from his sleep and said, "Surely the LORD is in this place—and I did not know it!" And he was afraid, and said, "How awesome is this place! This is none other than the house of God, and this is the gate of heaven."

—Genesis 28:16-17

*H*ere Jacob "wakes up" from his normal way of seeing the world—and also, therefore, from his normal way of living in it. He awakens to the knowledge that the world is the very dwelling place of God, and his response is one of awe. It is easy to understand why. Just imagine for a moment that for your entire life, you have lived in only one house. And one morning you roll out of bed and go downstairs to find a stranger sitting at your table, eating a bowl of cereal, drinking coffee, and reading the paper.

"What are you doing here?" you demand to know, astounded.

The stranger gestures toward a chair and invites you to sit down, calling you by name. "I'm eating breakfast," the stranger says, continuing to eat, "like I do every morning. Why do you ask?"

"But you don't live here."

"Of course I live here. I've been living here since long before you were born. It's just that you've never noticed."

Such a discovery would shake you up a bit, wouldn't it? And that is what Jacob learned: his world was actually God's house. Somehow he had never noticed. But now he knew that wherever he stood was the gate of heaven—the place where the ordinary ends and mystery begins.

Take time today to return to a place, or to discover a place, that inspires you with awe. (If you can't actually go, visit the place in your imagination.) Perhaps it is the quiet sanctuary of a church, where all you hear is the bubbling of water in the baptismal font. Perhaps it is an ancient burial mound which, built by a prehistoric culture, still survives in the shadow of skyscrapers. Perhaps it is the very top floor of one of those skyscrapers, from where the city looks unfamiliar, though you have lived in it for years. Or perhaps it is in the plot of grass that you recently transformed into a garden, where you are amazed by the wonder and beauty of growing things.

Wherever you go, experience the power of the place. Take in its richness with all your senses. Then begin to ask yourself, "Why is this place different from other places? Why does it fill me with awe?" Know that you can sustain the feelings you have in such a place after you leave it. Visit it in your imagination whenever you want to be lifted above the commotion of your life. It is one of the gates of heaven.

I stand at the gate of heaven.

Day 75   **God knows me.**

O LORD, you have searched me and known me. You know when I sit down and when I rise up; you discern my thoughts from far away. You search out my path and my lying down, and are acquainted with all my ways.

—Psalm 139:1-3

*T*he psalmist writes of a God who knows all of your thoughts, feelings, strengths, weaknesses, successes, failures, habits, whims, regrets and dreams—and whose love for you is not limited by any of them. God is a Friend whose love is perfect. This Friend is Love itself.

You have probably experienced the joy of being perfectly loved by another person, if only for a brief time. It is a privilege to have a friend who cares without conditions, without strings; a friend who cares about you simply because he or she does, and cannot do otherwise. Such a friend is a reminder of the Friend we have in God.

How would you describe the perfect friend? What qualities would the perfect friend have? How would the perfect friend treat you?

Try to describe your vision of the perfect friend in several sentences. Then magnify your vision a hundred times, a thousand times. Still it does not begin to resemble your Friend who is God. Though knowing everything about you, this Friend never abandons you. This Friend never holds you in contempt. This Friend never betrays you. You are truly, remarkably, perfectly loved.

God knows me.

Day 76   **God lives in me.**

Those who have been born of God do not sin, because God's seed abides in them; they cannot sin, because they have been born of God.

—1 John 3:9

*C*an a seed sin?

The question probably strikes you as absurd. But think about it. . . . A seed knows only one way to grow—the right way. No matter how you plant it, it will always sprout *up*, toward the light of the sun, and its roots will always go *down*, toward the nutrients in the soil. A seed always grows in the proper direction because it carries within itself a God-given knowledge of what it is and what it needs. So, the answer is "No." A seed cannot sin.

So it is with all in whom God lives. Just as a tender seed sprouts forth and grows until it blossoms, our spirits, too, unfold. The God who lives within us causes our spirits to take root in the soil of forgiveness. As they stretch toward the light, their beautiful petals slowly open, preserved by grace.

Find a place where you can spend some moments in quiet reflection. Relax your muscles, let your mind be at peace, and allow your body to "settle in." Close your eyes.

Now picture a field of sunflowers in front of you, bathed in the light of dawn. The sunflowers stand tall in straight rows. See the green of their stems. Notice the deep yellow of their flowers. As the sun rises higher, progressing slowly across the sky from east to west, watch what happens. The heads of the sunflowers move, too, so that they are always facing the sun. They tilt back to absorb its warmth and energy. Turning toward the light is in the sunflower's nature.

Turning toward the light is also in our nature. We are no less directed toward God than the sunflowers are toward the sun. The God who lives in us helps us grow toward the God in whom we live.

God lives in me.

Day 77   ## I am holy.

For it is written, "You shall be holy, for I am holy."

—*1 Peter 1:16*

*S*ay the word *holy* very slowly. Does it sound like another word?

To understand that you are holy, it is helpful to understand *wholly*. Why? When you see yourself as holy, you recognize that you are wholly—entirely—God's. You have no life apart from God; God is the starting point and destination of your journey, as well as your companion all along the way. Furthermore, when you see yourself as holy, you recognize that you are *whole*. Your spirit is not missing any pieces and is not divided into parts. It rests, well and good, in the Spirit of God.

Take out a sheet of paper (preferably construction paper), scissors, and a marker or pen. Let the paper represent the Spirit that gives you life. Now, cut the paper into at least a dozen differently-shaped puzzle pieces. Scramble the pieces, *being very careful not to flip them over*, then write on each of them a role that you play (for example, "supervisor," "parent"), a skill that you have ("musician," "carpenter"), or an admirable quality that you possess ("hardworking," "creative"). After you have identified each piece, put the puzzle of yourself back together, reminding yourself that every part of you is holy.

Once you have assembled your puzzle, sit back and reflect on it for a few minutes. Celebrate that all of the many pieces of your self mysteriously fit together in one complete picture. You have no gaps. You have no missing pieces. You are, indeed, a holy child of God.

I am holy.

Day 78   **I pray for peace.**

First of all, then, I urge that supplications, prayers, intercessions, and thanksgivings be made for everyone, for kings and all who are in high positions, so that we may lead a quiet and peaceable life in all godliness and dignity.

—1 Timothy 2:1-2

*P*eace is what we want. Inner peace. We want to rest in the knowledge that we are whole, just as God created us to be. We want to feel valuable, to understand that our lives are significant. We want to see God's plan for our lives and follow it. So, we pray for inner peace.

Peace is what we want. Peace with others. We invite the people around us to seek the path that leads to reconciliation. We challenge ourselves to let go of our demands and hold onto our dreams. Together all of us will find a way to live in harmony. So, we pray for peace with others.

Peace is what we want. Peace in a world troubled with wars and rumors of wars. One nation battles against another. One people hates another. God's children destroy one another. We long for the day when the world will be a place of peace with justice for all. We long for the time when all the false barriers that divide us will be removed. The peoples of the world are one people. God's people. So, we pray for peace in the world.

Create a simple affirmation that expresses your deep desire for peace. It might be as brief as "Let there be peace," or "Bring peace, O God," or "Thank you for the peace you give me." Next, list the areas of your personal life where you feel there is a sense of brokenness or discord. Add to the list those areas of your community life (work, school, neighborhood, church, and so on) where tensions exist. Finally, complete the list with specific happenings on the world scene that bother you.

Read the items on your list aloud, repeating after each the affirmation that you have created. Repeat your affirmation with confidence! Be bold in asking for peace and in believing that God will grant it.

Throughout this week, whenever you feel a touch of fear, a bit of anxiety, or a little worry, repeat your affirmation. Allow your life experiences to become a living prayer of peace.

I pray for peace.

Day 79   God is peace.

For God is a God not of disorder but of peace.

—1 Corinthians 14:33

In order for preschoolers to feel comfortable, limits must be set on their environment and behavior. Otherwise, they feel very insecure. If, for example, they are placed in a playground whose boundary is not well-defined, as with a fence, they will feel frightened. Putting up a fence will put them at ease. It will make clear to them where they are supposed to stay, and this certainty will give them confidence.

We adults also prefer to have things reasonably well-defined. For example, we want to know that the universe is orderly, and that the laws of nature by which it operates will not suddenly change. Without being able to depend on this, we would not be able to function. What if the law of gravity suddenly began to operate randomly? How would we ever know when or where we would be safe? To say the least, it is reassuring to know that the laws of nature give some predictability to our world.

Each of us also takes comfort in defining appropriate and inappropriate behaviors for ourselves. We set limits on our own behaviors not so that we can say we are "right" or "wrong," but so that we can have peace instead of chaos. These limits have to be reexamined and even changed from time to time, but having them helps us to bring order to our lives. This order creates a sense of peace. This peace is God.

The following exercise is a simple yet powerful demonstration of the peace that comes from having appropriate limits. Hold a pitcher of water (representing life) above a counter top. Slowly pour out the water. As it spreads across the counter with nothing to limit its movement, do you feel a growing anxiety?

Now, take out any container. Let it represent the appropriate limits that you define for your life. Your container might be smaller or bigger than someone else's container, depending, for example, on how willing you are to take risks.

Set the container on the counter top. Slowly pour water into it. As the water predictably fills it, notice that you feel much more relaxed than you did when watching the water spread across the counter. You feel relaxed, that is, unless the water starts getting close to the rim of the container. If you begin to sense that you might "go too far" and spill the water, stop pouring.

With God's help we can discern what limits are appropriate to our lives. If we respect those limits, we will be filled with an ever-deepening sense of peace. This is the peace that is God.

God is peace.

Day 80   **God gives me peace.**

Now may the Lord of peace himself give you peace at all times in all ways.

—2 Thessalonians 3:16a

The scriptures remind us that all good gifts come to us from God (James 1:17). If we were to try to list all the good things that God sends our way, we would find it impossible. Yet, in the process of trying to count our blessings, we would be made more aware of the great bounty that we have received. Such an awareness fills us with peace.

To be constantly aware of God's blessings is a challenge. But the challenge is made easier if we understand that God is as near to us as our breath. Enter into an attitude of prayer. Sit or lie down in a comfortable spot away from distractions. Slowly relax every muscle of your body. Allow all stress and tension to leave you.

Now, focus your attention on your breathing. As you inhale, imagine that the air that you take in is filled not only with life-giving oxygen but also with the goodness of God. As you exhale, imagine that the air you breathe out takes with it not only the carbon dioxide that your body no longer needs but all the stress and anxiety of your life. Breathe in, breathe out. Inhale the goodness of God and exhale the negatives of your life. Feel a deep sense of peace coming over you.

Whenever you feel the slightest bit of stress or tension today, take a few slow, deep breaths. Inhale the good, exhale the bad. Feel your body relax. Remind yourself of this blessing:

God gives me peace.

$\mathcal{D}ay$ 81 **Peace is mine in abundance.**

May grace and peace be yours in abundance.

—*1 Peter 1:2*b

$\mathcal{T}$he Bible is filled with conflicts. But it is also filled with the resolution of conflicts. Time after time, God leads people through incredibly difficult situations and brings them to peaceful ends. For example, in the Old Testament we read about the boy Joseph. He was something else! First he accepted a special robe from his father—one that meant he did not have to work like his brothers. Then he began telling his family about his dreams, in which his brothers were bowing down and worshipping him. No wonder his brothers sold him into slavery! But years later God was able to resolve the conflict between Joseph and his brothers in a way that helped the entire family. Joseph had risen from slavery in Egypt to a position of authority in the government, where he was able to help his family through a famine. He forgave his brothers when they sought his assistance, gave them what they needed, and eventually was reunited with all his relatives. So, what had once seemed like an impossible situation of conflict ended in peace.

In the New Testament we read about Saul, who later became Paul. He was something else, too! He was out to persecute and destroy the followers of Jesus. But then he saw the light! When his eyes were opened to the truth of who Jesus really was, his life turned around. God transformed him into a great missionary. Again, what had once seemed like an impossible situation of conflict ended in peace.

Today God is still working to bring peace to the world, even when peace seems to be totally impossible. Peace is God's in abundance. And it is ours. God will give us all the peace that we need.

Enter into meditative prayer. Find your comfortable spot and center yourself in the divine presence. As you become relaxed, stretch your hands out in front of you. Clench them as if you are holding onto all the conflicts and difficulties of your past. Now, open them and let go of the conflicts. Turn them over so that your palms are face-up. Imagine that you are waiting to receive all the gifts that God wants to give you. Now, picture God placing the gift of peace in your hands. As you look at it, it begins to grow. It grows and grows, but it doesn't become heavy. Celebrate the immensity of this peace, and know that it is freely bestowed by the One who created you.

Peace is mine in abundance.

Day 82   I rest in God's peace.

I will both lie down and sleep in peace; for you alone, O LORD, make me lie down in safety.

—*Psalm 4:8*

*W*hen you rock a child to sleep, you truly bless her. As you hold her in your warm, comforting arms, she senses that she is surrounded by your love, and that she cannot be harmed. In some strange way, you share in the peace she feels. As you sit together, rocking, your spirits find a common rest.

Just as you bless the child you rock to sleep, you are blessed by the God whose arms tenderly enfold you. You are surrounded by divine love and cannot be harmed. In God's presence, you find your rest.

When Jesus was about to complete his earthly ministry and return to God, he was concerned about those whom he loved and would be leaving behind. He knew that they would be anxious and fearful in the face of all that was about to happen. So, he promised to send the Comforter to them when he was gone, to wrap them in divine love and reassure them that they would never be alone. This same Comforter is sent to us. As we are wrapped in its folds, we are filled with peace. The Comforter reminds us of the arms of God that will embrace us forever.

Find a warm, soft blanket. Imagine that this blanket is the Comforter of God. Wrap yourself tightly in it. Feel how it surrounds you. Know that you are safe and secure. In an attitude of prayer, give thanks to God for the peace that comes to you through the presence of the Spirit. And if today you experience moments of fear or distress, wrap your arms around yourself and imagine that you are being comforted by the arms of God.

I rest in God's peace.

Day 83   # I am a peacemaker.

"Blessed are the peacemakers, for they will be called children of God."

—Matthew 5:9

A church in a small town had experienced many years of decreasing attendance and involvement. Trying to decide whether or not to close its doors, the congregation called in a consultant. When the consultant arrived, he went into the sanctuary and was immediately aware of a spiritual presence. The presence was positive. And it was powerful. The sanctuary felt as though it were filled with the joy from all the wonderful worship experiences that had ever been held within its walls. The consultant therefore advised the church to keep its doors open. He also suggested that the congregation shift its focus away from the gloom of the present to celebrate its vitality in the past. So, the members began to recall with satisfaction and joy many of the good things that had happened to the church in its long history. Favorite traditions that had died out were eventually restored. And gradually the congregation began to grow.

The catalyst in this church's revitalization was the consultant's being able to sense the true "spirit of the place." It was a spirit of joy and peace. But the spirit of a place is not always positive, is it? At some time you may have walked into an empty room and immediately sensed that something troubling had just happened in it. Or, you may have entered a friend's house and immediately sensed that something was wrong. Or, you may have gone to work and immediately sensed that you were in big trouble.

Like physical spaces, each of us carries with us either an air of peace or an air of conflict. This "air" is determined by our intention, which speaks louder than any words we might say. In any given situation, either we intend to promote peace, or we intend to thwart it. So, if we *want* to be peacemakers, we *will* be.

Set your intention on promoting peace today. *Live* peace, in whatever setting you find yourself. Do positive things for others, and an air of peace will surround you.

I am a peacemaker.

Day 84   **Peace endures.**

For the mountains may depart and the hills be removed, but my stead-fast love shall not depart from you, and my covenant of peace shall not be removed, says the LORD, who has compassion on you.

—Isaiah 54:10

$\mathcal{G}$reg and Tom had known each other for a long time. Back in third grade, they had declared themselves "blood brothers." In middle school, everyone had rightly called them "best friends." Now it was time for high school graduation, and with it would come the inevitable separation as the two of them moved on to different colleges and careers. The future of their friendship seemed bleak. Both boys were afraid that it would not survive across the miles and the years that were about to come between them. They sensed that their goodbyes might really mean *good-bye.* As graduation approached and their apprehension grew, they started to argue. Then they began to avoid each other. "Oh well," each seemed to be thinking, "nothing lasts forever."

Or does it?

After the graduation ceremony, Greg and Tom reconciled. They promised to stay in touch with each other, no matter what. Somehow they would keep their relationship alive. Years later, not only has their friendship survived, it has grown stronger.

These friends truly loved each other. Their relationship was powerful enough to cast out their fear about the future. When fear ceased to exist, peace rose up in its place, and that peace has endured. So it is with the love and peace of God.

All of us search for peace. Sometimes we search for it in the acquisition of possessions, only to find that even the greatest material prosperity leaves us feeling empty. And so we eventually grow restless. If we become wiser on our journey, we gradually shift our attention from the things of the world to the things of the spirit. We lose our attachment to our possessions and claim for ourselves the spiritual treasures that have lasting value. These are the things that endure. Greg and Tom learned early on just how valuable these things can be.

See if you can find a rock large enough for you to stand on. (If you can't, locate a place that represents security and permanence to you.) Stand there and remind yourself that nothing can shake the solid foundation upon which you stand. That foundation is the God who promises you a peace that will endure forever.

Peace endures.

Day 85 — Time is meaningless.

That which is, already has been.

—*Ecclesiastes 3:15*a

*H*ave you ever experienced *déjà vu*, the feeling that you are in a place where you have already been, doing what you have already done, but there is no way in the world that could possibly be? If so, you know how fuzzy our perception of time can be. The fuzziness isn't necessarily comfortable. When we are suddenly thrust into miracle-time—where past, present, and future are all rolled together into one—we don't always know what to make of it.

Most of us would prefer that time be precise and predictable. Then we can decide just what to do with it. Just think of how we talk about time. We *have* time, *lose* time, *gain* time, *pass* time, *take* time, *waste* time, *spend* time, *save* time, *appoint* time, *manage* time, *arrange* time, *improve* time, *change* time, *consume* time, *kill* time, *make* time, *use* time. We have truly set ourselves up as the great custodians of yesterday, today, and tomorrow.

But *déjà vu*, like today's scripture passage, reminds us that "time," as we know it, is ultimately meaningless. "Yesterday," "today," and "tomorrow" are our own creations, real only in human terms. God's time is not divided into past, present, and future. Instead, God's time is the "Eternal Now," as it was called by theologian Paul Tillich. It is a time beyond time, and therefore beyond description. It is this moment, in which all things are fully present, all at once—all things that ever were, and are, and ever shall be.

Try to capture a thought as it flits through your mind. Notice that even as you do, the thought is already past. You have not really captured anything but its shadow. And in the meantime you have split your mind between what was and what is.

This is the same thing that happens whenever you invest time with too much meaning. You split yourself. While part of your mind tries to focus on the present, other parts are still worrying about the past or starting to worry about the future. Yet it is only when you can keep yourself centered in the present that you can become more fully open to the joy of God's Eternal Now. To rejoice in the Eternal Now is to have the mind of Christ.

Whenever you catch yourself worrying about time, thinking that you have too little or too much of it, that it's going too fast or not fast enough—remember that you can look at things differently. Forget about time. Stay in the present. Think only of *now*. Remind yourself, over and over, that ultimately:

Time is meaningless.

Day 86 Things are not as they seem.

And the one who was seated on the throne said, "See, I am making all things new." Also he said, "Write this, for these words are trustworthy and true."

—Revelation 21:5

*W*hat is your corner of the world like? Do you see a great gap between the wealthy and the poor? Is there violence? Obscenity? Conflict? Abuse of power? Alcoholism? Broken families? Barrenness? Look, too, within your heart. Do you see hopelessness? Jealousy? Anger? Resentment? Sorrow? Longing?

It may seem so. But our God is a God of transformation, continuously at work. This is the promise that God has made us: "I will make all things new." Make things new *now*, not on some far-off day. To God, there is no such thing as a "far-off day." To God, time is meaningless. The future is now. God's wonder-working, life-transforming work is happening *now*.

Look at the picture below. Can you make sense of it? If not, hold the book level with your eyes and look again.

Answer: GOD IS HERE!

As you can see, things are not always as they seem. The meaningless chaos around us is not so chaotic as it appears. God is in the midst of it, bringing forth abundant life, tenderly, expertly. The divine presence is continually at work, but to see it we must focus on the things that reveal it rather than the things that obscure it.

Things are not as they seem.

Day 87   **All things are possible.**

Jesus looked at [his disciples] and said, "For mortals it is impossible, but not for God; for God all things are possible."

—*Mark 10:27*

    Pessimism: expecting the worst.
    Optimism: expecting the best.
      Realism: insisting on the need to face facts and be practical rather than visionary.
    Idealism: basing actions and thoughts on a belief about how the world ought to be.
    Cynicism: thinking that life has little value or meaning.

*H*aving read the scripture text and the definitions above, write responses to these questions:

(1) On a scale of 1 to 10, how (a) pessimistic, (b) optimistic, (c) realistic, (d) idealistic, and (e) cynical are you? Consider the results. Which would you regard as your basic life stance?
(2) Now, on the same rating scale, indicate how you imagine God to be for each item. Reflect on the results.
(3) Indicate how Jesus would have rated himself for each item. Compare the results to those in (1). What do you find?
(4) Do you believe that all things are possible? How does the way you live express your belief or disbelief?

"For God all things are possible." This is what Jesus taught his disciples. He was an eternal optimist and a radical idealist. And the mind that was in him is growing within you. Dare yourself to have a little more faith, a little more hope. Whenever you are in a difficult situation, silently say the words *all things are possible*. It is a very simple phrase, but it can quickly change your perspective.

All things are possible.

Day 88   **God delivers me from danger.**

"He delivers and rescues, he works signs and wonders in heaven and on earth; for he has saved Daniel from the power of the lions."

—*Daniel 6:27*

$\mathcal{G}$od did not rescue Daniel by killing the lions but by taming them. God can work the same miracle for you. What are your lions? What makes you feel trapped, with no way out? What makes you feel afraid? Intimidated? Hopeless? Would you like to have your lions tamed?

Choose one of your lions to subdue, with God's help. Your lion may be a longstanding phobia: of the dark, of heights, of spiders, of strangers. It may be a self-esteem issue: fear of being seen in a swimsuit, of showing your emotions, of being caught without your make-up on, of asking someone out on a date. It may be something that you have always wanted to do but were afraid to risk: skydiving, taking a vacation by yourself, falling in love, dancing, changing careers. Or, it may be a more tangible problem: surgery to be faced, a financial crisis, a cross-country move, a parent-child dispute, a spouse's alcoholism.

How might this lion be subdued? One suggestion that you might find helpful is to turn around and face it. Eye to eye. If you are afraid of the dark, go to a dark place and stay there awhile, asking God for courage. If you are afraid of showing your emotions, force yourself to share your feelings with a trusted friend or family member, asking God for courage. If you are afraid of changing careers, seriously entertain the possibility of doing so, asking God for courage. If you are afraid of your spouse's alcoholism, consider confronting it in an intervention, asking God for courage.

After you have decided on a strategy for taming your lion, talk to someone who might give you encouragement and further suggestions. Then ask her to check in on you now and then to find out how you are doing.

Have no doubt that God can deliver you from this, and every, lion. God has promised you this miracle. Accept your deliverance.

God delivers me from danger.

$\mathcal{D}ay$ *89*   God gives far more than I ask.

"But strive first for the kingdom of God and his righteousness, and all these things will be given to you as well."

—*Matthew 6:33*

$\mathcal{I}$magine that for your entire life, you have been bumbling about in a world that is as dark as night. Then one day, after running into a wall for the seventh time since breakfast, you suddenly realize that you have grown tired of it. Surely there must be more to life. "If only I had something to see by," you lament, rubbing your forehead. But there is nothing you can do but go on stumbling and fumbling about, until on another day you happen to stub your toe on something. For some reason, you reach down and grope around on the ground, and lo and behold, you find a candle.

Now you have in your possession what you had asked for: a little light to see by. But you also have much more. Your candle gives off a little heat, and a beautiful scent that you have never smelled before. When you set it on your windowsill, it invites visitors to your door. When you feel romantic, it creates an intimate mood. And, maybe best of all, it can be used to light hearth-fires, your own and your neighbor's too. Truly you have far more than you ever wanted.

This is the miracle of answered prayer. We ask for much less than we might, but somehow it doesn't matter. Ask for a little light, and God gives you a blaze of glory. Ask for a teacher, and God gives you a messiah. Ask for a place to live, and God gives you a kingdom. Ask for a kingdom, and God gives you the universe.

Yesterday you identified a lion that, with the help of God, you would begin to subdue. But sometimes lions can't be tamed all at once. Sometimes you have to be patient and tame them little by little. Think again about your lion. What one small, manageable step might you take today to further subdue it? Enter into prayer, asking God to help you take that step. As you do, know that God will respond by giving far more than you ask.

God gives far more than I ask.

Day 90   **God does the impossible.**

As they entered the tomb, they saw a young man, dressed in a white robe, sitting on the right side; and they were alarmed. But he said to them, "Do not be alarmed; you are looking for Jesus of Nazareth, who was crucified. He has been raised; he is not here. Look, there is the place they laid him."

—*Mark 16:5-6*

*W*e have entertained the notion that all things are possible. Today we push that idea further. If something seems *not* to be possible, it is because right now our minds are too small to conceive of it. How do we know that our minds are too small? *Because God goes ahead and does the "impossible" anyway.* God's miracles transform the world. God's work is not limited by the size of our imaginations. And so, it blows our minds. "Raise your expectations of me," God seems to be telling us as we stare in amazement at an empty tomb. "I am transforming the world! Change your perspective! Transform the way you think!"

Today's exercise celebrates the miracle of resurrection—not just the raising of Christ from the dead and the renewal of life, but the raising of our expectations and the renewal of our minds. Begin by reading or singing these verses from J. M. C. Crum's hymn "Now the Green Blade Riseth" (the tune is the same used for the Christmas carol "Sing We Now Noel"):

> Now the green blade riseth from the buried grain,
> Wheat that in dark earth many days has lain;
> Love lives again, that with the dead has been:
> Love is come again like wheat that springeth green.
>
> When our hearts are wintry, grieving, or in pain,
> Thy touch can call us back to life again,
> Fields of our hearts that dead and bare have been:
> Love is come again like wheat that springeth green.

Now identify the "dead and bare fields" in your life. Where have you been limiting your own growth? Where have you thought of making a change but then decided against it, saying, "I'm too old to change now," or "I'm not smart enough to do that," or "I can't afford it," or a million other excuses churned out by the "I-would-if-I-could-but-I-can't" mill?

Now, raise your expectations, not of yourself, but of what God can do through you. Allow your mind—and your life—to be renewed. Expand your ideas of what is possible. Remember:

God does the impossible.

Day 91   I expect miracles.

"For nothing will be impossible with God."

—*Luke 1:37*

*A*ll things are possible. Nothing is impossible. For God, everything in the world is the same. Everything is a miracle. You might say, then, that in the eyes of God—and in the mind of Christ—miracles are nothing out of the ordinary.

Unfortunately, our eyes are accustomed to seeing differently. They are used to keeping the ordinary and the miraculous distinct. So we must retrain them. We must teach them to see miracles where they are accustomed to seeing none.

When you were a child, did you ever go on a treasure hunt with some friends? An adult would hand each of you a grocery bag and a list of "treasures" that you were supposed to locate in your neighborhood: a piece of candy, a dandelion, a quarter-sized stone, an apple that had fallen from a tree, a neighbor's shoe. . . . Can you remember the excitement of the hunt? It didn't really matter what objects you were sent out to find; the joy was in the *looking*.

Go on a miracle hunt today. You don't have to go anywhere special. Just open your eyes and try to see your surroundings with the mind of Christ. Wondrous signs of God's creative presence are all around you. Look at a photograph of your niece, and recognize your deceased grandfather in her face. Listen to a musical recording that you love, and be amazed not only by the sound of it, but also by the technology that can somehow store it and play it back. Slice an apple sideways, separate the halves, and discover the star on the inside. Slowly curl your hand into a fist, then release it again; think of all the intricate connections of blood vessels, nerves, muscles, tendons, and ligaments that are working together to make that simple movement possible.

Expect miracles and you will behold them. Behold them and you will celebrate. The world is filled with spiritual treasures.

I expect miracles.

Day 92   **I expect to see the path.**

Stand at the crossroads, and look, and ask for the ancient paths, where the good way lies; and walk in it, and find rest for your souls.

—*Jeremiah 6:16*a

On a piece of paper, create a graph of your life. First, draw a time line across the middle. Label the left end "birth" and the right end "today." Now chart the most significant experiences of your life, putting the positive ones above the line and the painful below. Let the distance from the line indicate the intensity of your feelings. Draw a dotted line connecting these events. Next, chart a second set of highs and lows, only this time trace your spiritual development. Above the time line mark the times when you felt especially close to God (were growing spiritually). Below the time line indicate when you felt far from God. Connect these points with a solid line. Your graph will look something like this:

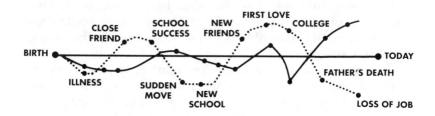

Reflect upon the two lines you have drawn. Where are they close together? Where far apart? Do you see a meaningful relationship between your experiences and your spiritual growth? What insights do you gain? Keep this graph of your life to use in later exercises.

Your spiritual growth—your inner path—is not dependent on your external circumstances but on your awareness of the closeness of God. Remain open to God's presence in your life, trusting that your path is unfolding as it should. Go through the day, confident that you will receive the guidance that you need. Say to yourself:

I expect to see the path.

Day 93 I see the path clearly.

Your word is a lamp to my feet and a light to my path.

—*Psalm 119:105*

*T*he path into the forest was clearly marked. Ruth began her journey with the anticipation of finding some spring wildflowers deep in the woods. She walked briskly, keeping her eyes intent on the ground. After a half-hour or so, she came across a beautiful patch of violets. She picked a large bouquet, then headed home. On the way, she met another woman. Excitement was written all over her face. "Did you see all the deer?" the woman asked. "I've counted thirty-seven so far." Ruth was surprised. She hadn't seen a single one, but then, she had not been looking for deer. Her eyes had been focused on the ground, searching for wildflowers.

Expectation helps to determine what you see. It is a light to your path that reveals what otherwise you might not see. If you walk through a forest hoping only to find wildflowers, it is likely that you will miss the deer. But if someone tells you before you set off on the path that this particular forest is full of deer, you will expect to see one. And chances are that you will not be disappointed. Your eyes will be attracted to the deer like to a lamp in the darkness.

Retrace a familiar path that you take frequently. It might be your typical way to work or school. It might be the route that you take to the store or to a friend's home. Whatever path you retrace, look for all the details that you might have missed in the past. What has been there all along that you failed to notice? What is there that usually isn't? What things do you see that you wonder about? Expect to be surprised by some of what you see. Expect what you see to have meaning. Let the light of your expectation make your path more clear.

I see the path clearly.

Day 94   **Christ makes my path clear.**

"For 'In him we live and move and have our being.'"

—*Acts 17:28a*

*J*esus journeyed through life responding to what was immediately in front of him. When he encountered a need, he tried to meet it. When he encountered conflict, he tried to resolve it. When he encountered pain, he tried to heal it. He dealt with the realities of life that were presented to him, *as* they were presented to him.

It is difficult for us to predict what will happen in the future. And the farther down the road we look, the more difficult it becomes. But having the mind of Christ, in which we live and move and have our being, we can see clearly what is immediately in front of us. We can identify the decisions we need to make, the questions we need to answer, and the tasks we need to accomplish *now*.

In any moment, the mind of Christ has only *one* guiding principle: *agape*. The mind of Christ asks only: "What must I do now in order to express the unconditional love of God?" Like Jesus, we are here to show the world what it wants to know—that God loves us and will never abandon us, no matter what. When we focus our attention upon the present moment and ask what *agape* would have us do, the mind of Christ makes our path clear.

You may be familiar with these lyrics by Daniel S. Twohig:

> I walked today where Jesus walked
> In days of long ago;
> I wandered down each path He knew,
> With rev'rent step and slow. . . .

Twohig wrote these lines in response to a trip through the Holy Land. And they can easily apply to our walking the path of life with the mind of Christ as our guiding principle. When we walk with our minds focused on seeing the present moment and with our hearts focused on expressing *agape*, we, too, are walking where Jesus walked.

As you walk through the routines of this day, do so with the mind of Christ. Do not complicate your path with worry about the future. Deal only with the decisions that need to be made today. And whenever you are confused, allow the law of *agape* to be your guide.

Christ makes my path clear.

Day 95   Waiting is a meaningful part of my journey.

Whenever the cloud was taken up from the tabernacle, the Israelites would set out on each stage of their journey; but if the cloud was not taken up, then they did not set out until the day that it was taken up.

—*Exodus 40:36-37*

*S*uppose that you are about to take a long flight to attend a conference. You make all the necessary arrangements for being gone, pack your bags, and head for the airport. When you arrive, you notice that your take-off has been delayed for two hours.

What do you do? Begin walking to your destination? Search frantically for another mode of transportation? Insist that the plane take off on time? Of course not. You wait! While you might puzzle over the cause of the delay, you trust that there must be a good reason for it.

You might willingly endure a flight delay if it will assure a safer trip. But how willing are you to endure delays on your spiritual journey even if they will assure greater personal growth? When you ask God for guidance, do you become impatient if you don't immediately receive clear direction? Might you be one who is likely to pray, "Lord, give me patience, and I want it right now"?

Waiting patiently for direction is a vitally important part of your spiritual journey. Perhaps the "delay" is meant to be a time of rest, when you can gather your strength before taking a tremendous step. Perhaps it is meant to be a time of preparation, when all that you need for the journey falls into place. Perhaps it is meant to be a time of reflection, when you gain perspective on where your path has brought you so far.

Today's scripture passage describes how the Israelites waited for God's cloud to show them the way. When the cloud moved, they moved. When the cloud stopped, they stopped. Even though they were anxious to get to the promised land, they did not rush on ahead. God's guidance was more important than their travel plans.

Reflect back over your spiritual path (Day 92). Were there times when you moved forward too quickly? Did your impatience hinder your journey?

Be patient in times of waiting. More than that, *value* times of waiting. They help to ensure that your journey will unfold as it should.

Waiting is a meaningful part of my journey.

Day 96   I move ahead without worry.

"Do not worry about tomorrow, for tomorrow will bring worries of its own."

—*Matthew 6:34*a

*W*orrying is looking backward. It is being afraid that the future may repeat some unpleasant experience that you had in the past. When you look backward, when you worry, you are dragging the burdens of yesterday into tomorrow. It isn't long before you have a kink in your neck and an ache in your back. Your pace slows down. Maybe you even stop moving altogether.

In Matthew 14:22-32, we read how Peter stepped out of the boat in the middle of the lake in response to Jesus' call. At first, stepping out in faith—thinking only of the moment—Peter was able to walk across the water. But then he felt the wind blowing against him. He began to be afraid. Why? Could it be that the fisherman in Peter began to remember times when the wind had placed him in danger? If Peter hadn't "looked backward," if he hadn't started to carry the weight of the past, he wouldn't have begun to sink.

Imagine that there is a tremendous magnet somewhere behind you. Imagine also that you are wearing a backpack. Each time that you worry over something that might happen, you must place a piece of metal in the backpack. As you try to move forward, carrying your worries, you feel the pull of the magnet. The more worries you store up, the harder it is to take a step forward. You keep glancing backwards in frustration. Progress is slow. You are growing tired of the struggle.

Now imagine that God removes your backpack of worries and drops it on the ground. Feel the freedom of being able to move ahead, unencumbered. What a relief it is to leave your fears about the future behind you!

Spend a few moments in praise to the God who offers you the opportunity to move ahead without having to look back and without having to bear the burdens of yesterday. Give praise to the One who lightens your load.

I move ahead without worry.

Day 97   I travel lightly.

He said to them, "Take nothing for your journey, no staff, nor bag, nor bread, nor money—not even an extra tunic. Whatever house you enter, stay there, and leave from there."

—Luke 9:3-4

*P*erhaps you have heard someone say, "You will have a headache for each key that you carry." This statement implies that the more keys you have, the more responsibilities you have, and the more difficulties you will have to deal with. More keys probably also means more possessions, which add complications of their own. Every possession makes demands: it must be maintained, repaired, supplied with whatever it may need to function, and, of course, protected from damage and theft. Sometimes what we acquire even demands that we acquire more. For example, you buy your first computer. It is very basic, using simple software programs. You pick up an inexpensive printer to go with it. Soon you discover that your software isn't powerful enough to do what you want it to do. So you decide to buy a new software package. Then you become aware that your computer's memory is too small to run it. So you must upgrade to a more powerful system, and you pick up a fancier printer to take advantage of your new fonts and graphics capabilities. And so it goes. . . .

Mother Teresa began her ministry to "the poorest of the poor" on the streets of Calcutta, India. Her personal ministry eventually grew into the Roman Catholic order of The Sisters of Mercy, whose work now reaches around the globe. One of their mission sites is in California, where a building was donated for that purpose. The first time that Mother Teresa visited the facility, she ordered that the pews, the wall-to-wall carpet, and the heating system be removed. She insisted that these would distract the Sisters from serving the community. Pews must be polished. Carpet must be cleaned. A heating system must be maintained. Doing all of these things would require time and money that would be better spent in ministry to others. Mother Teresa correctly perceived that the more things we have, the more complicated our journeys become.

What do you own that you do not really need? Think of the closets and drawers that may be jammed full of things that you haven't used in years. Think of the attic or basement where there may be boxes of things that you are keeping "just in case." Think of the shelves that may be piled high with books and games and hobby supplies that you hope to get to "someday." Pick at least one possession that you can let go of, and give it away.

I travel lightly.

Day 98 **The Spirit renews me along the way.**

But those who wait for the LORD shall renew their strength, they shall mount up with wings like eagles, they shall run and not be weary, they shall walk and not faint.

—*Isaiah 40:31*

$\mathcal{I}$magine that you are riding a bicycle across the country. Pedaling day after day, you begin to struggle. But then you reach the flat, smooth roads of the Plains states, and a steady wind blows up behind you. Now you are moving forward with very little effort on your part. This is a good image for the work of the Holy Spirit. When the going gets tough and your reservoir of strength is nearly depleted, the Spirit blows against your back and provides relief. It is no wonder that in the Hebrew language of the Old Testament, the word for "Spirit" also means "wind."

When you begin a long drive, you will have an idea of how much time it should take to reach your destination. Hopefully you will have taken into consideration that you must stop now and then to buy gas. Refueling is a necessary part of your trip. In the same way, it is important that you allow for "refueling" on your spiritual journey. You cannot push on ahead endlessly without letting the Spirit replenish your inner resources. Spiritual refueling happens through prayer, meditation, devotional readings, scripture study, exercise, spending time with nature, being part of a sharing group, and so on.

What are your ways of renewing your spirit for the journey? Where do you find the strength that you need? Identify one thing that particularly rejuvenates you, and plan to do it regularly.

The Spirit renews me along the way.

Day 99   **God is my light.**

Indeed, you are my lamp, O Lord, the Lord lightens my darkness.

—*2 Samuel 22:29*

$\mathcal{T}$oday's reading is a meditative prayer. Before you begin, identify a troubled area of your life, a problem you are trying to solve, a person or situation that worries you, or a matter of faith. Then sit or lie down in a quiet place, away from distractions. Breathe deeply and relax. Ask God to be with you. When you feel centered, let the following drama unfold in your mind. Take your time. Don't force anything. Let images and words come to you.

It is dusk. You are standing at a place where a path forks. Because the right-hand path seems somewhat familiar, you decide to take it. Follow it, paying careful attention to what is around you. Notice that as you go, the little light of dusk is fading. Soon it is quite dark. How does this make your journey difficult?

Now it has grown even darker, like a deep cave that knows no light. You stop moving. This pitch-dark place represents the problem you identified earlier. Acknowledge to God how you feel about it. Ask God to take away any negative emotions.

Now you see the glow of a lantern. It is carried by someone you love, whom God has sent to help you; identify who it is. This guide hands you the lamp and tells you to go back and take the left-hand path. There, the guide says, you will receive an important message. So you go back, grateful for the lantern's light.

As you turn onto the other path, notice that dawn is breaking. With each step you take, the light in the sky becomes more brilliant; soon it is dazzling. You stop, marveling at it. Wait here for the message you are to receive about the darkness in your life. Wait as long as it takes. The message may or may not come in words. Be open to the revelation, however it comes.

Once you have received your message, return back the way you came, offering thanks to God. Close your meditation with a time of quiet reflection.

God is my light.

Day 100   I am renewed by the light.

"The eye is the lamp of the body. So, if your eye is healthy, your whole body will be full of light."

—Matthew 6:22

*T*he eyes are truly the windows of the soul. Almost without fail, you can see in the eyes a person's spiritual vitality. When a person is full of life, there is a gleam, a twinkle, a spark, a shining in his or her eyes that comes from someplace down deep. And this light is but a glimmer of the light that seems to radiate from the person's entire being. Surely you have been around such a person, whose face is bright with contentment and joy, and whose presence in a room can gladden everyone else who is there. Name some people you have known who radiated the light of God. What were their eyes like? What was their demeanor? What other features or qualities did they have that especially moved you? Identify ways that these people either revealed God's light to you or renewed God's light in you.

Pay careful attention to the eyes of everyone you encounter today. Train yourself to notice the quality of light that is there. Be grateful that these persons allow the light of God to shine through and bless you.

I am renewed by the light.

Day 101   The light is not limited.

The people who walked in darkness have seen a great light; those who lived in a land of deep darkness—on them light has shined.

—Isaiah 9:2

*L*ightning flashes in the night sky. Your electricity flickers and goes off. What do you do? You scavenge until you locate a book of matches, then strike one to light a candle. At once the room reappears.

There can never be too much darkness for a match.

In the same way, there can never be too much darkness for the light of God. Let the darkness be thicker than the thickest fog, and still the light will overcome it. Let the darkness be deeper than the deepest ocean, and still the light will overcome it. Let the darkness be heavier than the heaviest mountain, and still the light will overcome it. Let the darkness be as dark as darkness can be—it will not matter. The darker it is, the brighter the light will shine.

To reinforce this idea, make plans to rise early one day soon and witness a sunrise. Be sure to rise when it is still dark so that you can see the sun actually coming up. As the sun rises, imagine that the light of God is rising within you. See its rays slowly but steadily overcoming the night. And when the dawn has fully broken in the sky and in your soul, praise God by reading aloud these words from the hymn "Light of the World, We Hail Thee":

> Light of the world, illumine
> This darkened earth of thine,
> Till everything that's human
> Be filled with the divine;
> Till every tongue and nation,
> From sin's dominion free,
> Rise in the new creation
> Which springs from love and thee. Amen.
> —John S. B. Monsell

The light is not limited.

108

Day 102   I never walk in darkness.

"To you has been given the secret of the kingdom of God."

—*Mark 4:11*b

*T*he light of God never burns out. Nor can it be extinguished. Therefore, none of us needs ever be lost in darkness. This is a secret of the kingdom of God.

Perhaps you have stood near the eternal flame at the grave of John Fitzgerald Kennedy. Perhaps you have driven past a house at night and noticed electric candles shining warmly in all its windows. Perhaps you have worshipped in a sanctuary where a presence light continually burns. Perhaps you know someone who keeps a "company candle" lit in a window twenty-four hours a day; it is a sign of welcome, and a reminder of the importance of offering hospitality to anyone in need.

When you have the mind of Christ, you know the power of the light that never goes out. You know the powerful message it sends and the powerful emotions it evokes. Whether or not anyone is there to see it, the light burns on. Whether or not anyone is there to tend it, the light burns on. And the light overcomes the darkness. You need not ever be lost.

Today you are encouraged to create a "kingdom candle" that you can burn daily. Let it be a sign that the illuminating presence is with you, and that you willingly share it with others. Your kingdom candle may be an actual candle; if so, a very safe seven-day devotional candle, available at many religious bookstores, is recommended. Alternatively, you might use an electric candle or choose a specific lamp to keep lit. Whatever your kingdom candle is, light it every morning before you begin your day's labors. As you do so, commit yourself to walking in God's light and to extending it to others.

Each day, allow your kingdom candle to burn as much as possible. Whenever you must extinguish it, remind yourself that the real light of God remains burning within you and will never go out.

I never walk in darkness.

Day 103   My awareness is not limited.

"I do not call you servants any longer, because the servant does not know what the master is doing; but I have called you friends, because I

have made known to you everything that I have heard from my
Father."

—John 15:15

*A*re you open to revelation?

By definition, revelation from God always brings change; if
things were meant to remain as they are, nothing would need to
be revealed. So revelation comes to let you know something that
you don't know, because you need to know it. What is made
known to you is meant to transform you.

So, how open are you to revelation? How willing are you to
make changes in your life?

Identify those matters regarding that which you are most
reluctant to change. Be as specific as possible. Here is a list of
topics to stimulate your thinking:

relationships	career	family time
personal habits	religion	household rules
finances	parenting	vacation
politics	social issues	health

When you have identified a specific matter that fits under one
of these categories, reflect carefully on why change seems so difficult for you. Is your reluctance to change due to fear? If so,
acknowledge what you are afraid of. Then think about how you
might regard this matter out of faith rather than fear. If your
understanding of the matter needs to be deepened, ask the Spirit for help. Be open to revelation.

The mind of Christ is committed to continual growth. Trust
your journey, even if it asks you to change. Remain open, and
allow God to expand your awareness.

My awareness is not limited.

Day 104   I know the truth.

I write to you, not because you do not know the truth, but because you
know it, and you know that no lie comes from the truth.

—1 John 2:21

*I*f you live in the Spirit, fully open to revelation, your awareness continually grows. You come to know the truth. According

to the scripture passage, even when you are filled with questions, you know the truth. You only need to be reminded of what you know.

What is your truth, as you now understand it? And how do you live through times of doubt? Today we must answer these questions. We cannot simply inherit all the answers of our ancestors like they were pieces of heirloom jewelry. God's truth is continually revealed; there is no end to it. Our journeying spirits must continually seek it out with the eyes of faith, guided by the wisdom of those who have sought it before us.

At the turn of the last century, a young man posed questions about truth and doubt to poet Rainer Maria Rilke. Below are two brief excerpts from Rilke's responses to the young man's letters (taken from *Letters to a Young Poet*). Read them carefully.

I want to beg you, as much as I can, to be patient toward all that is unsolved in your heart and to try to love the *questions themselves* like locked rooms and like books that are written in a very foreign tongue. Do not now seek the answers, which cannot be given you because you would not be able to live them.

And the point is, to live everything. *Live* the questions now. Perhaps you will then, gradually, without noticing it, live along some distant day into the answer.

Now write a response to Rilke, in which you address these questions:

(1) What things are "unsolved in your heart?" What are the big questions or doubts of your life?
(2) What do you think Rilke means when he warns, "Do not now seek the answers . . . you would not be able to live them"?
(3) How do you "live questions"? What does it mean to "live along into the answer"?

Rilke, like the author of today's scripture passage, writes to reassure us that if we have the courage to face our doubts and confront our fears, we can live fully in our knowledge of the truth. Remind yourself of this when you feel uncertain. The truth is yours. Seek to understand it.

I know the truth.

Day 105   **I know the way.**

"And you know the way to the place where I am going."

—*John 14:4*

*S*urely you have heard about the legendary dog who, by some misfortune, finds itself alone and hundreds of miles from home. Not to be dismayed, it sniffs the air, points its nose in the direction it thinks home should be, and bravely sets off. Weeks later, covered with burrs, its ribs sticking out, its foot-pads bleeding, the dog shows up at its owner's back door. She is simply amazed, having long before given up hope of ever seeing her dog again.

This is a familiar story, but it will never grow old and stale. Whenever a dog is lost, the story lingers in the back of our minds, giving us hope. Whenever a dog returns home, the story is told and retold with relish. It is the story of a loyalty that has no limits, a spirit that will not quit, and instincts that triumph in the end. It is a story of knowing the way home—a way that is known not with the head but with the heart.

This story is not unlike the story of a spiritual journey. Jesus said that, just like him, we know the way to God. So, if we trust our instincts, if we have a spirit that won't quit, and if our loyalty to God is without limits, we will find the way home. The mind that was in Christ is in us.

Promise yourself that today you will pay careful attention to your instincts. When you feel led in a certain direction, you will follow it. When you sense that you are moving too fast or too far, you will slow down or stop altogether. When something seems not quite right, you will check it out. When you have a hunch, you will act on it. Set off on your way to God, and you will find that the knowing is inside you.

I know the way.

Day 106   **The way is wisdom.**

When he established the heavens, I [Wisdom] was there, when he drew a circle on the face of the deep . . . I was beside him, like a master worker; and I was daily his delight, rejoicing before him always, rejoicing in his inhabited world and delighting in the human race.

—*Proverbs 8:27, 30-31*

$\mathcal{B}$efore beginning to make a window, a stained glass artist decides what the finished product should look like. Then, while cutting each small piece of glass, the artist tries to envision how it will fit into the total picture. Only if the artist keeps the pieces in perspective will the creative process accomplish its goal. Every stained glass window that the artist has ever made has helped to teach this truth. The artist has the wisdom of experience.

Wisdom helps us see the big picture of life. Sometimes we have trouble seeing more than "the little pieces of glass" that are in front of us. But if we are wise, we will work to enlarge our perspective. We carry with us a life-history that can help us to understand how things interrelate. We can try to see how the little pieces of the "stained glass window" fit together into a larger, more revealing whole.

Today's scripture text celebrates the wisdom of God that, like a master worker, creates the world. All of the little pieces and parts of the universe fit together, gloriously and wondrously, because God is wise. And God offers this same wisdom to us. This is the wisdom that is the way.

Locate a picture that has some fine detail in it. Now, find a piece of paper that will completely cover the picture. After punching a small hole in the paper, place it over the picture. What is visible through the hole? Now, gradually lift the paper, still looking through the hole. Move the hole up to your eye and peer through it. Now what do you see? The whole picture!

As your spiritual journey proceeds, you will become wiser. Gradually you will be able to see more and more of the big picture. And when you can't seem to see beyond the little pieces of life, trust that the Master Artist has things in proper perspective.
The way is wisdom.

Day 107 Creation reveals the wisdom of God.

For lo, the one who forms the mountains, creates the wind, reveals his thoughts to mortals, makes the morning darkness, and treads on the heights of the earth—the LORD, the God of hosts, is his name!

—Amos 4:13

*N*ancy once noticed that ants were crawling all over her peonies. In an effort to protect her plants, she sprayed them with ant poison. The ants died, but unfortunately, much to Nancy's amazement, the buds of the flowers never opened. She hadn't realized that ants play an integral role in the opening of peony buds, loosening them in search of their sweet juice. God had planned it to work that way, and Nancy had unwittingly interfered with the plan.

Have you ever wondered about the logic behind a particular part of nature? How does the earth know that it should orbit the sun and rotate on its axis at the same time? (Sounds like trying to simultaneously rub your head and pat your tummy!) Why doesn't gravity ever get tired of the work that it does? Why don't the seasons ever become confused and come out of turn?

And what about dreaming? Why did God create us in such a way that our sleep is filled with strange stories? Dream research has determined that all of us must dream during sleep in order to think clearly during our waking hours. How this process works is not completely understood, but that it *does* work is beyond debate. So all of us have dreams, every night, even when we can't recall them.

All of creation reveals the wisdom of God. At times, that wisdom may be beyond our comprehension. We may misunderstand how the different parts of creation fit together. Then, thinking that our actions will have little or no consequence, we run the danger of doing things that will upset the balance of nature. Only later do we discover that our choices have had great and lasting effects.

Think of an aspect of creation that puzzles you. Is there, for example, a particular animal, plant, weather condition, or astrological phenomenon that you don't understand? See what you can discover about its purpose. Learn why God may have chosen to include it in our world.

Creation reveals the wisdom of God.

Day 108   **All creation is light.**

All things came into being through him, and without him not one thing came into being. What has come into being in him was life, and the life was the light of all people.

—John 1:3-4

114

*A*ll the colors of the rainbow are present in white light. When a beam of white light hits a prism, the colors are separated, and we can see them individually. So, light is color—all colors at once.

Everything that we see has color. The color of an object is determined by which colors it absorbs from the light and which colors it reflects. We see the colors that it reflects.

Over the centuries, we have come to associate certain colors with specific feelings. For example, sometimes we are "green with envy" or "in the pink" or "in a blue mood." Such descriptions indicate that we respond to color on an emotional level. Our mood can, for example, be influenced by the color of a room. Why else would so many fast-food restaurants be decorated in orange, a color that stimulates the appetite?

Today is an awareness day. Begin by re-creating this chart of the rainbow colors on a paper that you can carry with you.

COLOR	OBJECTS	FEELINGS
Red		
Orange		
Yellow		
Green		
Blue		
Indigo		
Violet		

Take time as you go through the day to notice the colors that surround you. Write down at least one object for each color on the chart. Then, look closely at that object awhile. Notice any feelings that arise in you, and add them to the chart. Begin to become more aware of how the colorful light of God's creation can influence you. And give thanks that this wonderful array of color was created just for you.

All creation is light.

Day 109   **Creation dances with joy.**

Praise him with tambourine and dance; praise him with strings and
pipe! Praise him with clanging cymbals; praise him with loud clashing
cymbals! Let everything that breathes praise the LORD! Praise the LORD!

—Psalm 150:4-6

Have you ever stopped to watch snowflakes falling? Sometimes they appear to be dancing their way to the earth. They
swirl up and around in a beautiful ballet, then finally and grace-
fully settle on the ground.

Have you ever watched a gentle rainfall? The rain comes
down, soft and steady. The puddles on the street seem to reach
up to welcome every drop. Spiderwebs, sheltered in the trees,
sparkle with moisture. The windowpanes stream with water.

Have you ever observed the effects of a breeze? It catches the
leaves of the trees and gently turns them over. It flutters the flag
at the top of the pole. It causes the wheat fields to ripple and the
flower beds to sway.

All of creation dances with joy, and God is its partner.

For today's activity, you will need a scarf (or a piece of lightweight fabric) and a musical recording. Select music that is
uplifting and filled with movement. As the recording begins to
play, hold the scarf in one hand and begin to move it in response
to the music. Allow it to float through the air; let it dance up and
down and swirl around—whatever the music leads you to do.
Gradually you will feel your body dancing with the scarf. Let
them be one, and continue to dance with the scarf until the
music stops.

God dances with a joyous creation and invites you to do the
same. Dance with creation, and you dance with God!

Creation dances with joy.

Day 110   **Joy is my home.**

Even the sparrow finds a home, and the swallow a nest for herself,
where she may lay her young, at your altars, O LORD of hosts, my King
and my God. Happy are those who live in your house, ever singing your
praise.

—Psalm 84:3-4

116

$\mathscr{W}$e often use the words "happiness" and "joy" interchangeably, as though they have the same meaning. But they don't. Happiness usually depends on the presence of a particular person or the experience of a particular success. So, it is a temporary state, there one moment and gone the next. But joy comes to stay. It is not dependent on external circumstances. It is a deep inner contentment that comes from knowing, beyond a shadow of a doubt, that we are loved by God. Our joy in being perfectly loved is only heightened whenever we glimpse the same quality of love in our relationships with other people.

We also tend to use the words "house" and "home" as though they mean the same thing. But they, too, are different. A house is a physical structure in which we happen to live. A home, on the other hand, is where we feel like we belong. To feel "at home" is to feel joy. It is to feel loved, accepted as we are, comfortable and safe. Our home may be a specific place, or it may be a feeling that we carry with us wherever we go.

Quickly write down all the places where you have lived. Now put a star beside those places that felt like "home." List the reasons why they felt like "more than just a house." Ask yourself such questions as, "What made this place feel comfortable? Peaceful? How did it express who I was?"

Finally, go over your list of characteristics. These are some of the qualities that help to make a "house" a "home" for you. They bring you not just happiness, but joy. Realize that this joy can be carried with you wherever you go. Loved by God, you are always at home.

Joy is my home.

$\mathscr{Day}$ *111*   **Joy is my name.**

For this reason I bow my knees before the Father, from whom every family in heaven and on earth takes its name.

—Ephesians 3:14-15

$\mathscr{T}$hink for a minute about your given name. Do you know why your parents named you what they did? Perhaps they appreciated your name's meaning. Perhaps they wanted to name you after a relative, a dear friend, a biblical figure, or a famous person. Or, maybe they just "liked the sound of it."

To give someone a name is a powerful thing to do, because

names carry messages with them. And we who have been called "children of God" carry with us a message that is divine. Our name reveals that we belong to the greatest family imaginable—the family of the Creator. We could have been given no better name. We know exactly what it means. Our name means Joy. How could "child of God" mean anything else?

Concentrate today on feeling the power of your name. Remember, Joy is a deep and abiding feeling of contentment. As you go about your routine, do each task Joy-fully. Do the dishes Joy-fully. Pay the bills Joy-fully. Turn in your report Joy-fully. Mow the lawn Joy-fully. Do the shopping Joy-fully. Drive home from work Joy-fully. Carry Joy with you wherever you go, and know that it is the meaning of your God-given name.

Joy is my name.

Day 112 Joy is God's promise.

God said, "This is the sign of the covenant that I make between me and you and every living creature that is with you, for all future generations: I have set my bow in the clouds, and it shall be a sign of the covenant between me and the earth."

—*Genesis 9:12-13*

*I*f you can locate an old yearbook from your high school or college days, read some of the things that your friends wrote in it. Did they promise undying loyalty? Did they promise never-ending friendship? What happened to those promises? Where are those friends today? Even though our intentions may be good, the realities of life do not always allow us to keep the promises we make.

According to Genesis, the rainbow is a reminder that God has promised to stay in relationship with us, no matter what. It is not a reminder to God. God does not forget. Rather, it is a reminder to us of the one thing in life that we can count on. Seeing the rainbow in the sky, we can rejoice, knowing *for certain* that God will never forsake us.

Across the top of a sheet of paper write: MY LIFEBOOK! Below this, write the promises of God that you treasure most—promises made in the past (for example, "I'll always keep in touch with you") and promises being made to you today (for example, "I'm still listening to you, and I always will be"). Carry this paper with you throughout the day. Realize that while your friends may have written their promises in your *year*book, God's promises are written in your *life*book. Celebrate the joy that comes to you because you can trust God's promises to be fulfilled.

Joy is God's promise.

Day 113   God is my salvation.

Surely God is my salvation; I will trust, and will not be afraid, for the LORD GOD is my strength and my might; he has become my salvation.

—*Isaiah 12:2*

*A*ngie stands alone at the top of a human pyramid, high above the basketball court. Her feet are planted on the stout shoulders of two other cheerleaders. She is smiling; her gestures are crisp and precise, radiating confidence. Apparently she is unconcerned that her safety is entirely dependent upon the strength of the five people in formation beneath her. Finally, the stunt over, she dismounts with a double-twisting back flip and lands in the cradled arms of two of her fellow squad members.

When Angie was in elementary school, she used to stand halfway up the stairs in her family's house and call for her father to "Come catch!" The moment her father had positioned himself at the bottom of the stairs, she would leap into the air, to land in his waiting arms. He caught her every time. She knew that he would never drop her—not because she had proof, but because she had belief. Her belief had grown with experience. That first jump had been a leap of faith, but he had been strong and quick enough to catch her. With every jump that followed, she had learned to trust him more.

You learn to trust God in the same way. At some point, you take that initial leap of faith. You decide that you will take a chance on God, that you will hope that God will love you and protect you. And, as your life becomes a collection of stories which all have the same ending—"It was tough, but with God's help I got through it"—your trust in God becomes more complete. Eventually you are doing your own double-twisting back flips through the air, and God never fails to catch you.

Write a description of a specific leap of faith that you have taken. Maybe it was a situation that required you to take a risk, or to venture into the unknown, or to put your trust in someone of whom you were unsure. What made you decide to take the leap? Conclude by writing about how this experience made you more or less willing to trust in subsequent situations.

Sometimes when we trust other people, they fail us. However, God will not fail us. That is why *God*—and no other—is our salvation.

God is my salvation.

Day 114   **My salvation is a gift.**

Immediately the father of the [epileptic] child cried out, "I believe; help my unbelief!"

—Mark 9:24

It is safe to say that the father of the child in this story had been through the mill. His son had been afflicted with epilepsy since childhood. Seizures had caused him to fall into fires and be burned, to tumble into the lake and almost drown. For years the father had been on guard, day and night, wanting to keep his son from harm. And year by year he had watched the joy of living fade from his son's eyes.

Worn down by time, this father had given up all but a smidgen of hope. But that little hope was big enough that he could ask Jesus for help, even though he could hardly imagine that help would ever be had.

But help *was* to be had. Salvation came. Not because the son had earned it. Not because the father expected it. It simply came. A gift. An unmerited, unforeseen, and joyously welcomed gift. Through Jesus, God closed the gap between what the father could believe and what the boy could receive. With the gap closed, the believing and the receiving became one, and father and son were healed together.

On a piece of paper, make three columns. In the first column, list several situations in which you need God's help right now. Then, in the second column, list the outcome that you would hope for in each case. Finally, in the third column, list any doubts or worries that are undermining your hope. Here is a brief example:

Need God's Help	Hoped for	Doubts or Concerns
Baby is due.	My baby and I are healthy after the delivery.	Afraid that the birth will be breech. I feel helpless. Can I trust the doctors? Can I trust God? Will I be able to stand the pain?

When you have completed your outline, enter into prayer, asking God to help you overcome the gap between your hopes and your doubts. No matter how wide the gap is, take the leap of faith and believe in God's saving action. Without fail, you can trust that God's arms will catch you.

My salvation is a gift.

Day 115   The more I believe, the less I fear.

But overhearing what they said, Jesus said to the leader of the synagogue, "Do not fear, only believe."

—*Mark 5:36*

The mind of Christ is characterized by faith. In the midst of turmoil it trusts God to provide all the help that is needed. It remains unafraid, centered in the quiet power of its belief.

By contrast, the mind that has lost its spiritual center is characterized by fear. It is divided against itself. Its belief is at war with its worries, its faith is at war with its doubts. Rather than hoping for the best, it can only struggle not to expect the worst.

Consider the leader of the synagogue. (The synagogue was a meeting house where the Jewish community would regularly gather to pray and study the law of God.) An important man, the leader of the synagogue had many decisions to make, many matters to attend to. Day in and day out, he was under constant pressure. And now he had been informed that his sick daughter had just died. The worst had come to pass. His grief was overwhelming. He should go home, they told him; no one, not even this healer named Jesus, could help his daughter now.

But Jesus reassured the distraught man, saying, "Do not fear, only believe." Have a little faith, in other words. Center yourself. Put more trust in God.

Before too long the man and his wife were staring at their daughter in amazement as she sat up in bed, eating. "She is not dead," Jesus had told them, taking her hand in his. "She is only sleeping."

For today's exercise, take out a clear drinking glass. Drop in ten drops of yellow food coloring to represent an overwhelming fear. Fill the glass with water and stir. Now add a single drop of blue food coloring to signify the entrance of a little faith. Do not stir, however. Just watch what happens. After a few minutes, leave the glass sitting on the cupboard. Return to it a half-hour (or more) later. Observe what has happened. Remember that the new color is the traditional color of healing and life. What does this exercise demonstrate to you?

Use today's main idea as a silent reminder whenever you start to feel worried, anxious, or insecure. Have a little faith.

The more I believe, the less I fear.

Day 116 I am not ashamed of my belief.

Now there was a Pharisee named Nicodemus, a leader of the Jews. He came to Jesus by night and said to him, "Rabbi, we know that you are a teacher who has come from God; for no one can do these signs that you do apart from the presence of God."

—John 3:1-2

*N*icodemus came to Jesus *by night*. Why, do you think?

It appears that Nicodemus was afraid of how people would react if they saw him with Jesus. To say the least, Jesus was quickly becoming a source of controversy. If Nicodemus acknowledged him as a teacher from God, there could be grave consequences, not only for Nicodemus but for those he represented. Reputations could be stained. Leaders could be ousted. Families could be torn apart. Businesses could be boycotted. Friends could be betrayed. Lives could be ruined and, if the controversy grew, possibly even lost. So, Nicodemus came to Jesus in secret, wrapped in a cloak under cover of darkness.

Respond to the following questions, being as honest with yourself as possible:

(1) Are there ways in which you keep your spiritual life "under wraps"? What are they?

(2) Do you have certain beliefs that you do not share with other people? If so, what are they, and why do you keep them to yourself?

(3) Do you regard spirituality as basically "a Sunday thing," not to play a very obvious role the rest of the week? If so, why? For example, do you think that spiritual truths don't really work in the "real world"?

Do not be afraid of believing what you do. Do not be afraid of living what you believe. Let the mind of Christ grow within you, and allow your believing and your living to become one.

I am not ashamed of my belief.

Day 117   I do not hide the truth.

The woman said to Peter, "You are not also one of this man's disciples, are you?" He said, "I am not."

—John 18:17

*J*esus has just been arrested. Peter, who only hours before had professed his undying loyalty to the "troublemaker" from Nazareth, now denies knowing him. And he will deny him twice more before the cock crows. His fear of being implicated in Jesus' offenses is greater than his shame at being untrue. So, what will it matter if he hides the truth? If he tells a little white lie, or two, or three?

Hiding the truth out of fear can have serious consequences. To illustrate this, take out two eggs. Place one of them in a cup filled with water, the other in a cup filled with white vinegar. Notice that, sitting there in their cups, the eggs look exactly alike. Now, leave them, and don't look at them again until the end of the day. *(Stop reading here. Continue reading at the end of the day—or the following morning.)*

What do you find when you return to the eggs? In one cup, the acid in the vinegar has been eating away the calcium in the eggshell. If this egg were soaked in vinegar long enough, the structural integrity of its shell would continue to weaken, leaving the yolk and white increasingly vulnerable.

In the same way, your spirit is eaten away when you lie or hide the truth out of fear. At some point, evidence of this "corrosion" becomes detectable in your voice, your actions, your manner.

But, more importantly, your personal integrity, as well as the integrity of your relationships, begins to weaken. You become more and more vulnerable and, therefore, even more afraid.

Commit yourself to honoring the truth. Be unflinching when afraid, unswerving when scorned, undaunted when accused, and unyielding when tempted. To honor the truth is to have the mind of Christ.

I do not hide the truth.

Day 118   I am not intimidated.

Do not fear what they fear, and do not be intimidated, but in your hearts sanctify Christ as Lord.

—*1 Peter 3:14b-15a*

Usually when we talk about a "genealogy," we are referring to family history: what's-his-name was the father of what's-her-name, who later became the mother of so-and-so, and so on. But you might say that emotions, too, have a genealogy. They come to be, they live, they produce offspring, and they die.

Take fear, for instance. How is it born? What feeds it? What are its effects? What causes it to die?

There are many "families" in the family of fear. During your lifetime you will be adopted by many of them. They will try to teach you to fear what they fear. You may have already proven to be an apt learner.

On the list that follows, indicate the fears that you now have, rating each on a scale of 1 to 10 ("10" being "very strong"):

_____ Fear of death	_____ Fear of the unknown
_____ Fear of what is different	_____ Fear of failure
_____ Fear of suffering	_____ Fear of change
_____ Fear of not having enough	_____ Fear of being known as you are
_____ Fear of growing old	_____ Fear of a certain group
_____ Fear of the future	of people
_____ Fear of intimacy	(specify: _____)
_____ Fear of expressing feelings	_____ Fear of being in a relationship
_____ Fear of rejection	_____ Fear of losing

_____ Fear of a certain idea   _____ Fear of success
     (specify: _____)   _____ Fear of living
_____ Fear of being alone   _____ Other: _____

Now, for one of your strongest fears, do an "emotional genealogy," answering as many of these questions as you can:

(1) When did you begin to be afraid of this? Why? Did someone "teach" you to be afraid of it? How?
(2) How has this fear been reinforced over time?
(3) List the advantages of having this fear.
(4) List the disadvantages of having this fear.
(5) Looking at its "offspring," would it be wise for you to continue having this fear? What might you do to "lay it to rest"?

Let your "emotional genealogy" be a revelation to you. Do not willingly accept the fears that others wish to pass on to you. Instead, accept the faith that is your inheritance through Christ.
I am not intimidated.

Day 119   **I rejoice!**

Give thanks in all circumstances; for this is the will of God in Christ Jesus for you.

—1 Thessalonians 5:18

The mind of Christ does not distinguish between the best of times and the worst of times. Rather, it sees every time as a time to give thanks. Birthing and dying, planting and reaping, breaking down and building up, weeping and laughing, mourning and dancing, seeking and losing, keeping and casting away, rending and sewing, speaking and being still, doing battle and making peace—all of it happens in one season, and that is the season of thanksgiving.

To always give thanks and rejoice is to always affirm life, despite what the circumstances of life throw at you. It is a choice that you make daily, to resist the temptation to fear and to embrace the presence of God.

On a piece of paper write down eight worries or problems that you have right now (for example, "getting through my final exams," "looking for a better job," "helping Mom through her mastectomy"). Then use your list to compose a prayer of joy. Plug your worries into the following lines, concluding each with today's central idea. (You may have to fine-tune the wording a bit.) Close this prayer with an affirmation of your trust in God:

O Spirit,
In the midst of _____, I rejoice!
Even when I am _____, I rejoice!
Despite _____, I rejoice!
Whenever _____ seem(s) too much to overcome, I rejoice!
And though _____ tempts me to fear, I rejoice!
Against all odds, even _____, I rejoice!
And in the face of _____, I rejoice!
Regardless of _____, I rejoice!

O God, I choose to rejoice because you (conclude with an expression of trust and praise).

I rejoice!

Day 120   The mind of Christ transforms my values.

Then they came to Capernaum; and when he was in the house he asked them, "What were you arguing about on the way?" But they were silent, for on the way they had argued with one another who was the greatest. He sat down, called the twelve, and said to them, "Whoever wants to be first must be last of all and servant of all."

—*Mark 9:33-35*

Each of us has a deep longing to know that we are valued. As we journey through life, we try a variety of ways of satisfying this longing. We may try the path of popularity, hoping that if enough people—or the right people—call us "friend," we may gain a larger sense of importance. We may travel the path of acquiring material possessions, hoping that if we surround ourselves with enough things—or the right things—we will attain a higher sta-

126

tus. We may go down the path of collecting titles and degrees, hoping that if we get enough credentials—or the right credentials—we will become somebody.

What we forget is that we are somebody already. We are unique and wonderful creations of God. We were each made with the blessing of the Creator already stamped on us. We don't have to find greatness. It is already ours. And so, God does not require us to be successful. Instead, God asks us to be true to our identity as children of God and faithful to our callings as human beings. Notice that we are called human *beings* and not human *doings*. Our self-worth is to be based not on what we do, but who we are. Therein lies our greatness.

Today, find at least one opportunity to defer to someone else, allowing this person to take the position of privilege or honor. This might be as simple as letting someone park in the space that you have spotted or allowing someone to move ahead of you in the checkout line. As you defer to this person, notice the good feelings that well up in you. Remind yourself that both of you are valued totally and unconditionally by God.

The mind of Christ transforms my values.

Day 121 **In every conflict I have a choice.**

"But I say to you that listen, Love your enemies, do good to those who hate you, bless those who curse you, pray for those who abuse you."

—*Luke 6:27-28*

*I*magine that you have a teenage daughter who is late coming home. She is already a half-hour past her curfew. You wait at the door, ready to pounce on her when she arrives. The later it gets, the more upset you become. When she finally walks in, you quickly reassure yourself that she is safe, then jump all over her for being irresponsible.

What was happening here? Let's look at how the incident developed. When your daughter did not come home on time, you chose to believe that she was deliberately late because she had no respect for your authority. Then came your emotional reaction. Mixed in with your worry was annoyance, resentment at being taken advantage of, and frustration at having your authority challenged. Now you were really ready to let her have it, and you did!

"But I couldn't help it," you might have said later to your spouse. "That's the way I felt." Many of us believe that we have a choice about our actions but not about our feelings. However, this is a misunderstanding of how our emotions are produced. Our interactions with other people involve at least four steps, repeated over and over: a triggering event; our belief about the triggering event; our feelings in response to the belief; and, finally, our response action or reaction, which usually becomes a new triggering event. We might diagram the interaction process like this:

Event ⟶ Belief Statement ⟶ Feelings ⟶ Response

As you can see, our feelings are produced by our thoughts, very early in the interaction. Therefore, if we control our thoughts, we *can* help what we feel, and thereby prevent or defuse a conflict.

Go back to the example. Suppose that when you noticed your daughter was late, you chose to believe, "She is usually on time. She must have been delayed for an important reason." Then, instead of anger and frustration, you would have felt trust in your daughter and concern for her safety. And when she finally entered the door, safe and sound, you would have expressed relief while calmly inquiring about her delay.

Take time today to analyze at least one troubling encounter that you have with another person (keep this analysis for future reference). See if you are able to identify what was happening at each step of the interaction process. Remember:

In every conflict I have a choice.

Day 122   **I choose to do good.**

See that none of you repays evil for evil, but always seek to do good to one another and to all.

—1 Thessalonians 5:15

*R*eview the analysis you did yesterday of a troubling interaction. If you were able to discover what was happening in each step of the interaction process, you now understand how your initial beliefs about a triggering event influence your feelings. You also know how your feelings help to determine your response action.

Of the four steps, most of us tend to overdo either the belief statements or the feelings. If we emphasize beliefs, the interaction process is short-circuited to become: triggering event → belief → response action. (Your daughter is late → you think she is being disrespectful → you let her have it.) As a result, we react to situations without an awareness of how our feelings are influencing us.

On the other hand, if we emphasize feelings, the short-circuited process becomes: triggering event → feeling → response action. (Your daughter is late → you are angry at her → you let her have it.) As a consequence, we react by saying and doing things that make little sense.

Whether we overdo beliefs or feelings, our hasty reactions are usually not helpful. Which of these "short-circuit" patterns are you most likely to follow? Are you more likely to ignore your feelings and respond only on the thinking level? Or are you more likely to skip over the thinking and get right to your feelings? Identify your most typical short-circuit pattern and reflect on how it limits your ability to respond in the most helpful way.

Concentrate today on your interactions with others. Choose to do good to everyone.

I choose to do good.

Day 123 I will listen only to God.

Beloved, do not believe every spirit, but test the spirits to see whether they are from God; for many false prophets have gone out into the world.

—1 John 4:1

*B*eware of the tongue! Scripture suggests that it is easier to tame the creatures of the sea than to tame the human tongue (James 3:7-8). Remember times when you have wounded someone with careless words. Remember times when your feelings have been hurt by the words of others. How important it is to choose our words carefully! And it is just as important to listen for the truth in what other people say. The truth they speak is the voice of God.

Review the diagram of the interaction process on Day 121. As you can see, words begin to play a role at step four, after a triggering event has been filtered through beliefs and feelings. If someone's words don't "ring true," or if they don't seem to fit the situation, it may be because the interaction process has been short-circuited. Then you might ask yourself where the words might be coming from. Are they loaded with the speaker's beliefs? The speaker's feelings? If you sense no truth in them, allow them to return to the speaker. Do not hold onto them. If, on the other hand, you sense that the words are true, take them in and understand how God might be speaking to you through them.

Today, listen for truth and only for truth. Allow everything else to pass by.

I will listen only to God.

Day 124　　　　　　**Let God's will be mine.**

"Father, if you are willing, remove this cup from me; yet, not my will but yours be done."

—Luke 22:42

$\mathcal{J}$esus could see the handwriting on the wall. His faithful witness to God—his teachings, his healings, his acts of compassion for those who were commonly neglected and despised—had rubbed some very powerful people the wrong way. He was faithless, in their eyes. He broke laws. He kept bad company. He said he was someone he couldn't possibly be. He was a threat to the kind of religion that they believed people should practice, to the kind of community that they believed people should live in. So they would have no choice, Jesus knew. They would have to do away with him.

Jesus didn't want to die. But somehow he found the courage to pray, "Not my will but yours be done." It was God's will that Jesus continue doing what he had always done—witnessing to what was good and just and right. It was God's will that he remain true to his identity and his calling, *no matter what.* And if that meant his death, then his dying would be consistent with the way that he had lived.

For most of her seventy-odd years, Dorothy had defined herself as a teacher. It was her deep conviction that teaching was part of her God-given purpose in life, and she had remained true to that calling. She taught school and Sunday school. She taught in the very living of her life. She looked for opportunities to teach. Even when she learned that she had terminal cancer, she regarded her illness as an opportunity to educate others. She invited family members and friends to participate actively in her care; to talk openly about the dying process, about faith, about feelings; to be with her as her bodily life ceased and her spirit's life was transformed. Dorothy's dying was truly consistent with the way that she had lived. Even in the face of death, she found a way to be the "teacher" she had felt called to be.

What is God's will for your life? Like Jesus and like Dorothy, you may be aware of directions that God wants you to go. Who has God called you to be? If you were to someday have an epitaph on your gravestone, how would you want it to read? How would you want to be remembered? Dorothy's epitaph might have read, "She was a teacher whose curriculum was life itself."

From among several that might be appropriate, choose an epitaph for yourself. Let it be a statement describing who God has created you to be and what, ultimately, your life is about. Let its words be a challenge to you to live consistently within God's will for your life.

Let God's will be mine.

Day 125   Out of conflict may come righteousness.

Then they came to Jerusalem. And he entered the temple and began to drive out those who were selling and those who were buying in the temple, and he overturned the tables of the money changers and the seats of those who sold doves; and he would not allow anyone to carry anything through the temple. He was teaching and saying, "Is it not written, 'My house shall be called a house of prayer for all the nations? But you have made it a den of robbers.'"

—Mark 11:15-17

Jesus entered the house of God. What he saw made him very sad—and very angry. A place of prayer had become a shop of horrors. He was saddened and angered by what he saw. "This will not be," he declared, and, putting his anger into the service of God's truth, he turned the tables on corruption. He confronted the moneychangers. He entered into conflict with the temple authorities, demanding that they be more consistent with their calling as servants of God.

Most of us are not very comfortable picturing Jesus trashing the courts of the temple. But it is a picture that we must try to understand. This picture shows us that in the face of wrong, God calls us to witness to what is right. The greater the wrong, the greater the chance that our witness will meet with resistance. But we take the risk, knowing that out of conflict God's righteousness may come.

We are surrounded by much that is wrong. Violence has raised its fists and aimed its guns; its knuckles are well-scarred, and its bullets have left many victims. How shall we resond to it? Shall we hide behind our doors, lamenting, "There is nothing we can do"? No. Shall we pick up guns of our own? No. Let us put our sadness and our anger in the service of God's truth, whenever and however we can. Let us call our community back to *agape*.

Identify at least one way that you will refuse to participate anymore in violence. Perhaps you will no longer watch TV programming that places a cheap value on human life. Perhaps you will no longer buy toys for your children that encourage them to imagine killing and being killed. Perhaps you will no longer remain silent when someone expresses a prejudice. Perhaps you will no longer talk callously about "those people." Commit yourself to doing what is true, to saying what is true, to living what is true, *no matter what*. Commit yourself to *agape*. This is your calling. This is what it is to have the mind of Christ.

Out of conflict may come righteousness.

Day 126   **Out of conflict may come renewal.**

"Do not think that I have come to bring peace to the earth; I have not come to bring peace, but a sword."

—*Matthew 10:34*

*Y*esterday we discussed how righteousness may come out of conflict; how, if we are willing to take a risk and confront wrong in our community, our witness may help God's truth and love to grow. Today we look at how *renewal* may come out of conflict; how, if we are willing to risk confronting wrong *in ourselves*, our spirits may not only grow, but flourish.

Think for a moment about a large tree that has very thick foliage. Hardly any sunlight can pass through its leaves. The seedlings that are growing in its shade do not receive enough light. Unless someone takes a saw in hand and thins the branches of the tree, the seedlings will never survive. Now think about a human body with a major artery that is nearly 100 percent blocked by plaque. Hardly any blood can pass through. The tissue on the other side of the blockage is not receiving enough oxygen. Unless someone takes a scalpel in hand and restores the flow of blood, the tissue will not survive.

In order to flourish, we must be ready to cut out whatever is obstructing our growth. So the Prince of Peace comes, sword of truth in hand, that we may clearly identify and then remove the source of our inner conflicts. Thin out the branches that the seedlings might grow. Clear out the plaque that the blood might flow. Then our lives will be more consistently open to the will of God.

Identify at least one obstruction to your growth that has been creating conflict within you. Examples would be too much pressure at work, lack of sleep, an addiction, loneliness, anger at your parents or your children. Now, what steps might you take to remove the obstruction? Commit yourself to doing whatever is necessary, and begin today. May this spiritual "surgery" lead to your renewal.

Out of conflict may come renewal.

Day 127　　　　　**Forgiveness renews me.**

And be kind to one another, tenderhearted, forgiving one another, as God in Christ has forgiven you.

—Ephesians 4:32

Living in relationship with others is like walking a spiritual high-wire. It requires a tremendous sense of balance. You must work hard to keep yourself steady. On the one hand, if you wrong someone, you must allow yourself to receive forgiveness. On the other hand, when you yourself are wronged, you must allow yourself to forgive. You must be equally ready to do both. Otherwise, if you are unwilling to forgive, the weight of your resentments will eventually cause you to lose your balance. Or, if you are unable to receive forgiveness, your step will falter beneath the weight of your guilt. In either case, your spirit may easily fall. Thank God for the net of grace that gently catches us below, that we might climb back up on the high-wire, center ourselves, and try again!

Today's exercise is meant to affirm this delicate spiritual balance that must be maintained. Create a mobile of forgiveness. To begin, cut four small circles out of construction paper or medium-weight cardboard (use more circles if you want to make a more elaborate mobile). On the first two circles write down specific ways that you have forgiven others; on the other two, specific ways that you have been forgiven. Attach each circle to the end of a length of string.

Now make the mobile itself, working from the bottom up. Tie a string of forgiveness to each end of two lightweight rods that will serve as horizontal arms in your mobile (for rods, you might use pencils, dowel sticks, or lengths of wire). Next, tie an empty string at the balance point of each arm. Lift each arm by this string to make sure that the assemblage hangs level.

Finally, tie the balance-point strings of both horizontal arms to each end of a third arm. Attach an empty string to the balance point of this arm. Now check to make sure the entire mobile hangs level from it. If it does, your mobile is ready to display. Hang it where it can move freely.

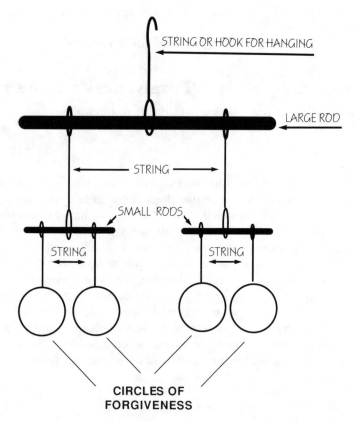

STRING OR HOOK FOR HANGING

LARGE ROD

STRING

SMALL RODS

STRING

STRING

CIRCLES OF
FORGIVENESS

Over the next few days, observe your mobile of forgiveness. Air currents, gravity, and other forces will affect the balance of its parts. Adjust them regularly, and know that in relationships, such adjustments bring renewal.

Forgiveness renews me.

Day 128 **Forgiveness is letting go.**

No longer shall they teach one another, or say to each other, "Know the LORD," for they shall all know me, from the least of them to the greatest, says the LORD; for I will forgive their iniquity, and remember their sin no more.

—Jeremiah 31:34

The Hatfields and the McCoys, now *they* could hold a grudge. No one knows for sure how the infamous feud between these two families got started. Some say it was over a stolen hog; others say that it was over a rebel Hatfield killing a yank McCoy in the Civil War. However the feud began, by the time it ended, generations later, perhaps a hundred lives had been lost, and the governor of West Virginia (on the McCoy side of the creek) and the governor of Kentucky (on the Hatfield side) had almost declared war on each other. Not exactly a shining example of forgiveness.

Forgiveness is letting go of the past, and letting go of wounded pride. It is not necessarily forgetting, for all things, when remembered, may add to wisdom. However, a forgiving spirit will remember not the transgressions it has suffered but the lessons it has learned. Carrying these lessons through life is not a burden but a blessing.

Stand in a narrow hallway with your arms held out from your sides. Press the tops of your wrists hard against the walls. Remain this way for a full minute or two without relieving the pressure. Think of this pressure as the emotional strain that you experience when either you refuse to forgive or do not feel forgiven.

At last, relax. You should feel a sudden lightness, even a "lifting" sensation in your arms. This only begins to suggest the release that comes through the act of forgiveness, whether you are granting it or receiving it. Remember this feeling when you are tempted to hold on to grudges, and find the humility of spirit to let go.

Forgiveness is letting go.

Day 129   **Forgiveness is love.**

For you, O Lord, are good and forgiving, abounding in steadfast love to all who call on you.

—Psalm 86:5

Forgiveness is *agape*, and *agape* is forgiveness; the two cannot exist apart from each other. As *agape*, forgiveness is patient and kind. It does not insist on its own way; it is not irritable or resentful. Bearing all things, believing all things, hoping all things, and enduring all things, forgiveness never ends.

Indicate which of these "rules" you tend to play by when deciding whether or not to forgive someone who has hurt you:

_____ He/She should apologize first. (Or: I shouldn't have to be the one to apologize.)

_____ He/She should take back any words that were offensive.

_____ He/She should promise to change offensive behavior.

_____ He/She should do something special to make up for the offense.

_____ If he/she repeats the offense, I will be justified in reacting more severely.

_____ I should be able to bring up the offense in the future to make a point.

_____ If I just "forget it," I don't have to forgive the offense.

_____ If I forgive him/her, he/she should be grateful.

_____ I should not have to forgive him/her over and over again.

_____ I should not have to forgive the same offense over and over again.

_____ Others: _____

_____

Now indicate the rules that you tend to expect God to play by when forgiving you:

_____ God should be willing to forgive me, even before I apologize.

_____ If I say I'm sorry, God should be satisfied. I shouldn't have to change.

_____ If I say I'm sorry, God should go easy on me. I shouldn't have to make up for what I did.

_____ God should regard each of my offenses as an isolated incident.

_____ God should forget my offense after forgiving me, and not keep lording it over me.

_____ If I make the same mistake again, God should still forgive me.

_____ God should be patient with me. After all, I'm only human.

_____ Others: _____

_____

Compare what you marked on the first list to what you marked on the second. Do you see any ways in which you have a double standard? Do you tend to forgive others more or less easily than you expect to be forgiven by God?

The problem is, *all* of these rules are creations of our own minds. They are not creations of the mind of Christ. God's forgiveness—and ours—is free of rules, just as God's love is without conditions. Begin *now* to strive for the day when you can look again at these lists of rules and check none of them as yours.

Forgiveness is love.

Day 130   # Forgiveness restores relationships.

"I do not judge anyone who hears my words and does not keep them, for I came not to judge the world, but to save the world."

—*John 12:47*

The big day has arrived. Everything is in place, the food is ready, the guests have taken their seats. . . .

And then it is over, in the blink of an eye. It leaves you feeling a little flat. The event went off exactly as planned, but somehow it wasn't quite what you had expected it to be. It didn't quite measure up, and you begin to pick it apart, trying to figure out why.

Know the feeling? You set your expectations so high that the grandest event in the world wouldn't be able to live up to them. "If you expect nothing, you won't be disappointed," we are warned. But we go on expecting, and go on being disappointed, even when things go well.

The same is true when we have expectations of other people. No matter how well they do, sometimes they just don't measure up. And sometimes they fail miserably, in our judgment. But *judgment* is the key word. *Judgment* injures relationships. It produces an environment in which fear, anger, and shame can grow. These eventually block out the light of *agape*, and then, like plants without sunlight, our relationships wither and fade.

Forgiveness, on the other hand, restores relationships. It offers *agape* unconditionally, regardless of expectations that are disappointed, rules that are broken, and standards that are not met. It creates an environment in which trust, appreciation, and respect can grow. The light of *agape* passes through these to our relationships, which are thereby helped to flourish.

Assume an attitude of prayer. Silence your mind. Be alone with God, without distraction. Let your spirit bask in the unconditional light of God's acceptance. Rejoice that you are forgiven. Rejoice that your relationship with God is uninjured. You may sometimes fail God, but God will never fail to love you. God's love is not dependent on what you do. It is dependent only on who you are. You have always been, and will always be, God's child. Return to this inner sanctuary of joy whenever your spirit begins to weaken and stumble beneath the weight of expectations and judgments. Receive forgiveness, and celebrate your freedom.

Forgiveness restores relationships.

Day 131   I am here to forgive.

When they kept on questioning him, he straightened up and said to them, "Let anyone among you who is without sin be the first to throw a stone at her." And once again he bent down and wrote on the ground. When they heard it, they went away, one by one, beginning with the elders; and Jesus was left alone with the woman standing before him. Jesus straightened up and said to her, "Woman, where are they? Has no one condemned you?" She said, "No one, sir." And Jesus said, "Neither do I condemn you. Go your way, and from now on do not sin again."

—John 8:7-11

Forgiveness is an essential part of our life's mission. We must learn to do more, however, than not cast stones. It is relatively easy to drop a rock, shove our hands deep into our pockets, and walk away from one who has given offense, all the while condemning her in our hearts. It is a far harder thing to stand alone with her and be

138

a forgiving presence: to look her calmly in the eye and acknowledge her, to find the words that will lift her up rather than put her down.

Today, if possible, go and be with someone you have found it difficult to forgive. (If actually visiting someone is impossible, call on the person in your mind. If you have a photograph of the person, keep it nearby.) Go to this person carrying no stones. Go without expectations. Go without words that must be said. Simply go and be. Spend time together and allow the forgiveness of God to flow through you.

Make forgiveness your mission today. Cast no stones. Refuse to walk away. Choose to be a forgiving presence, remembering:
I am here to forgive.

Day 132 I forgive those who do not understand me.

Then Jesus said, "Father, forgive them; for they do not know what they are doing." And [the soldiers] cast lots to divide his clothing.

—Luke 23:34

*T*hey do not know what they are doing."

"If they only understood, this would not be happening."

Sometimes, like the soldiers who crucified Jesus, people just don't understand. Parents don't understand their children; children don't understand their parents. Husbands don't understand their wives and wives don't understand their husbands. Friends, colleagues, neighbors, strangers, even entire groups of people stare at each other, utterly baffled, their eyebrows raised, and too often their fists raised as well.

Sometimes people will *never* understand you, for reasons beyond your control. No amount of time, no amount of talking, no amount of tears, no amount of good faith—nothing you do will ever get through to them. When this happens, forgive them. Let go of your need to *make* them understand. Their lack of understanding probably stems from fear. It is not your problem. It is not an attack against which you must protect yourself, unless you choose to regard it that way. Remember that, centered in the Spirit, you are always safe.

Sit down and write a letter to someone whose inability to understand you has caused you pain. Describe your experience of the relationship and explain why you have felt misunderstood. Express your deepest feelings. Then, go on to summarize what you suspect the other person's thoughts and emotions might have been, and why he or she might have had them. Show that you are trying to understand this person. Finally, declare your desire to move past the misunderstanding. Communicate forgiveness. Even if you don't feel like forgiving this person, make yourself write the words, and thereby plant the seeds of forgiveness in your heart.

When you have finished the letter, decide what to do with it. You may keep it and reflect upon it later. You may want to actually send it. You may want to destroy it as a sign of spiritual release. Whatever you do, view this as a first step in understanding and forgiving one who does not—and may never—understand you.

I forgive those who do not understand me.

Day 133 The way of forgiveness leads to unity.

Then [the thief] said, "Jesus, remember me when you come into your kingdom." He replied, "Truly I tell you, today you will be with me in Paradise."

—*Luke 23:42-43*

*J*esus' forgiveness of the criminal who was dying beside him united their spirits forever. "You will be with me," he promised, "in Paradise." Forgiveness restores relationships. It joins what has been asunder. It can heal the most irreconcilably divided, the most dreadfully damaged relationship that one can imagine. But the work of forgiveness is hard. It requires you to have a heart that is brave, eyes that can envision a miracle, and a spirit that will never despair until the miracle has come to pass.

Today you will focus on the "envisioning" aspect of forgiveness. Prepare yourself for meditative prayer. Get comfortable, relax, breathe deeply, rest in your spiritual center. When you feel calm and aware of God's presence, imagine yourself sitting in a breathtakingly beautiful place. Take careful note of how it looks, sounds, smells, and feels. Fill yourself with its grace.

After a time, imagine someone coming toward you. It is someone with whom you are angry, or someone in whom you are disappointed. Who is it?

The person sees you and stops. Get up and go to the person. Offer forgiveness in a way that is appropriate. Notice that, as you do, your surroundings become even more radiant. Realize that God is with you in this paradise, healing both of you and uniting your spirits in a way that transcends all hurts and all differences.

Continue this meditation as long as you would like for other persons who come to mind. Visualizing like this is one way to pray for the miracle of forgiveness. Align your will with God's, and remember:

The way of forgiveness leads to unity.

Day 134   **My neighbor and I are one.**

For the whole law is summed up in a single commandment, "You shall love your neighbor as yourself."

—*Galatians 5:14*

*M*any of us seem to cut the last part of this verse short, to read, "You shall love your neighbor." Of course, we generally accept that we are to love our neighbors. But we sometimes find it harder to accept that we are to love ourselves. We find it hard to accept ourselves. Yet, the summary of God's law tells us that we love others *as* we love ourselves. Our ability to love ourselves will determine how well we love others.

If you were to pick up a pane of colored glass and look at the world through it, everything you saw would be colored by the glass. That pane of glass represents your feelings about yourself. They control your perceptions of your neighbors. If you have little love for yourself, if you are critical and demanding of yourself, so you will be of others. On the other hand, if you have deep love for yourself, if you are gentle and forgiving of yourself, so you will be toward those around you.

Think about someone who easily annoys you. Jot down this person's personality traits and behaviors that get on your nerves. Now, examine your list. Which personality traits are you afraid of having in yourself? Which behaviors do you find yourself either doing or guarding against doing? How similar are you to the person who annoys you? Could it be that your perceptions of this person are being colored by your feelings about yourself?

Whenever you feel annoyed by someone today, stop and ask yourself how you might be like this person. Then offer only *agape*. In doing so, you will be offering *agape* to yourself.

My neighbor and I are one.

141

Love is the only law.

Love does no wrong to a neighbor; therefore, love is the fulfilling of the law.

—Romans 13:10

Agape is the only law.

Amazing, isn't it? *One law*. When we allow *agape* to influence our interactions with other people, we simultaneously fulfill the spirit of all other spiritual laws. *Agape* is all that is required of us.

God has made it easy for us, at least in theory. With only one law to follow in our interactions with others, we are not as apt to get confused. God's will is made more clear, as we see in the loving life of Jesus. Jesus healed on the Sabbath without hesitation, though other laws forbade it. Jesus kept company with sinners, though other laws forbade it. Jesus respected the full personhood of women, though other laws forbade it. Jesus followed only one law, and that was *agape*.

We often allow our own rules and regulations to become more important to us than the law of *agape*. For instance, we sometimes make house rules so rigid and their enforcement so strict that no one in the family can enjoy living in the house. *Rule*: The house must be kept neat and orderly at all times. What if taking time to clean the house begins to take priority over the family's taking time to talk with one another? *Rule*: The children can't have dessert until they finish all the food on their plates (even if their parents were the ones who put it there!). What if forcing a child to clean a plate turns what could be a time of family fellowship into a battle of wills?

To help you keep your spirit focused on the law of *agape*, you might want to use an acrostic. Create your own, or use this one:

> Love
> Openly
> Values
> Everyone

Whenever you are puzzling over what is important in a relationship, repeat your acrostic as a reminder of the law of *agape*. Feel its power. Know that in openly valuing everyone, you will fulfill every spiritual law.

Love is the only law.

Love opens my eyes.

As he came near and saw the city, he wept over it, saying, "If you, even you, had only recognized on this day the things that make for peace!"

—Luke 19:41-42a

In today's scripture, Jesus laments that the people of Jerusalem could not see with the eyes of love. Right in their midst was the Prince of Peace, the personification of *agape*. But all they saw in him was a troublemaker! They could not perceive his love or his forgiveness, let alone envision a world transformed by it. No wonder Jesus wept. He recognized what was being lost because of their blindness.

Take a good look at Peter. Would *you* have called him a "rock"? He was impetuous. He would often run his mouth before putting his mind in gear. He would boldly step out of a boat and walk on the water, full of faith, and begin to sink a few moments later because he was afraid. He would vow to stand by Jesus no matter what, then almost immediately turn around and deny ever having known him. He was not exactly someone you could count on. But Jesus looked at him and said, "You are the solid rock upon which I will build my church" (Matthew 16:18). This is seeing with the eyes of love. This is seeing beyond the reality of the moment to the possibilities of the future. This is believing that God is not finished with us, yet.

Look today with the eyes of love. Think about someone you know well. Imagine what he or she might become in the future. See all the negative possibilities falling away and only the positive ones remaining. See this person reaching full potential, becoming all that he or she is meant to be. Even as Jesus looked at an impetuous Peter and saw a rock, look at your friend and see the person he or she may one day become.

Love opens my eyes.

Day 137 **Love sees beyond difference.**

I led them with cords of human kindness, with bands of love. I was to them like those who lift infants to their cheeks. I bent down to them and fed them.

—Hosea 11:4

$\mathcal{A}$ preschool class was shown a series of pictures of different families and the dwellings in which they lived. The families were from many cultures and races. Some of them included both parents, some had only one; some of them had several children, others had none. The children studied all the pictures and then were asked to talk about them. At one point, they were specifically asked to identify differences they had noticed among the pictures. In response, the children pointed out differences in family size and configurations. They talked about differences in the structures that the families called "home." But not one of them mentioned the families' differences in physical appearance.

Prejudice is something that we are taught. It is not naturally a part of our thinking. By nature, we are more prone to see our similarities than our differences, but society teaches us early on that we are not all alike, and that some of us are better than others. We are shown the lines that are supposed to divide the human family and are strongly encouraged to accept them. We are also shown how to draw our own lines.

Agape erases all of those dividing lines. It teaches us to see beyond differences, so that once again we might see all the ways in which we are alike. It joins together what we have so artificially put asunder.

Identify a person who you would consider to be very different from yourself—someone who is different in appearance, culture, personality, or lifestyle. Now invite *agape* to renew your vision. Focus on all the ways that you and this "different" person are alike. Make a list. What do you have in common? How are you similar in desires and dreams? What needs do you both have? What feelings do you share? Today, look upon every person you meet with the eyes of love, and celebrate that both of you are loved by a God who bends down and feeds us all, who lifts us up in a parent's embrace.

Love sees beyond difference.

Day 138   **Love gathers in.**

"How often have I desired to gather your children together as a hen gathers her brood under her wings, and you were not willing!"

—*Luke 13:34*b

144

A young couple agreed to become foster parents. They were willing to accept any child into their home. Soon a biracial infant came to live with them. When they told their relatives about its arrival, one woman immediately expressed her objections. However, when that woman actually saw the child for the first time, it was suddenly just a "baby." The "biracial" label disappeared. Rather than an abstract issue that could be argued, the child was now just an infant in need of love.

Love does that. It erases the little circles that we draw around ourselves to exclude people, and then draws another circle in their place—a circle larger than the universe, so that all might be included. Love openly values everyone. It is not afraid of differences, even those differences that are not understood. It is not afraid to meet another's needs, but protects and nurtures and shelters that person.

In today's scripture text, Jesus likens himself to a mother hen who lovingly gathers her little ones under her protective wings. This is how Jesus loves us, no matter who we are. In the shelter of his wings, each of us is valued as we are and nurtured to become all that God intends us to be.

Find a comfortable place for a time of meditative prayer. Close out anything that might distract you. Relax every part of your body, letting go of all tension and concern. Feel yourself surrounded by the love of God. Now, imagine that you are in a great grassy meadow filled with beautiful flowers and sunshine. Jesus is standing in the center of it, reaching out to you. He is inviting you to join him. A sense of security comes over you. You know that there is no danger here, that you are always safe when you are near Jesus. Walk toward him. His outstretched arms are still waiting for you to come closer. Finally they surround you. You are filled with great comfort and peace. Then you realize that you are not alone with Jesus. There are countless others enfolded in his arms. You do not feel crowded, though. There is plenty of room for everyone. There is plenty of love for everyone. Feel *agape* uniting you not only with Jesus but with every other person who is there. Stay as long as you wish. When you are ready to leave, take with you the peace and love that you found.

Love gathers in.

Love comforts.

"Come to me, all you that are weary and are carrying heavy burdens, and I will give you rest. Take my yoke upon you, and learn from me; for I am gentle and humble in heart, and you will find rest for your souls."

—*Matthew 11:28-29*

*I*magine for a moment that Jesus is standing right beside you. You are bound together by a yoke which rests upon his shoulder and yours. Suddenly you realize that you will never have to bear any more burdens alone. Jesus will always be there to help you, bearing the weight with you. This yoke is permanent, yet gentle. It is a great source of strength.

You might say that the yoke of Christ is similar to a hug for a couple of reasons. In the first place, both a yoke and a hug connect us to someone else. And then, that connection gives us the comfort and strength that we need to bear our burdens.

Psychologists tell us that in order to remain emotionally healthy, we need the touch-equivalent of eight hugs a day. When a hug is appropriately and lovingly given, it can be a powerful healing agent. When our day has been long, our load has been heavy, and our stress has been constant, there is nothing like it. It can relax us almost instantly. We can feel the love and peace from the other person flooding through us. It is almost as if the hug reminds our body of all the loving touches that it has ever received. We are calmed. We are comforted. We are renewed.

Today, look for appropriate times to comfort and strengthen the people around you with a hug. Do not be afraid. And do not be overly concerned about how they will respond. Just offer your hugs, realizing that you can never give too many of them away. As you give one, you receive one back. Your supply is constantly replenished.

Love comforts.

Love grows.

When they had finished breakfast, Jesus said to Simon Peter, "Simon son of John, do you love me more than these?" He said to him, "Yes, Lord; you know that I love you." Jesus said to him, "Feed my lambs."

—*John 21:15*

*F*rom the little flame of a single match can come a wonderful fire that will warm an entire room. Once the kindling has been lit, the flickering flame quickly grows into a blaze.

Agape grows like that. Take friendship circles, for instance. Its members often find their fellowship so rewarding that they begin to invite additional friends to join it. The group gets larger and larger, and after awhile, when the entire circle gathers, the house is hardly large enough to comfortably hold everyone.

Jesus knew that Peter's love for him would continue to grow and eventually would reach out to others. He didn't try to pressure Peter into that growth, but simply let him know that by loving others he would be loving his master. This invitation could have only positive results, because the more love Peter gave, the more he would have to give. *Agape* grows like that.

Think of someone you love dearly. How has your love for this person grown since you were first introduced? And, has your relationship with this person added other people to your circle of friends? Celebrate all the good that has come from your relationship. Acknowledge the joy that comes in experiencing the spread of *agape*.

Love grows.

Day 141   **Love creates community.**

"I have other sheep that do not belong to this fold. I must bring them also, and they will listen to my voice. So there will be one flock, one shepherd."

—*John 10:16*

*C*ommunity is not something you are born with, like your family line. It is not limited by geography, like your neighborhood. It is not defined by its rules of organization, like your favorite club. Community is a process. It is living with compassion, so that you and others are drawn together. It is being in communion, in a circle of unity where everyone is welcome. It is joining in commemoration of common values, common stories, common struggles, common joys. It is making a commitment to be taught and supported and comforted by one another. It is deepening communication, so that you can fully understand one another.

Make a loaf of bread whose recipe uses yeast. (For a quicker alternative, you might buy a frozen loaf of *unbaked* yeast bread to use for this exercise.) Let the process of creating the bread be a parable of community. Knead the dough and let it rise. Watch it grow under the influence of the yeast, just as surely and mysteriously as community grows under the influence of *agape*. Finally, bake the bread, and, while it is still warm, break it with a friend, remembering:

Love creates community.

Day 142 The community is my family.

And looking at those who sat around him, he said, "Here are my mother and my brothers! Whoever does the will of God is my brother and sister and mother."

—*Mark 3:34-35*

*Y*our birth family is something that happens to you. But community is something that you help to make happen. You create community by sharing your life with people who want to share their lives with you. And your community becomes your family when you "reframe" the family picture in spiritual rather than biological terms.

Who is your spiritual family? Identify its members. (Persons in your biological family may, of course, be included.) Write their names on a chart and, if possible, gather and attach their pictures. Who have been your "parents" and "grandparents"—the elders who have served as role models, mentors, counselors, and teachers of your heart? Who have been your "brothers and sisters"—those of your own generation with whom you have shared most? Who have been your "children," your "nieces and nephews"—those younger ones who have looked to you for guidance and support? Reflect on some of the qualities that the members of your spiritual family have in common. Which of these "family traits" have become yours?

Give thanks to God for surrounding you with such a family. Acknowledge that while you are one with all people, these people have touched your life in especially significant ways. Finally, close your prayer with an expression of hope. Ask that your spiritual family might continue to grow, and that you might bless their lives as they have blessed yours.

The community is my family.

Day 143   # I sacrifice for community.

We know love by this, that he laid down his life for us—and we ought to lay down our lives for one another. How does God's love abide in anyone who has the world's goods and sees a brother or sister in need and yet refuses help?

—1 John 3:16-17

*D*id you know that when geese are flying in formation and one of them has to drop out because it is sick, tired, or wounded, two other geese will fall out of formation and go down with it, to help any way they can? We might take a lesson from these friends of ours. They have never once been heard to say:

"Oh, it's Harold again. I'm so tired of helping Harold!"

"I won't go with Harold. Can't you see there are hunters down there?"

"I'd rather not go down. I'll have to fly twice as hard to catch back up, and I'm feeling a bit frazzled today."

"Don't look at me. It's not my turn to go."

"I'm not really very good at helping wounded ducks. You do it."

"There's a good tail wind, and I've really been looking forward to this trip to the lake. Couldn't somebody else stay behind?"

Geese make sacrifices for one another because it is in their nature to do so. In community, we make sacrifices for one another because it is in *our* nature. God's love abides in us. It consecrates us, joining us together in holy relationship. Therefore, we are willing to sacrifice for one another. Moved by God's love, we withhold nothing from someone whose need is greater than our own.

So, are you more like the goose that flies down with its weakened friend, or more like the goose looking for some excuse not to? Which goose better represents your attitude toward responding to the needs of those around you? Complete the following statements, being as honest and specific as possible:

I act like an "excuse goose" when . . .
When I act like an "excuse goose," I feel . . .
When I act like an "excuse goose," others probably feel . . .
I act more like an "I'll go" goose when . . .
When I act like an "I'll go" goose, I feel . . .
When I act like an "I'll go" goose, others probably feel . . .

I sacrifice for community.

Day 144   **The community works together.**

The one who plants and the one who waters have a common purpose, and each will receive wages according to the labor of each. For we are God's servants, working together.

—1 Corinthians 3:8-9a

*I*n community, the labor of each member contributes equally to the life of all. Today's exercise will symbolize this simple but powerful truth.

Begin today to plan a meal that you and some members of your community will prepare and eat together. Invite as many people to participate as you wish. After you have a guest list, choose someone to help you create the menu. Select labor-intensive, though not necessarily time-consuming, recipes (stir-fry, for example). Let there be plenty of work for everyone to do, as well as plenty of fun to be had. Ask each participant to bring some ingredients and/or supplies to the event. You might even ask a musician-friend to bring a guitar instead of groceries, to enter-tain the guests; or, arrange for someone to bring a boombox and a few favorite cassettes or CDs.

When the participants arrive, let the food preparation and cooking begin! Indicate what tasks need to be accomplished and ask for volunteers. As the work proceeds, stay in the background and coordinate the work. Try also to observe the interactions going on around you.

Finally, put a couple of people in charge of setting the table and presenting the meal. Supply them not only with table set-tings but also any candles and other decorations that will help to make the meal as pleasing to the eye as to the palate.

At last, when everything is ready, gather the group around the table. Join hands. As host, offer a blessing upon the food and each person who helped to prepare it. Give thanks for the dignity of work and the fellowship that is enjoyed when working *together*.

The community works together.

Day 145   **The community has one purpose.**

Now I appeal to you, brothers and sisters, by the name of our Lord Jesus Christ, that all of you be in agreement and that there be no divisions among you, but that you be united in the same mind and the same purpose.

—1 Corinthians 1:10

*I*magine that your car is stuck deep in mud along the side of a road. When you press on the accelerator, the tires just spin. A couple of sympathetic motorists stop to help. They lean against the rear bumper and start to push. The problem is, they have no rhythm. When one is pushing, the other is letting go. When one is letting go, the other is pushing. And you, sitting there behind the wheel, don't know *what* is going on, so you just press on the gas whenever you feel like it. Mud flies through the air. How long do you think your car will be stuck?

A community is able to work together because it has unity of purpose. To the degree that its members have a common vision and are agreed on what must be done and how, its life and work will be coordinated.

If possible, listen today to a recording of a symphony, such as Beethoven's Ninth, which ends with the familiar "Ode to Joy" (the tune of the hymn "Joyful, Joyful, We Adore Thee"). As you listen to the symphony you have selected, try to isolate the sounds of different instruments. Deepen your appreciation of how they unite to form *one* sound, alive and moving and full of power. Understand the unity of purpose that must bind one musician to the next to create the beautiful music that you are hearing. This demonstrates what can happen when a community serves a common vision.

The community has one purpose.

Day 146 **The community has one mind.**

If then there is any encouragement in Christ, any consolation from love, any sharing in the Spirit, any compassion and sympathy, make my joy complete: be of the same mind, having the same love, being in full accord and of one mind.

—Philippians 2:1-2

A community which is united in mind is also united in spirit and in power. Never is this power more apparent than when the community is united in prayer.

Identify a current need of someone in your spiritual family. Ask permission from that person for you and a number of other "family members" to pray on his or her behalf. If permission is granted, invite others to join with you in prayer for this person *at a specific time each day,* wherever they may happen to be. For example, say that a friend shares with you that she is very frustrated with her career. She consents to being the focus of prayer; she wants God to give her a sign of whether she should stay in her current job or make a change. You consult with your group, and all of you agree to pray for her from 10:00-10:05 P.M. each evening until she receives direction. You make sure that everyone in the group understands exactly what they have been asked to pray for.

United in prayer, a community can help bring its members to greater awareness of God's guidance as well as inspire them to follow it. And so its members find encouragement in Christ, consolation through love, and sharing in the Spirit.

The community has one mind.

Day 147   **The community praises God with one voice.**

May the God of steadfastness and encouragement grant you to live in harmony with one another, in accordance with Christ Jesus, so that together you may with one voice glorify the God and Father of our Lord Jesus Christ.

—Romans 15:5-6

*S*ome people worship God through chanting. After years of chanting God's praises, they can gain exceptional control of their vocal chords, to the point where they can actually split their voices and simultaneously chant high tones and low tones. One voice singing two parts at once, in perfect harmony. It is like a gifted soprano standing up to perform a solo and throwing in a superb alto line for good measure.

The community is much the same in its praise of God. It has one voice that is heard as simultaneously singing many unique, harmonizing parts.

Make a list of persons whom you appreciate for their special contributions to the "voice" of your community. Think of the musicians, the leaders, the mentors, the visionaries, the educators, the humorists—the persons who "sing" the high and the low parts, the demanding and the easy parts, the quiet and the striking parts. Praise God for their faithful "singing" by repeating the following declaration of praise for each person on your list:

I glorify you, O God, for the part sung by (name),
who blesses the community by . . .

Conclude by praising God for your own voice, trusting that it is joining with all the voices of the community in one harmonious song of praise.

The community praises God with one voice.

Day 148   I know the Spirit.

"Righteous Father, the world does not know you, but I know you; and these know that you have sent me. I made your name known to them, and I will make it known, so that the love with which you have loved me may be in them, and I in them."

—*John 17:25-26*

At the beginning of our spiritual journeys, we are not well-acquainted with God. We may not even know what to call God, beyond a few of the most common names. Through studying the scriptures and listening to the faith stories of other people, we come to know more about God. But what we really want is to *know* God, in a very personal way.

We can begin to move beyond just knowing *about* God to knowing God personally when we start to realize that God, being Spirit, is always with us, and within us. God can be *experienced*. And the experience of God cannot be fully analyzed or explained. It is a spiritual, not necessarily physical, phenomenon.

Many people, including numerous saints in the church's history, have had mystical experiences of the divine. These experiences take various forms—visions, dreams, encounters with angelic presences, the hearing of mysterious voices, and so on. Some of them come in response to specific or repeated requests on the part of the person who receives them. Others come completely uninvited, and sometimes are not even welcomed, at first. But over and over again, these experiences bring the same message: "Do not be afraid." They comfort the person's spirit, and they change the person's life.

153

Do you want to know God more personally? Are you open to having an encounter with the divine? Take a moment for meditation and prayer. Allow your whole being to relax and let go of any worry or anxiety that you might be feeling. Center your thoughts on the wonder of God being with you, right where you are. Sense the Spirit of God surrounding you. Ask God to come to you in a way that will bring you the comfort that you need. Open yourself to experiencing something that you may not have experienced before. Do not be afraid. Do not try to determine what God will say or do. Just allow yourself to receive the Spirit of God. Be still and know.

I know the Spirit.

Day 149 The Spirit changes my mind.

For those who live according to the flesh set their minds on the things of the flesh, but those who live according to the Spirit set their minds on the things of the Spirit.

—*Romans 8:5*

*L*et's say that you are up in the attic one day and you run across a cardboard box that your mother gave you years before. Inside you find many old family pictures, including a large portrait of your great-great-great grandmother. Being very interested in family history, you are excited by your discovery, but dismayed at its condition. Beneath the dusty, cracked glass of the fragile frame, the portrait looks quite yellowed and faded and covered with water stains. You are not sure that it can be salvaged. However, once you take it downstairs into the light and get it out of its rickety square frame, you begin to feel more hopeful. Maybe it won't look so bad, after all. You decide to put it in a beautiful oval frame that (just by coincidence!) you recently purchased on a whim. You shape the picture to fit the new frame by trimming off its tattered edges. With some of the background now cut away, your grandmother's face is highlighted even more. Once you reframe the portrait, you are ecstatic. It looks like a totally different picture!

When things look bad, "reframing" them can make all the difference. Looking at them in a different light, seeing them at a different angle, you may find that they aren't quite so unsalvageable as you had thought.

Consider the case of eighty-year-old Dottie. She had been sick all winter. Deciding that she was going to die before long, she asked a longtime friend to drive her to the coast for one last visit to her relatives. Not far from their destination, she happened to look up in the sky and see someone parasailing. "I always thought that would be fun," she said, her voice heavy with regret. Well, Dottie's friend immediately headed off to find the parasailing site. In a short time the two of them were sailing high above the ocean—so high that they could hardly see the boat to which they were harnessed. When Dottie finally returned home from her trip, she decided that she probably wasn't going to die very soon, after all.

With the help of her friend, Dottie was able to "reframe" her life's picture. So, do you have a picture that needs to be reframed? Identify a problem that has been frustrating you. Try to view it in a new way. For example, might the problem be offering you some sort of opportunity? Might you be able to turn it to your advantage?

Let the Spirit change your mind, and your world will begin to change as well.

The Spirit changes my mind.

Day 150   The Spirit shows me another way.

He came to Simon Peter, who said to him, "Lord, are you going to wash my feet?" Jesus answered, "You do not know now what I am doing, but later you will understand."

—John 13:6-7

Do you remember all the rules that you had to follow when you were little? Early on, they probably made very little sense to you. Why *shouldn't* you play with matches? They were exciting little things. Why *shouldn't* you talk to strangers? People were good, weren't they? As you grew older, though, you began to understand that these rules were meant to protect you from harm.

Similarly, as you grow in the Spirit of God, you begin to understand truths that at one time would have made little sense. For example, in today's scripture text, Peter had no clue why Jesus was washing his disciples' feet. He had not yet grown enough in the faith to see that Jesus was trying to teach a lesson in humility. Although Jesus was their master, he was willingly doing the work of a servant. He was showing his friends another way—a truer way—of living: living in service of others. Serving others not out of obligation but out of love. In such a life there is no teacher and disciple, no master and servant. There is only brother and sister. Like Peter, the disciples didn't get the point, but, as Jesus said, "Later you will understand."

It is important to allow the Spirit of God to show you truths that you may not have understood before. So, today, try looking for deeper meanings in your interactions. For example, if someone complains to you about something that you have done (or not done), ask what this person might be saying about himself or herself rather than about you. Perhaps something in his or her mind or heart—something that has little to do with you—has prompted this complaint. If so, think about how you might lovingly respond to his or her inner concern rather than just the surface issue. Do not become defensive. Instead, regard the person in the spirit of *agape*. Let the Spirit show you how best to *serve*.

The Spirit shows me another way.

Day 151

The Spirit bears fruit through me.

"Abide in me as I abide in you. Just as the branch cannot bear fruit by itself unless it abides in the vine, neither can you unless you abide in me."

—John 15:4

If in the early spring you were to cut a branch from a fruit-bearing tree, bring it indoors, and put it in water, it would eventually blossom, but it would not go on to produce any fruit. Such a branch can only bear fruit if it stays attached to the tree. Otherwise, it cannot get the nourishment it needs to bear fruit. It cannot fulfill its purpose. In the same way, we cannot fulfill our purpose—reaching out to others through *agape*—unless we stay connected to our spiritual source, from which we gain our nourishment. If we are removed from it, our spirits wither and die. They are unable to produce any fruit, let alone the finest fruit possible.

In recognition of our capacity to bear spiritual fruit, select a favorite fruit to eat. Find a comfortable place to sit down and enjoy it. Prepare it slowly. Then, as you eat it, admire its distinctive taste and texture. Remember who gave the necessary soil, sunlight, and rain to the plant that produced it. Give thanks for those who tended and harvested it. Rejoice in the fact that there were fruit-bearing branches which remained attached to the tree so that it might come into being. Praise God for its nourishment of your body, and then go and produce bountifully.

The Spirit bears fruit through me.

Day 152 **In the Spirit I lack nothing.**

Jesus said to her, "Everyone who drinks of this water will be thirsty again, but those who drink of the water that I will give them will never be thirsty. The water that I will give will become in them a spring of water gushing up to eternal life."

—John 4:13-14

This scripture passage contrasts the water that we must go looking for with the water that springs up within us. When we must go searching for water to drink, there is no end to the task. We may locate a source of cold, clear water, drink deeply, and satisfy our thirst. But not long after we walk away from the well, our thirst will return. And so, we will have to search for another well. Over and over again.

Jesus offers us living water from a spring that lies within us. Therefore, it is always readily available to us. This spring is the Spirit. Without it we have an endless search for satisfaction; with it, we have an source of endless satisfaction. So, our thirsting and our searching can be over, if we so choose.

How much of the Spirit do you allow to spring up within you? How often do you "put a cap on it," and seek to satisfy your thirst somewhere else? Enter into a period of confessional prayer. Acknowledge to God any ways in which you are still searching outside yourself for something that your life seems to lack. Then, ask for greater openness to the Spirit's flow, that you might drink daily of the water that offers abundant life.

In the Spirit I lack nothing.

There is plenty.

On the last day of the festival, the great day, while Jesus was standing there, he cried out, "Let anyone who is thirsty come to me, and let the one who believes in me drink. As the scripture has said, 'Out of the believer's heart shall flow rivers of living water.'"

—*John 7:37-38*

*E*arlier this century, there lived one of the greatest minds of all time. His name was Buckminster Fuller. Among other things, he was the inventor of the geodesic dome (of which the Epcot Center structure is an example). The opera house of Sydney, Australia, was also his design.

Fuller understood his life purpose to be the study of the planet's resources and their wise use. He wanted to share his knowledge with others and make "spaceship earth" (his designation) a better place to live. In the course of his studies, he discovered that there is always enough wind blowing across the surface of the earth to produce all the electricity that the people of the world could ever want. All we had to do was find a way to harness it. So, he created the three-bladed windmill, which is still the most effective tool we have for capturing the energy of the wind.

What amazed Fuller was that there is actually no shortage of any of the natural and replenishable resources that we need. There is plenty to go around. All of us on the planet could live at a comfortable standard of living if we would only learn to cooperate with each other and wisely use what we have been given.

The problem is that so many of us are unwilling to work together and to share. We have drawn artificial lines across the surface of the earth to divide us from one another. We have invented the concepts of "we" and "they" and convinced ourselves that there are not enough resources for both groups to enjoy. If we would only open our hearts to each other and to the wonderful creation that God has given us, we would truly experience the rivers of living water that never stop flowing.

Find something that you own and that you treasure. Think of someone else who might also enjoy owning it. In your heart, begin to understand that you do not have to possess it in order to enjoy it; what you share with another person is not really lost to you. When you have mentally let go of "owning" the item, give it away. As you do, celebrate the good feeling that you have as it brings joy to the other person. You have lost nothing and you have gained much. **There is plenty.**

Day 154   In the Spirit there is no death.

Jesus said to [Martha], "I am the resurrection and the life. Those who believe in me, even though they die, will live, and everyone who lives and believes in me will never die. Do you believe this?"

—John 11:25-26

If you were to put a few ice cubes in a saucepan and allow them to melt, they would turn into water. The same oxygen and hydrogen molecules and atoms would still be present, but in a different form. If you then heated the water, those molecules would change into yet another, invisible form: steam. Finally, under the right conditions, you could condense that steam back into water, freeze the water back into ice, and begin the cycle all over again. In all of these transformations, nothing would ever be lost.

The mind of Christ knows that nothing is ever lost.

The mind of Christ knows that there is no death.

Get into a comfortable position and enter into meditative prayer. When your mind is quiet and your body is relaxed, picture an insect egg on a green leaf. The sun gently warms the egg until finally you see it hatch. A little caterpillar crawls out. Watch the caterpillar eat the leaf and then wiggle away. Feel the joy of having witnessed another creature coming to life.

Now see the caterpillar returning. It crawls out on a twig and suspends itself upside down. As you watch, it slowly spins a cocoon around itself, eventually disappearing from view. The cocoon doesn't move, not even a quiver. The caterpillar is dead. Or so it seems.

But now you see that the appearance of death is an illusion. Right before your eyes, a beautiful monarch butterfly breaks out of the lifeless cocoon. It rests on the twig, drying its orange and black wings in the sun. Finally, it flutters away on the breeze. Feel the joy of its life! The caterpillar was not dead—only changed! And one fine day, the butterfly that it became will find a leaf, and lay an egg, and begin the endless cycle of transformation all over again.

Conclude your meditation with a period of reflection. What

159

does the transformation of the caterpillar into the butterfly teach you about life and death?

Nothing of the essence of life is ever lost. It is only changed. When we die, we simply shed the physical shell that we have carried around on our earthly journey. Our spiritual journey continues. Like the caterpillar that becomes the butterfly, we do not die but go on in a new and freer form.

In the Spirit there is no death.

Day 155   The Spirit heals.

So if anyone is in Christ, there is a new creation: everything old has passed away; see, everything has become new!

—2 Corinthians 5:17

The Spirit is hard at work. Its mission is very straightforward: It heals what is not whole. This mission is endless, and takes many forms: the renewal of the old, the rehabilitation of the weak, the reconciliation of the estranged, the refreshment of the weary, the repair of the broken, the restoration of the lost, the revival of the ill, the resurrection of the dead. . . .

We can assist the Spirit's healing work by sharing its vision. The Spirit's vision is not limited by time; it sees past, present, and future all wrapped up together. Therefore, whenever the Spirit sees brokenness, it also sees wholeness, already accomplished in some form. Whenever we are able to do the same, we help to bring healing about.

Consider the case of Judy, who was diagnosed with breast cancer. Tests revealed that the disease had spread to many of her major organs. The doctors gave her little hope, but she followed their recommendations and began to undergo different treatments. During chemotherapy, she grew progressively weaker under the attack of the powerful drugs. She sometimes felt that she couldn't go on fighting anymore. Then a friend advised her to change her way of looking at things. "Don't think of it as a battle," she told Judy. "Picture the drugs in your IV as a source of God's healing light, and imagine each drop entering your body not to attack its disease, but to fill it with love. Feel the light making you strong and well. *See* yourself strong and well." So Judy did. Almost immediately she felt the terrible effects of the drugs on her body beginning to subside. Her spirits lifted. She started to recover. Today, two years later, she feels whole again. While a small amount of the cancer still remains, she rejoices in the physical and spiritual healing that she has experienced. And she attributes the change, in large part, to the "change in her vision."

Teach yourself to see the world as the Spirit does. Whenever you see brokenness, change your perspective and envision wholeness in its place. See the old as made new; the weak as made strong; the estranged as made one; the weary as made fresh; the lost as made found; the ill as made well; the dead as made living. Join the Spirit's healing mission. Having the mind of Christ, help to bring forth the new creation!

The Spirit heals.

Day 156   # I believe in healing.

When he entered the house, the blind men came to him; and Jesus said to them, "Do you believe that I am able to do this?" They said to him, "Yes, Lord." Then he touched their eyes and said, "According to your faith let it be done to you." And their eyes were opened. Then Jesus sternly ordered them, "See that no one knows of this."

—Matthew 9:28-30

A recent news story told about a man, blind since birth, who, thanks to a new surgical procedure, acquired the ability to see. The man awakened from the operation to find that his entire world had changed. The things and people around him were now not only visible, but they had color and depth. His mind was overwhelmed. He tried to adjust, but even as he did, his other senses, on which his survival had once depended, became dull. More and more he felt confused, unsure of himself and his perceptions of the world, until finally he asked to have the surgery reversed. He wanted to go back to being blind.

Who knows whether this man made the better choice? The world of the blind is no less beautiful than the world of the sighted. Yet this man's story lends itself to comment. Healing changes things. Whether the healing is physical, spiritual, emotional, or relational, it will not come and go and leave things as they were before. So, if healing is to happen, you have to believe not only that it is possible, but that it is desirable. You have to trust it, to want it fully, to accept it gladly, with every fiber of your being, no matter how it will change your life. You cannot receive the new when you are clinging to the old. You have to open your hands.

Brainstorm on paper some of the possible benefits of not being healed. Why might someone wish to remain broken? What advantages might there be? What privileges? Do you see how tempting it might be, in certain circumstances, to remain unwell?

Believe in the possibility of healing. Believe in the benefits of being healed. And let there be no limits to your belief.

I believe in healing.

Day 157   All who believe are healed.

After the people of that place recognized him, they sent word throughout the region and brought all who were sick to him, and begged him that they might touch even the fringe of his cloak; and all who touched it were healed.

—*Matthew 14:35-36*

*O*ur belief in healing may sometimes be shaken. "It doesn't always come when it's needed," we may observe. A rock-solid marriage falls apart. A new mother dies of breast cancer. Why does healing come to some and not to others?

But all of us *can* be healed. We can, in the most painful circumstances of our lives, come to a sense of wholeness. The process of healing may take time, and it may not always happen in the way we have requested. Unlike most of us, God does not differentiate one form of healing from another and then rank them in order of significance. Healing is healing, and it is available to us all.

When a marriage falters, we desire the obvious—reconciliation—and if it doesn't happen, our faith is shaken. When a woman discovers a tumor in her breast, we look for a cure, and if it isn't found, we question God. In the absence of the outcome we had wanted, we feel that either our faith has been too little or our God has been too small. With our blinders set firmly in place, we do not see that healing may have happened in another, unexpected way. Perhaps divorcing was healing for the husband and wife who had been trapped for years in an endless cycle of spousal abuse. Perhaps dying was healing for the woman whose dignity had been destroyed by disease. Perhaps

162

in the end all of these people came to feel the wholeness they had longed for.

Think about a particular situation in which you believe healing, physical or otherwise, is needed. Now make a list of ways in which you have limited your understanding of how that healing should happen (as in "the problem should just disappear"). What preconceived ideas about healing do you have? For example, are some forms of healing more significant to you than others?

All who believe are healed.

Day 158   I ask for healing.

Then Jesus answered her, "Woman, great is your faith! Let it be done for you as you wish." And her daughter was healed instantly.

—Matthew 15:28

*Y*esterday we affirmed that healing is available to everyone. Healing is a process in which we achieve a sense of wholeness in the painful circumstances of our lives. It may not always happen as quickly as we might want or in the way we might expect.

Take out four pieces of paper, and give each of them one of the following headings: Physical Healing, Emotional Healing, Spiritual Healing, and Relational Healing (add or substitute other kinds of healing, if desired). For each category, identify specific needs, small or large, that you have for healing.

After you have created your lists, being as thorough as possible, enter a period of prayer. Begin by affirming your faith in the healing process. Then ask God to lead other persons to a deeper involvement in your healing. Request that, even as the woman in the scripture text went to Jesus on her daughter's behalf, someone might intercede on yours. Maybe you need someone's prayers or presence, someone's counsel or cooperation—whatever it is, ask for it, and trust that God will hear.

I ask for healing.

Day 159   I am healed by touch.

When Jesus entered Peter's house, he saw his mother-in-law lying in bed with a fever; he touched her hand, and the fever left her, and she got up and began to serve him.

—Matthew 8:14-15

$\mathcal{A}$ husband and a wife are having an argument. The war of words is escalating, when suddenly the husband reaches out and gently takes his wife's hand. The couple ceases their yelling. They become calm. Their problem is not yet resolved, but the touch has reminded them of what matters most.

A man lies in a hospital bed, agonizing with back pain. He cries out when he is moved; he wants no one to touch him. Then his minister, whom he trusts implicitly, offers to bathe him. The man agrees. Soon the man's pain begins to subside, and he sleeps soundly for the first time in many days.

A woman listens to her dying father fighting for breath. Deep in a coma, he will not let go. She knows that he is afraid. She goes and sits near him. She begins to stroke his hair, tenderly, there at his temple, where he had stroked hers when she was little and trying to go back to sleep after a bad dream. She sees his body relax. Before too long, his spirit quietly slips into the light.

Touch is powerful; it can heal in many ways. The problem is, since many of us are not comfortable being touched, we often hinder the Spirit's work. Today's exercise is meant to help you become more comfortable with your body and more sensitive to the power of touch.

The skin contains thousands of nerves that are connected to every part of the body. A light massage, especially in the morning before your bath or shower, will stimulate your entire nervous system while also relaxing you. (You may use warm oil for the massage, but it is not necessary.) *Important*: As you massage each part of your body, prayerfully affirm, time and again, "I am healed by touch." Don't hurry. Concentrate on what your body feels like. Concentrate on what it feels. Start by massaging your scalp, using small, circular strokes. Move on to your face, giving special attention to your temples and the back of your ears. Proceed to your neck, front and back; then to your shoulders and arms, using circular strokes at the joints and back-and-forth strokes on the long parts. Use larger, more gentle circles on the chest, stomach and lower abdomen; go up-and-down over the breastbone. The back should also be massaged up-and-down, as far as you can reach. Do your legs as you did your arms. Finally, vigorously rub your feet and toes.

This full-body meditative massage should take 5-10 minutes. You may want to incorporate it into your daily routine. If you do and are sometimes in a rush, massage only your scalp and feet. Again, when doing the massage it is essential to affirm:

I am healed by touch.

Day 160   I am healed by prayer.

And he cured many who were sick with various diseases, and cast out many demons. . . . In the morning, while it was still very dark, he got up and went out to a deserted place, and there he prayed.

—Mark 1:34a, 35

*P*rayer is a door through which you return to the Source that heals all wounds. Quiet yourself now, and open that door. Enter into prayer, and imagine that you are ascending the stairs that will lead your soul to the high places of God. Leave behind all of your worries, all of your fears, and all of your sufferings, and begin to feel the Spirit's reassuring presence.

As you climb the stairs, thank the Spirit for being with you, more faithful than the most faithful friend. Express appreciation for your healing process, and ask that your journey toward wholeness might proceed with joy.

Now the stairway suddenly opens up into the outdoors. You are now walking on a path, about halfway up a gently rising mountain. The mountain stretches up and up. For as far as you can see, it is covered with brilliantly colored trees and wildflowers. A stream sparkles and sprays over a bed of ancient rocks. Continue your ascent, taking in everything around you, until you reach a place where you want to stay. After spending a comfortable time there, conclude your prayer for healing with these lines taken from a hymn by Mary S. Edgar:

> God who touchest earth with beauty,
> Make my heart anew.

I am healed by prayer.

Day 161   I am healed.

For in him every one of God's promises is a "Yes." For this reason it is through him that we say the "Amen," to the glory of God.

—2 Corinthians 1:20

Amen: We sing it, we say it, we shout it, but do we really pay any attention to what the word *means*?

"So it is!" This is the "amen" that glorifies God; this is the "yes" that drowns out every "no." "So it is!" Right now, right here, "so it is!"

You have asked for healing. Amen. So it is. In some way, you are being healed, right now, right here. Yes. You. Do you see it? Do you believe it? Do you praise God for it?

For today's exercise you will need old newspapers and/or magazines, scissors, a large sheet of heavy paper or cardboard, and glue or tape. Begin by cutting out words and pictures that somehow describe or represent aspects of your life *as you want it to be*.

Now create a montage of your healed life. On the heavy paper or cardboard, arrange the words and images you have chosen into a larger, composite picture. Glue them into place. Be sure to leave no empty space in the montage. You are a whole person. You have no lack that is not being filled, no wound that is not being healed, no brokenness that is not being repaired. "Amen!" God declares. "So it is, and so it shall be!"

Keep this montage in a place where you will see it often. Let it be a reminder of who you really are:

I am healed.

Day 162   **I feel empowered.**

I can do all things through him who strengthens me.

—*Philippians 4:13*

A seed carries within it a genetic code that directs its development into a plant. While its growth is influenced by environmental conditions, for the most part what the seed becomes is determined by that code. We do not fully understand how this miracle of life happens, but we do know that after it sprouts, the seed grows by utilizing a process called photosynthesis. The plant absorbs light through its leaves and mixes it with nutrients and water absorbed through its roots. From this mixture comes the energy of growth.

We are very much like the seed that grows into a plant. We are born with tremendous spiritual potential. Our growth and development are dependent upon the spirit, which empowers us. It is our light and our living water. We absorb the Spirit, mix it with the ingredients of life, and thereby receive the energy to remain faithful to what God wants us to do.

We are empowered to do what *God* wants us to do. This is important to understand. Today's scripture does not suggest that we can defy the physical realities of life. If we are children, we should not expect God to give us the strength to do the work of adults. If we haven't done our homework, we should not anticipate that God will empower us to get an "A" on our exam. If we have not taken care of our bodies, we should not look for God to help us win a triathalon. We are empowered by the Spirit to do what we are called to do—to listen patiently to someone in pain, to teach a Sunday school class, to forgive an enemy, or to support a neighbor during a crisis. If we remain true to our calling, whatever potential God has placed within us will be empowered to grow and flourish.

Take time for a period of meditative prayer. Once you are comfortable and completely relaxed, picture yourself in the midst of a lush garden. All around you are plants of every kind. Some are flowering; others are food-producing; some have beautiful foliage. You can sense the energy of this place. It is alive with possibilities. Now, look at a leaf and imagine that you can see it absorbing the sunlight. Notice the plant quivering as its energy increases. Feel that same sunlight being absorbed by your body. Feel how powerfully you are connected to the earth. Know that every cell of your body is being nourished and empowered by the light that the Spirit provides. Affirm that the Spirit has placed you in this time and place and has given you whatever you need to live faithfully. Carry the Spirit's strength with you throughout the day.

I feel empowered.

Day 163   I experience God in children.

Then he took a little child and put it among them; and taking it in his arms, he said to them, "Whoever welcomes one such child in my name welcomes me, and whoever welcomes me welcomes not me but the one who sent me."

—*Mark 9:36-37*

*A*n old man sat in the dentist's waiting room, his eyes downcast. He would not look up for anything. His frowning face and sagging shoulders made him appear bitter and discouraged. A woman entered, glanced at him, then found a seat across the room. He didn't look up. A few minutes later, a middle-aged couple came into the room. They smiled at the old man, greeted the woman, and sat down to wait their turn. Still the old man didn't look up. Then, a mother arrived with her three-year-old son. The little boy went over to the old man, put a tiny hand on his bony knee, and said, "Hello. What's your name?" The man smiled, lifted the boy into the chair beside him, and entered into a lively conversation. The transformation in him was astounding.

A woman in a nursing home had reached the amazing age of 101. Now her physical health and memory were beginning to fail. Though she had always been a very outgoing person, she could hardly sit up in bed and visit. Her minister called on her regularly, but as soon as he would leave, she would forget that he had been there. One day he brought the children's choir to sing for her. A great lover of music, she thoroughly enjoyed the children's performance. But on the minister's next visit, not long after, she could not remember who he was. He reminded her that he served the church where she had been a member all her life, but even that made no impression. Finally, he mentioned how he had brought the children to sing for her on his last visit. At once her face lit up. She remembered very well the children and their joyful songs.

Children in our midst can create amazing transformations. They call forth the very best in us. If we are discouraged, bring us a child and we perk up. They remind us of the hope and vitality that God wants us to experience in life.

Look at the children around you today. Notice their enthusiasm and joy of life. Take time to talk with a child. Listen to whatever is on his mind. Find out what excites him. Allow a bit of his energy to rub off on you. Experience the Spirit of God that is in him.

I experience God in children.

Day 164   **Everyone is a child of God.**

Beloved, we are God's children now; what we will be has not yet been revealed. What we do know is this: when he is revealed, we will be like

him, for we will see him as he is. And all who have this hope in him puri-
fy themselves, just as he is pure.

—1 John 3:2-3

If you receive a gift from a friend but decide for some reason
not to open it, it will be of very little use or value to you. Or, if
you open the gift and then put it on a shelf and that is the last
you see of it, it will do you no good. A gift has its significance in
its being received, opened, *and* used.

God has given us a tremendous gift: the knowledge that everyone is a child of God. If we do not receive, open, and use this gift,
it will have little or no significance to us. Everyone is a child of
God. This is an affirmation that can change the world.

When a child is baptized, the liturgy reminds us that she is a
child of God. Because we recognize this fact, we vow to treat the
child in such a way that she may grow up to understand this
truth and be able to affirm it for herself. We pledge ourselves to
love her, no matter what. If we were to regard her as anything
less than a child of God, we might sometimes feel justified in
ignoring her or even in being unkind toward her. But, instead,
we try to treat her with kindness, gentleness, and understanding.
By doing so, we receive, open, and use the gift of knowledge that
God has given us.

Find a small hand mirror and tape this message on it: "You are
a precious gift from God." Put the mirror in a box and gift-wrap
it. Address the tag to a friend, and include this note: "A gift to
you from God." Give your gift away, and realize that you are presenting it to a child of God.

Everyone is a child of God.

Day 165   I am a child of God.

His divine power has given us everything needed for life and godliness,
through the knowledge of him who called us by his own glory and goodness. Thus he has given us, through these things, his precious and very
great promises, so that through them you may escape from the corruption that is in the world because of lust, and may become participants
of the divine nature.

—2 Peter 1:3-4

*Y*ou may find that yesterday's main idea was easier for you to affirm than today's. You may be comfortable celebrating the fact that others are children of God, but, like all too many of us, you may have difficulty accepting that you are, too. You have been made in the image of God. You have been created to reflect the divine presence in your life. You have been brought into the world to become "a participant of the divine nature." Ponder this for a moment.

Are you ready to say that you are a participant in the divine nature? You may be used to thinking of the divine nature as something completely separate from yourself. Perhaps you could say that you feel close to God. You might even say that the Spirit dwells within you. But do you believe that *you are a participant in God?* Can you affirm that there is no real separation between God and you?

Picture a water droplet in an endless ocean. That water droplet and the ocean are inseparable. Although it is very small, the droplet participates fully in the ocean's life. In the same way, you participate in God as God creates and sustains the world. The more fully aware you are that you are part of God, the more creative and sustaining you become.

Today's exercise is meant to be a simple yet powerful reminder of how, as a child of God, you are a participant in the divine. Fill a large bowl with cool water. Take the bowl and a hand towel to a quiet place. Enter into an attitude of prayer. When you are calm and relaxed, dip your fingertips into the water. Play in it a little. Feel it, as if for the first time. Then cup your hands, dip them in the water, and lift them up. Listen as the water flows gently back into the bowl, until droplets fall one by one from your hands. Know that the waters of your life are God's, and that the waters of God are yours.

Now, gently lay your wet hands on the sides of your face. As you feel the water on your cheeks, affirm that you are a participant in the divine nature. Affirm that you are, indeed, a true child of God, saying aloud:

O God, renew me by this water. Increase my faith, confirm my hope, and perfect me in love. Let the mind of Christ grow strong within me, until your grace is my grace; your peace, my peace; your freedom, my freedom; and your power, my power. Amen.

I am a child of God.

Day 166   # I feel nurtured.

He will feed his flock like a shepherd; he will gather the lambs in his arms, and carry them in his bosom, and gently lead the mother sheep.

—*Isaiah 40:11*

A pet requires constant care. Water, food, exercise, baths, cage cleaning, periodic checkups at the veterinarian, and, of course, some personal attention. This is the basic stuff of tender loving care.

From time to time, we may forget to provide everything that our pet needs. But God does not forget to provide what *we* need. God nurtures us constantly, providing our basic necessities and also reassuring us that we are loved, no matter what. There is no gap between our needs and God's willingness to meet them. That is because there is no division between us and our Creator. All that God has is available to us at any moment.

Today's scripture text describes God's care for us as being like a shepherd's care for the sheep. There is a tenderness in the passage that speaks volumes about the tenderness of God's care. God's arms reach out to us, offering all that we need. God holds us closer than we can imagine, gently leading us in the right ways. Truly God nourishes and nurtures us.

Take time to get in touch with the tender, loving care that God offers you. Relax. Sense the presence of the divine surrounding you. Know that you are receiving the very best that God has to give. As you breathe in, imagine that the air is filled with the goodness of God provided for your nourishment. Breathe out any feelings of loneliness or despair. Breathe in the love of God that tenderly holds you. Breathe out any pain or weakness. Pay attention to your breathing. Breathe slowly and deeply, taking into yourself the goodness of the Creator. If you wish, slowly repeat this affirmation as you meditate: "All that I need, God provides."

I feel nurtured.

Day 167   # I feel protected.

"For it is written, 'He will command his angels concerning you, to protect you,' and 'On their hands they will bear you up, so that you will not dash your foot against a stone.'"

—*Luke 4:10-11*

It was 3:00 A.M. George couldn't sleep. But then, he hadn't slept soundly in months. He was trying to find a way to save the family store. His whole life was staked on it. It had been his father's store before him, and when his father had retired, George had been proud to take it over. He loved serving the townspeople, and he catered to their needs and their whims as best he could. And the townspeople loved him, he knew. It wasn't their fault that times had changed and "left the little guys behind," as he would so often say. No, he thought, it was *his* fault. He should have either expanded or gotten out of the business long ago. Now, tonight, he knew that he was ruined. He was embarrassed. He was afraid.

George got out of bed and went downstairs. He began pacing the floor. Painful minutes went by. Then, suddenly, it occurred to him to turn on the TV. A strange thought, for him, because he never watched TV. And what could possibly be on the air at that hour? Still, the thought kept nagging him. Finally, he sat down on the couch and picked up the remote. He flicked on the set. And, in that dark half-second before a picture could appear on the screen, George heard a deep voice on the TV say, "Everything will work out." When he heard those words, George immediately flicked the TV off again. He couldn't help smiling to himself. Four simple words, coming from God-knew-what middle-of-the-night programming. But they had changed everything for him. "Everything will work out," the voice had said. Somehow he now understood that even if he lost the store, he would still have what mattered most—his family, his friends, his life. And that would be more than enough. He was safe. Those words coming from the dark screen of the TV might as well have come from an angel.

George received a message of protection even in the midst of feeling alone in his problems. However, many times we receive such messages in the presence of other people. In whose presence do you feel protected? Is there someone with whom you feel safe and free from danger? Name one person who provides this sense of security for you. This person is a messenger from God who has been sent especially to protect you. Give thanks to God for so richly blessing you.

I feel protected.

I have eternal life.

Let what you heard from the beginning abide in you. If what you heard
from the beginning abides in you, then you will abide in the Son and in
the Father. And this is what he has promised us, eternal life.

—*1 John 2:24-25*

*P*lease don't pinch me. If this is a dream, I don't want to wake
up!"

Suzy had waited a long time for this moment. Finally, she was
living in the cabin in the woods that she had dreamed about for
years. Granted, she would only be living in it for a two-week
vacation, but right now that two weeks felt as good as forever.
There was no one around, no TV, no telephone; only the trees
and the animals to keep her company. This is what she needed to
refresh her spirit. *This* is what life was all about.

Suzy's experience can help us to understand the concept of
eternal life. We tend to think of "eternal" in terms of length of
time, as "lasting forever." But length of time has no meaning to
God. What is "forever" to one who was, and is, and always shall
be? No, "eternal" refers not to a quantity of time but a quality of
life. You might say that it is what we experience when the life
we are living is so wonderful that we would want it to go on forever.

The scripture lesson for today tells us that this quality of life
is ours when we abide in Jesus. What does it mean to "abide" in
Jesus? It is to have the mind of Christ. It is to understand that
every moment we live is part of God's plan. Having the mind of
Christ, our living becomes consistent with the will of God. And
whenever we experience life as being consistent with the will of
God, eternal life is ours. Eternal life is here now, in part, and it
is coming someday in its fullest expression.

Write about a time or an experience that you wanted to last
forever. Describe it in detail. Note the qualities of that experience
which were most important to you. These qualities help to
describe eternal life. Go through your day looking for these same
characteristics in your surroundings. Be intent on experiencing
the eternal today.

I have eternal life.

Day 169   **Peace is born within me.**

For a child has been born for us, a son given to us; authority rests upon
his shoulders; and he is named Wonderful Counselor, Mighty God, Everlasting Father, Prince of Peace.

—Isaiah 9:6

$\mathscr{T}$he celebration of a child's birth is incomplete if the child's
name is not known. A name somehow makes the child real in a
way that even the child's loudest cries cannot. Indeed, the scriptures tell us that a name has the power to shape the child's character and destiny. Being well aware of this, the prophet Isaiah
christened the long-awaited messiah with many names: "Wonderful Counselor, Mighty God, Everlasting Father, Prince of
Peace."

Today you carry God's peace inside you, just as a mother carries a child within her womb. We celebrate its quickening in your
soul. As you look forward to its "birth," think about the many
possible names that you might give it. Brainstorm on paper at
least ten words and images for peace—more, if you can. For
example, perhaps you have experienced a sense of peace while
working on a volunteer mission project; so, one name that you
might give to peace is "helping." Or, if you have come to know
peace while on a quiet spiritual retreat, you might name peace
"solitude." When you have finished your list, keep it to use with
tomorrow's reading.

Know that your outpouring of names "christens" the peace
that lies within you, thereby helping to make it real. You are both
acknowledging the life of peace that is growing inside you and
giving it nourishment. Celebrate this day with joy, repeating
again and again:

Peace is born within me.

Day 170   **Peace is everywhere.**

"Glory to God in the highest heaven, and on earth peace among those
whom he favors!"

—Luke 2:14

$\mathscr{O}$ne day a woman acquires a cat, her first pet, from the
Humane Society; the next day, every other person at work sud-

denly seems to be telling "My cat likes to . . . " stories. One day a man purchases a Nissan Sentra; the next, every other car on the highway suddenly seems to be a Sentra. One day a couple christens their child with the name Kylie; the next, every other baby in the birth announcements suddenly seems to be a Kylie.

One day something new comes into your life, and suddenly you begin to experience the world in terms of it. The world itself hasn't changed, but your participation in it has.

This is exactly what happens when you open yourself to the message of God's peace. Your awareness of its presence is heightened. You sense it inside you. You experience it outside you. *Peace is what claims your attention.*

Begin today to focus your attention on the things that reveal the peace of God. Quickly review the list of names for peace that you brainstormed yesterday. Select one of the names—"helping," for example—and set your intention to be aware of its presence around you today. Watch for it, let it claim your attention, and you will begin to see it everywhere.

Peace is everywhere.

Day 171 I find peace.

Therefore, since we are justified by faith, we have peace with God through our Lord Jesus Christ.

—Romans 5:1

As we give peace our attention, our intention to see it becomes stronger every day. Eventually we find that even when we are not consciously thinking of peace, we are sensitive to its presence. Nevertheless, it can often catch us by surprise, popping up when we least expect it. It isn't that peace comes and goes. *We* come and go, or at least our minds do. Our attention wanders to other things, and sometimes we don't notice peace until something or someone reminds us of it.

Take out a couple of sheets of paper, preferably in an eye-catching color. Cut out 25-30 small slips. On each slip, write the word "peace," or use the various names for peace that you listed on Day 169. Now put the slips in drawers, cupboards, cabinets, in the refrigerator, in the glove compartment of your car, in a magazine—places where you will be likely to casually find them over the course of the next few days. Better yet, ask someone else to plant the slips, but request that she or he not hide them *too* well!

Whenever you come across a slip, let it be a reminder of the way in which the mind of Christ chooses to see the world. *Expect* to find peace. Such expectation is an expression of faith, and you will not be disappointed.

I find peace.

Day 172   **Peace reconciles.**

For he is our peace; in his flesh he has made both groups into one and has broken down the dividing wall, that is, the hostility between us. He has abolished the law with its commandments and ordinances, that he might create in himself one new humanity in place of the two, thus making peace, and might reconcile both groups to God in one body through the cross, thus putting to death that hostility through it. So he came and proclaimed peace to you who were far off and peace to those who were near; for through him both of us have access in one Spirit to the Father.

—Ephesians 2:14-18

*T*his scripture passage teaches us, first, that conflict is a wall that divides us from one another, and, second, that Christ breaks down the wall, proclaiming peace to us all. This is a powerful idea. Spend some time exploring it in writing. Respond to these questions:

(1) Long ago Jesus abolished the religious laws that were creating conflict between Jews and Gentiles (non-Jews). Today we have "rules" and "laws" that create hostility between us and other people. What are some of them? Are you willing for them, too, to be abolished, so that all peoples might be reconciled?

(2) In what specific ways can conflict be like a wall?

(3) What have been some of the higher, thicker walls in your life? What walls are you facing right now?

(4) According to the scripture text, when a wall comes down and two hostile parties are reconciled, "a new humanity" results. What do you think this means?

Keep today's main idea firmly in mind, especially when there is disagreement or outright hostility between you and another person. Add no more bricks or mortar to any wall. Do what you can to tear walls down. Do not forget:

Peace reconciles.

Day 173   **Peace unites.**

Above all, clothe yourselves with love, which binds everything together in perfect harmony. And let the peace of Christ rule in your hearts, to which indeed you were called in one body. And be thankful.

—*Colossians 3:14-15*

*I*t is very appropriate to think of a peaceful relationship as a healthy body, because the quality of our interactions with other people is quickly translated into physical symptoms. Friendly exchanges and trusted connections give us positive energy—they make us more vigorous. Experiences of hostility and betrayal, on the other hand, not only steal our vigor but leave behind negative energy in its place. The symptoms of this negativity can range from clenched teeth to migraine headaches to serious illness. The lack of peace we feel in our relationships can create a lack of wholeness in our bodies.

So, let's think of a relationship as a "body," and let's say that the measure of its health is the degree of unity and peace among its members. It thrives so long as its members are able to understand and work with one another. On the other hand, when its members lack the ability to communicate and cooperate, it suffers.

When you get dressed today, drop several coins into the bottom of one shoe. Wear that shoe throughout the day. Notice how at first the presence of the coins affects your gait as well as your attitude. Then notice how you gradually adjust to them, until you may even forget that they are there. However, even after you have adjusted to their presence, they continue to have a quiet but irritating effect on you. This is just how stress in a relationship continues to affect you even when you try to "keep busy" or "forget about it."

So, tend your relationships well. Where one member of your relational body is at odds with another, do the things that make for peace. Have no fear. Be willing to forgive. Show compassion. Offer healing. Welcome a miracle.

Peace unites.

Peace triumphs.

The God of peace will shortly crush Satan under your feet. The grace of our Lord Jesus Christ be with you.

—*Romans 16:20*

*S*atan is the name we give to that which opposes the grace of God with all its might, that resists the peace of God with all its power. It is that which rears up within us to start petty disagreements and world wars. It is that which will not prevail against the peace of God.

Peace triumphs. In the beginning, there is peace. In the middle, there is peace. In the end, there is peace. Satan arises, but to no avail. This is the promise of God.

Enter into meditative prayer, asking that God be with you. Imagine that you are outside on a beautiful day, wandering through a large grove of flowering trees. You wander around, amazed at the indescribable loveliness of the blossoms, which represent all the positive things happening in your life right now.

Suddenly, though, a storm blows up. Observe its approach with all of your senses. This storm stands for all the negativity in your life: fears, worries, troubled relationships, temptations, health problems, whatever. Watch the storm hit the grove at full strength, trusting that it cannot harm you; watch the clouds blot out the sun until only darkness remains, interrupted by frequent flashes of lightning.

Gradually the storm subsides. When the warm light of the sun returns, survey the scene. All of the trees have been stripped of their blossoms; the ground is littered with the remains. What emotions do you feel?

Now you hear the voice of God. "Walk among the trees," it says. You suddenly realize that you are not wearing shoes or socks. You are afraid that you will step on the thorns of the ravaged flowers, but you trust the voice. You begin to walk. And to your surprise, the flowers cushion your feet, like rich velvet. "Breathe deeply," the voice of God says, and you do. The fragrance of the flower blossoms is heavenly, and with each step you take it grows stronger. It buoys you up. Soon your feet cannot help it—they make you dance and skip and run and leap like you never have before. The flower carpet is endless; it stretches on and on before you, as far as your eyes can see. And in the tri-

umph of peace over the rage of the storm, you feel tremendous relief and joy. Nothing has been lost. Everything has been transformed. And everything, now, is beautiful.
Peace triumphs.

Day 175   In peace there is no fear.

"Peace I leave with you; my peace I give to you. I do not give to you as the world gives. Do not let your hearts be troubled, and do not let them be afraid."

—John 14:27

The Spirit's peace is not like the world's peace. The peace that the world gives is little more than a balance of power. Whether on the home front or the job front or the community front or the national front, it demands that we accumulate enough strength and resources to keep an opposing force from becoming a significant threat. The balance of power is fragile, indeed, and for some of us, achieving it becomes both the purpose of life and the definition of success. Yet the "peace" that comes from this balance is based totally on fear.

This is not the Spirit's peace. In the Hebrew language of the Old Testament, the peace of God is referred to as *shalom. Shalom* is so rich in its meaning that no single English word can translate it. It is a state in which nothing is lacking. *Nothing.* No need exists—no physical, spiritual, emotional, mental, social, cultural, or international need. This is because everything exists in perfect unity with God.

In the New Testament we are taught that through Christ, and through the body of Christ, *shalom* is ours, *now.* We have no more reason to fear. We have no more reason to struggle for power over another.

Take out two identical cups. Put in each of them a tablespoon of white flour. Then, to one cup, add a teaspoon of baking soda. Stir it completely into the flour. The contents of the two cups should look identical. Now switch the cups around until you don't know which is which. Pour a small amount of vinegar into each. Watch what happens.

These cups represent two hearts. The flour is God's peace; the baking soda is the fear that makes of God's peace the false peace of the world. The vinegar is the circumstances of life. When the vinegar of life is poured out, the heart that is filled with the peace of God remains steady. But when the vinegar is poured out on the heart that is filled with false peace, there is a reaction. The fear that had been hidden bubbles up. The heart is disturbed. Peace is lost.

Which of these hearts is yours?

Enter now into a time of prayer. Begin by confessing ways in which your heart is sometimes filled with false peace. Acknowledge secret and hidden fears that bubble up within you when touched by the vinegar of life. Ask that your fears be cast out by love.

Conclude your prayer with celebration. Recognize those ways in which your heart remains steady and calm when experiencing the difficulties of life. Be filled with *shalom*, the true peace of God, in which you know that all your needs are perfectly and mysteriously met.

In peace there is no fear.

Day 176 The miracle is seeing without fear.

When he had entered, he said to them, "Why do you make a commotion and weep? The child is not dead but sleeping."

—*Mark 5:39*

At about the age of eighteen months, a child begins to have stranger anxiety. For a period of time, anyone who is not familiar to the child is frightening to him. The parents are only able to leave him with family members or babysitters that he knows well and likes. He also needs consistency in his surroundings in order to feel safe. If there is to be a change in his environment, he must be introduced to it as gradually as possible.

As adults, we, too, can become very fearful of anything that is new or different. Change can be very disconcerting. It makes us wonder what might be coming next. It makes us ask what we can count on. Just think, for example, of what happens when a church's order of worship changes. Usually there is an immediate outcry of concern.

However, when confronted by change, we could choose to look at the situation in a different way. We could focus our attention on whatever has *not* changed. In the case of the change in the worship service, how much of its order has remained the same? What familiar parts of the service are still there? By acknowledging these, we will be less afraid.

Make of a list of all the things about your faith in God that do not change—the promises of God that you especially count on, the ways that God is always there for you. Be specific about what remains the same no matter what happens in your life. Now, identify an area of your life that has been troubling you lately. Keep it in mind as you review your list. Focus on the faith which remains constant in your heart, despite all changes that you might endure. Dismiss your fear. Know that, just as a child grows beyond stranger anxiety, you too can learn to trust. **The miracle is seeing without fear.**

Day 177 The answer comes with the question.

And this is the boldness we have in him, that if we ask anything according to his will, he hears us. And if we know that he hears us in whatever we ask, we know that we have obtained the requests made of him.

—*1 John 5:14-15*

*W*ithin nature, many plants are grouped together so that if one plant causes a particular problem, an antidote plant grows nearby. For example, a plant called jewelweed usually grows near poison ivy. Its juice can prevent the eruption of a poison ivy rash if it is immediately rubbed on exposed skin. Many gardeners use "companion planting" to take advantage of such natural pairings. If one plant tends to be bothered by insects, they will set out another plant nearby that will repel them. They may, for instance, plant mint among tomato plants so that they will not be bothered by tomato worms. Or, they may plant marigolds among their bean plants so that they will not be plagued by bean beetles.

In the plant world, a solution is available for virtually every problem that presents itself. This is also true in our lives. Whenever we are faced with difficulty, we will find a way through it, if we are open to seeing the way. This means that we must remain centered in the Spirit. Otherwise, our anxiety and fear may prevent us from seeing a path even if it is right in front of us. If we constantly affirm that a path will be found, we will be more likely to discover it.

Have fun with this maze. Find the way from the question to the answer. As you play with it, be reminded that even though you may travel down wrong paths for a time, the right path will always be available to you.

QUESTION

ANSWER

The answer comes with the question.

There is no scarcity.

Then he ordered the crowds to sit down on the grass. Taking the five loaves and the two fish, he looked up to heaven, and blessed and broke the loaves, and gave them to the disciples, and the disciples gave them to the crowds. And all ate and were filled; and they took up what was left over of the broken pieces, twelve baskets full.

—Matthew 14:19-20

*O*ne Sunday during worship, a minister dug deep into his pocket and found several pieces of candy. He tossed them into an empty offering plate. Then he started the plate around the congregation, inviting people to either add to the collection of candy or take a piece from it. To everyone's amazement, by the time the plate reached the back of the sanctuary, it was filled to overflowing with a wide variety of candies.

Have you ever puzzled over the story of the feeding of the 5,000? Have you ever entertained the possibility that the problem that day might not have been a lack of food, but rather a lack of willingness to share? The people may have had plenty of food, but also plenty of fear that giving it away would leave them hungry. Perhaps the real miracle that day was a miracle of generosity, which began with the one who shared the basket of loaves and fish. Did that act of sharing inspire the rest of the crowd?

However the feeding of the 5,000 happened, Jesus demonstrated that, in God's kingdom, there is no scarcity. When the crowd had eaten, there were twelve baskets of leftovers. The twelve full baskets, a symbol of the twelve tribes of Israel, let us know that there is enough "food" for all of God's children. God is the God of plenty. Scarcity is *our* problem, created by our fear of not having enough.

Sometimes we are afraid that we don't have enough time. But think about it. The amount of time that we have doesn't change. There have been twenty-four hours in a day, seven days in a week, and fifty-two weeks in a year for a very long time. We have plenty of time. The question is, do we use it wisely?

Create a pie graph showing how you use your time. Draw a circle and section off wedges of the "pie" to represent how you typically spend the hours in a day. Make the wedges larger or smaller, depending on the amount of time you give the activity. After you have divided the pie, put a "+" on one piece to which you would like to devote more time. Put a "-" on one piece to which you would like to devote less time.

Begin today to use your time in ways more consistent with your values. Whenever possible, shift time from the "-" to the "+" wedges.

There is no scarcity.

Day 179   **The miracle is gratitude.**

As he entered a village, ten lepers approached him. Keeping their distance, they called out, saying, "Jesus, Master, have mercy on us!" When he saw them, he said to them, "Go and show yourselves to the priests." And as they went, they were made clean. Then one of them, when he saw that he was healed, turned back, praising God with a loud voice.

—Luke 17:12-15

In today's scripture text, ten people were healed of a dreadful disease that had ruined their lives. But only one of them praised God for having healed him through Jesus. This man's willingness to give thanks was all it took for his story to make it into Luke's gospel. The author of this gospel obviously knew the power of a simple "thank you," which has softened many a hard heart. He knew the power of a kind word, which has opened many a closed mind. In short, he knew the power of gratitude.

One day, during her lunch hour, a woman dropped into a health food deli to buy an avocado supreme sandwich, her usual. She was not in the best of moods; the day was overcast, she was stressed out by her workload, and now she was running late. The Egyptian proprietor greeted her with a smile. "Isn't it a lovely day?" he remarked. "It's gray," she replied. "Oh, but the sun will come out again," he said. He turned away, and, without her asking him to, began to prepare her "usual," though she had only been in the deli twice before. The woman drummed her fingers on the counter, glad that the deli wasn't busy. There was only one other customer, a man sitting a few feet away. After a few minutes he introduced himself, and quickly they discovered that they had both spent time in Central America. Stories of political upheavals and amazing wood sculptors and adventures in the jungle flew back and forth between them until the proprietor finally returned to the counter. Handing the woman her sandwich platter in a carry-out bag, he said, with great emphasis, "I am very sorry to say that your food is now ready." She stared at him in amazement. "Your presence is very much appreciated

184

here," the proprietor continued. "We would wish for you to come by more often."

The woman who left the deli was not the same person who entered it. She felt for all the world as if she had been blessed. And, of course, she *had* been blessed, by the miracle of gratitude.

Take time today to write at least five notes of appreciation to others. Make at least two of the notes anonymous. Notice how good it feels to express your gratitude. And imagine how your notes of gratitude will change the day of those who receive them!

The miracle is gratitude.

Day 180   **I hear more than is said.**

Jesus said to her, "Go, call your husband, and come back." The woman answered him, "I have no husband." Jesus said to her, "You are right in saying, 'I have no husband'; for you have had five husbands, and the one you have now is not your husband. What you have said is true!"

—John 4:16-18

In this scripture passage, Jesus speaks with a woman who is also a Samaritan. According to the rules of his religion, these were two good reasons for keeping his distance. Yet, he not only talked to her but also heard and understood much more than the words that she said. In her statement, "I have no husband," he perceived the guilt and pain of her life story. His ability to hear her emotions made possible a miracle of spiritual healing for the woman, who immediately ran to tell others about this man she had met at the well.

Are you willing to listen to more than is said? If you are, you can participate in making miracles possible in the lives of others. When you do depth listening (hearing the story beneath the surface story) and when you respond to the real issues in a person's life, you open new possibilities for this person.

Say that you telephone a recently widowed friend and invite her to join the "old gang" for an evening out. She declines. You might accept her decision, say goodbye, and hang up. Or, you might accept her decision, and then go on to indicate that you understand how difficult it must be for her to think of doing something alone that she and her husband had once done together. Your compassion may touch her at a deeper level and open the way to a more meaningful conversation.

Today, listen to other people with two sets of ears. One will hear the words that are being spoken. The other will be sensitive to whatever underlying feelings or issues might be present. By your willingness and ability to truly listen, you will be inviting a miracle to happen in the lives of others.

I hear more than is said.

Day 181 I am closer to God than I know.

Immediately aware that power had gone forth from him, Jesus turned about in the crowd and said, "Who touched my clothes?"

—Mark 5:30

*J*esus was surrounded by a crowd. Why should he have wondered who had touched his clothes? Why did it matter? But Jesus was aware that this touch had not been just any touch. This touch had caused a shift in his power. It had had a purpose. Whoever had touched him had wanted to be healed.

Sometimes just being close to a person who is powerful can be healing to us. And, if we can't actually be with that person, we can draw comfort and strength from touching something that was once his or hers. Spend a moment remembering a person who was once a powerful influence in your life. Reflect upon the ways that this person left a positive mark on you. If you have an object that once belonged to this person or that you associate with this person, hold it in your hand or touch it. Feel your memories of the individual grow stronger, as if he or she were there with you. This object is a powerful and healing reminder of the influence this person had in your life. Now, find an object that reminds you of the powerful and healing presence of God in your life. It might be a cross, a Bible, a picture, or something from the natural world. Hold it in your hands. Sense the nearness of God. Celebrate all that God has done for you over the course of your life.

If possible, carry this reminder of God's presence with you today. Keep it in sight as you go about your routine. Whenever you feel in need of God's healing, reach out and touch the object. Let it be a powerful reminder that God's power is available to you.

I am closer to God than I know.

The best is now.

Jesus said to them, "Fill the jars with water." And they filled them up to the brim. He said to them, "Now draw some out, and take it to the chief steward." So they took it. When the steward tasted the water that had become wine, and did not know where it came from (though the servant who had drawn the water knew), the steward called the bridegroom and said to him, "Everyone serves the good wine first, and then the inferior wine after the guests have become drunk. But you have kept the good wine until now."

—John 2:7-10

In the book of John this is the first miracle that Jesus performs. It foretells exactly what his life and ministry will be all about—changing the ordinary into the extraordinary! Here he transforms plain old ordinary water into wine. But not just any old wine—the best wine of the party! This is a parable of how life is transformed when we allow the mind of Christ to work in us. What has been dull, everyday, and nothing spectacular suddenly becomes something worthy of our attention and our enthusiasm. Life—the present moment—becomes much more than we could ever have imagined!

Janet's life had been fairly typical. She was busy with the constant demands of owning a successful company. But most of her emotional energy was spent in regretting things that had happened in the past or in worrying about what would happen in the future. Then she was diagnosed with cancer. When the doctors told her that she had less than three months to live, her perspective on life changed, instantly and dramatically. She decided then and there to make the most of each moment she had left. Her first step was to sell her share of the business to her trusted partner. With the money that she received, she took a trip that she had put off for years because she had been too busy. Upon her return, she found that she was feeling better than she had before leaving on the trip. So, since she had always wanted to learn how to paint, she found a private instructor and began taking lessons. Devoting herself to her painting, she seemed to gain physical strength. A checkup with the doctor indicated that her condition had actually improved. Encouraged, Janet decided to take on a part-time job as an activities director at a nearby retirement center. Before she realized it, three months had passed. She continued to gain in strength, as she daily continued to do whatever brought her satisfaction and joy. Now it has been years since the doctors gave her months to live, and she is doing better than ever.

Living each day to the fullest is exactly what God means for us to do. As you move through the hours of this day, boldly repeat the following affirmation:

The best is now.

Day 183   I walk by faith.

For we walk by faith, not by sight.

—*2 Corinthians 5:7*

*G*oals, objectives, plans, policies, programs, procedures, structures, schedules, strategies, systems—all of these have a place in our lives. But especially on the journey of the spirit, we must use them with caution. Each of them is an attempt to determine tomorrow, either by making it different from today or by keeping it the same. But a spiritual journey is not about tomorrow, and it is not about our being in control. It is about this moment, and about yielding control of this moment to God. Our journey is, in short, about faith, about walking a path that cannot be foreseen.

An old proverb suggests, "When you come to the edge of the light you have been given and you are asked to take one more step, and all that might be there is a chasm, one of two things will happen. Either your foot will find firm ground, or you will learn to fly." This is walking by faith. This is being prepared to soar—to be spontaneous, adaptable, unpredictable, flexible, whimsical, and full of adventure.

Today's exercise is simply and ironically this: *plan to be spontaneous*. Do at least one thing, just for the fun of it, that you had not planned to do. In fact, your spontaneous activity may be choosing *not* to do something that you had planned to do! For instance, if you have set an agenda for the day that keeps getting interrupted, try to appreciate the interruptions. Pay attention to them instead of resenting them, and you may discover that they are somehow more important, in human terms, than your original agenda.

Whatever you choose to do, ease up. Open your entire day to faith, and as much as possible let the Spirit chart your course.

I walk by faith.

Day 184   **I listen for direction.**

And when you turn to the right or when you turn to the left, your ears shall hear a word behind you, saying, "This is the way; walk in it."

—*Isaiah 30:21*

*E*lementary school classrooms. Holiday dinners, with all the aunts and uncles and cousins. A car carrying a family on vacation, its members wrangling over which tourist spot to visit next. An office where the secretary is on one phone line as the second and third lines are ringing, two guests are waiting at the desk to be helped, and the boss has just asked for dictation to be taken.

What do all of these have in common? Everybody trying to talk all at once!

Such times can be confusing, to say the least. But just as confusing are the times when all the chatter you are hearing is inside your own head. So many voices. Which choice to make. Which lead to follow. Which way to turn. What words to say. And in the midst of all that chatter, you are actually supposed to hear the voice of the Spirit?

Part of listening for spiritual direction is learning to turn down the chatter or tune it out altogether. Then, no matter where the chatter is coming from, you can still hear the Voice telling you which way to go. Today's exercise is meant to help you with this. Begin by turning on as many things as possible in your home that make noise: every radio, boombox, television, stereo, dishwasher, oven timer, alarm clock, and so on. Now sit down in the middle of this chaos and begin to center yourself. Let the sounds be. Let your spirit rise above them. Enter into an awareness of God's presence. Do not worry if you can only achieve prayerfulness for a brief time. Even a moment is a triumph. Even a moment shows you how your spirit can learn to tune out the chatter and tune in to God, any time, any place.

In the midst of any chaos, you can center yourself in silence, and you can hear the Voice saying, "This is the way; walk in it."

I listen for direction.

Day 185   **My actions express God's guidance.**

The human mind plans the way, but the LORD directs the steps.

—*Proverbs 16:9*

*N*o doubt you have seen Secret Service agents on the news. You have probably noticed that they usually wear a radio receiver in one ear. Through this device their superiors give them up-to-the-minute instructions as to how they should carry out their assignments in protecting the President.

It is not so different when you tune in to the voice of the Spirit. You receive its bidding; then, you go and do.

Today's exercise asks that you keep a "Spirit diary." Be especially mindful of significant things that you do and say throughout the day, and, when the day is over, describe what happened in a diary entry. However, do so pretending that you are the Spirit. What did the Spirit say and do through you today? For example, "I (the Spirit) went into the store, and I saw a child who was crying and appeared to be lost. I was able to calm her down enough that I could go find a security guard." Or, "I (the Spirit) had to fire Bob today. But I refused to treat him like he had no feelings. We have our differences, but I treated him with respect." Some things that you write may sound strange coming from the Spirit's pen, but go ahead and write them down anyway: "I (the Spirit) had a huge argument with Madelyn about which TV program to watch"; or, "I (the Spirit) talked with Kenny about taking a trip to Bermuda." After you have chronicled the day's events, spend some time in quiet reflection. Which of your actions and words actually seemed to express the Spirit's guidance? Which did not? Why do you think you were more tuned in to the Spirit at some times than at others?

Always remember that, insofar as you are tuned in to the Voice, your journey proceeds under divine supervision. Let every action you take and every word you say give human form to the guiding force of your life.

My actions express God's guidance.

Day 186　　　　　　　　　　**God is always with me.**

"The hour is coming, indeed it has come, when you will be scattered, each one to his home, and you will leave me alone. Yet I am not alone because the Father is with me."

—John 16:32

*Y*ou look out into space through a telescope, and for the most part the sky seems empty. But scientists theorize that this apparent emptiness amongst the planets and stars is actually filled with invisible "black matter" which accounts for much of the mass of the universe. Indeed, you might say that, in terms of physics, this black matter holds the universe together. You can't see it, but you can certainly observe the powerful effects of its presence.

So it is with God. God holds your life together. You can't see God, exactly, but you can see—and feel—the powerful effects of God's presence. God's strength carries you when you are too tired to go on. God's love comforts you when your heart is breaking. God's hope sustains you when your world is falling apart. God's joy lifts you higher than you thought you could go. The ways that you see and feel God's presence are infinite in number and definite in their effect.

Write in response to these questions:

(1) How do you become aware of God's presence? How does God's presence make itself felt?
(2) When is it easiest to feel God's presence?
(3) What gets in the way of feeling God's presence?
(4) How does feeling God's presence on your path help you?
(5) Do you want or need to be more intentional about opening yourself to God's presence? How might you do that?

Throughout your day, no matter what happens, be mindful of this truth, and let it be a source of both celebration and comfort:
God is always with me.

Day 187 **God prepares a way for me.**

The LORD went in front of them in a pillar of cloud by day, to lead them along the way, and in a pillar of fire by night, to give them light, so that they might travel by day and by night.

—Exodus 13:21

*E*very morning on their journey toward the promised land, the Israelites arose from their beds to see a pillar of cloud in the sky. This cloud went ahead of them all day long, leading the way. Just a stroke of luck, do you think?

Sometimes the Israelites journeyed on through the cool hours of the night. Then a pillar of fire would light up the sky, showing them which way to go. Just a coincidence, or something more?

The Israelites knew better than we that "coincidences" are not really coincidences at all. They are God acting on our behalf, preparing our path. God is *always* acting on our behalf. And when we begin to view coincidences as instances of the divine presence at work—as *God-incidences*—they become marvelous "ah ha!" moments by which we can find our way.

"Pillars of cloud and fire" come to us when we need them most. For example, a vivid rainbow, a brilliant sunset, or a favorite animal may appear to remind us of God's presence. Or we may be comforted when we hear, at just the right moment, a favorite hymn or scripture verse. Or we may bump into a friend who has been on our mind and find that the encounter gives us a lift.

Such God-incidences grab our attention because of their timeliness. They make us sit up and take notice. And they often point us in a direction that otherwise we might not have taken. But we have to keep our eyes open. Pillars of cloud and fire will do us little good if we never notice them in the sky.

Make a list of God-incidences that have caught your attention lately—the timely things that you have heard or seen or experienced. Then enter into prayer. Express your gratitude for God's acting on your behalf. Then ask that you might be made more aware of the divine signs and wonders that mark your path. Trust that your prayer will be answered.

God prepares a way for me.

Day 188 **Nothing stands in my way.**

He has told you, O mortal, what is good; and what does the LORD require of you but to do justice, and to love kindness, and to walk humbly with your God?

—Micah 6:8

Trevor Ferrell, a twelve-year-old boy living in Philadelphia, saw a report about a homeless man on TV. Moved by the story, he went to his father and asked if he might have some money to purchase a blanket for the man. His father reacted by listing all the reasons why he shouldn't. But Trevor persisted. Not only did he manage to purchase the blanket, but he eventually started

"Trevor's Campaign," an all-out effort to offer support to homeless persons. Today, among other things, Trevor's Campaign collects and distributes clothing and food, and also runs a halfway house where homeless men and women can begin to change their life situations.

Trevor Ferrell let nothing—not even his father's cynicism—stand in his way of doing justice. His faithfulness is a lesson to us. Nothing but our own littleness of spirit and narrowness of mind can prevent us from doing the good that God would have us do.

If Trevor's faithfulness is a lesson to us, it is also a challenge. Like the words of the prophet Micah, his example summons us to join him in doing God's justice. So, identify a kind act that you may have thought of doing on behalf of another person, but then found reasons not to do. Find a way to do it now, and allow nothing to stop you. When you have accomplished it, celebrate the miracle of how simple such tasks can be when we do them without hesitation!

Nothing stands in my way.

Day 189 My path is filled with joy.

You show me the path of life. In your presence there is fullness of joy; in your right hand are pleasures forevermore.

—Psalm 16:11

Have you ever noticed that the world is filled with a great many people who seem sad, tired, gloomy, angry, worried, or bored? It is almost as if they are postponing happiness until their kids move out or their retirement comes or their lottery number is picked. Their lives seem to be living them instead of the other way around.

What about you? Are you passive, letting life happen to you? Or are you actively living it to its fullest?

Take out a piece of paper and some crayons, colored pencils, or markers. Draw a path on the paper, complete with details like rocks, weeds, streams to be crossed, and so on. Include any obstacles that have complicated your way. Let this path represent, in general, the more recent days of your spiritual journey.

Now, in the space around the path, draw simple images of whatever has given you joy lately: people, events, animals, the weather, good food, problems that you have resolved. Use especially bright colors when drawing them. Be specific and include as many things as you can.

When you are finished, observe that, despite any difficulties you have faced, your path has been filled with abundant pleasures. Give thanks to God for every one of them, and try today to be aware of all the sources of joy that sustain you. Do not forget: **My path is filled with joy.**

Day 190   I am becoming more fully aware.

For now we see in a mirror, dimly, but then we will see face to face. Now I know only in part; then I will know fully, even as I have been fully known.

—1 Corinthians 13:12

*I*t is frustrating to know that what we are seeing of our lives is only a part of the total picture. We want to see life clearly and completely—*now*. But as the mind of Christ grows within us, we become increasingly aware of the big picture. Our vision takes on a broader perspective.

Learning to see how the individual parts of our lives might fit together is a lot like putting a jigsaw puzzle together. We might begin by identifying the outside edges of the puzzle and linking them together. This shows us the overall size of the picture and also begins to suggest where certain colors or patterns will be found. Then, we might want to separate the remaining pieces by some distinguishing characteristics. After that comes the time-consuming and often confusing task of putting all the pieces together. We can get so focused on the individual pieces that we can't see how they combine to form the bigger picture. But gradually, by much trial and error, we learn how to fit everything together. With every piece that we hook up, our awareness grows.

Locate a jigsaw puzzle that you can begin to put together. If you are a beginner, you might want to select a puzzle with fifteen hundred pieces; if you like a challenge, try a bigger one. Find a spot where you can leave the puzzle pieces lying out until you have completed it. Allow the process of putting it together to become a parable of your own growth in spiritual insight.

I am becoming more fully aware.

Day 191   # I am learning the power of the light.

The light shines in the darkness, and the darkness did not overcome it.

—John 1:5

*S*uppose that it is after dark and you have gone for a drive around town. In the sky you notice the circling of a searchlight. Your mind begins to race through the possibilities of what the search light might mean. Maybe there is a festival or carnival nearby. Perhaps a store is having a grand opening or a huge sale. Finally you decide that the only way to find out for sure is to follow the light to its source.

Light is powerful. It can certainly get your attention. And the smallest amount of light can dispel a tremendous amount of darkness. As the light increases in intensity, the darkness can be completely eliminated, and even the shadows of objects can disappear.

We say that God is light, in whom there is no darkness. One way that you can experience the light of God is to combine it with the law of substitution. The law of substitution, as you may recall, states that it is much more effective to substitute a positive thought for a negative one than to simply eliminate the negative.

Take a moment to jot down a typical negative (dark) thought that often passes through your mind. Now, substitute a positive (light-filled) affirmation for it. For example, if you often think, "I am a worthless person," you might substitute, "I am a child of God." Today, try to recognize the moment when that dark thought pops into your mind. Then immediately replace it with your light-filled statement. You will begin to feel the light of God dispelling the darkness within you.

I am learning the power of the light.

Day 192   # I am a child of the light.

Jesus said to them, "The light is with you for a little longer. Walk while you have the light, so that the darkness may not overtake you. If you walk in the darkness, you do not know where you are going. While you have the light, believe in the light, so that you may become children of light."

—John 12:35-36

*J*esus teaches an important lesson in this passage: What we believe influences what we become.

Western medicine is beginning to understand this. For example, evidence is mounting that if we believe we are unable to adequately give or receive love, we may quite literally experience "heartache," "heartbreak," or "heart attack." Or, if we believe that the troubles of life are eating us alive, we may quite literally be consumed by cancer. On the more positive side, if we believe that we are capable of maintaining loving relationships, and of growing and learning through our difficulties, our physical health will be enhanced. This is certainly not to suggest that every instance of disease has an emotional cause, and that, if it does, it should not be treated by medical professionals. However, much disease does seem to be related to emotional *dis-ease,* and all disease is probably best treated by more than Western medicine alone.

What we believe influences what we become. In spiritual terms, if we intentionally cultivate the mind of Christ within us, we will become Christ-like. We will become children of the light.

Identify some troublesome areas of your life that seem to be filling you with darkness. Be as specific as possible.

Now, prepare yourself for a time of meditative prayer. Get in a comfortable position, close your eyes, relax your body, calm your mind. When you feel ready, imagine that a powerful beam of light is shining forth from you. Let this image grow strong in your mind. Then picture the beam of light penetrating the "dark spots" of your world, illuminating them, making them brighter and brighter until even shadows disappear. Feel the joy that comes in being filled with the light. Feel the assurance that comes in radiating the light, and in knowing that the darkness cannot overtake you.

As your time of prayer comes to an end, hold fast to these feelings. Commit yourself to believing, throughout the day, that you are a child of the light. Commit yourself to being the light. Be confident, wherever you go, that you can dispel the darkness. Remind yourself, again and again:

I am a child of the light.

Day 193   **I am given greater vision.**

Then Jesus laid his hands on [the blind man's] eyes again; and he looked intently and his sight was restored, and he saw everything clearly.

—*Mark 8:25*

196

*W*hat a world! Such details! Such definition! Wayne had never imagined that the world might look like this. When he stepped out of the optometrist's office wearing his glasses for the first time, he was overwhelmed. Now he could look at the trees and see individual leaves. He could look at streetlights and not see huge, undefined spots of light. He could look in the direction of a bird's song and actually see the bird. A whole new world was unfolding before him.

Wayne's experience of getting his first pair of glasses is symbolic of how our spiritual vision can increase. At first, we may see only dimly the world that is waiting for us. But our vision of that world changes as the mind of Christ becomes *our* mind. We are like the blind man in today's scripture passage. When Jesus first restored his sight, the man could see only forms of people that looked like trees. But then he looked intently, and he gained full vision. The mind of Christ invites us to look intently at life and to see clearly all that God has provided.

Find a pair of eye glasses that are not your own (or are not your current prescription). Wear them for a few minutes and notice how blurry the world becomes. If you are unable to locate a pair of glasses, you can get the same effect by looking through drinking glasses. Try moving about with this restricted vision. When you have begun to feel the frustration of not being able to see clearly, return to your normal vision and experience the relief that comes to you. Celebrate that on your spiritual journey, your vision is increased, day by day by day.

I am given greater vision.

Day 194   **My senses are sharpened.**

"'For this people's heart has grown dull, and their ears are hard of hearing, and they have shut their eyes; so that they might not look with their eyes, and listen with their ears, and understand with their heart and turn—and I would heal them.'"

—*Matthew 13:15*

A sensory awareness activity that many children enjoy is the "feelie box." A feelie box is made by cutting a hole in the side of a small box and then filling the box with several different objects. The child reaches into the hole and grasps one of them. After feeling it for a few minutes, he guesses what it might be, and then pulls it out to verify his guess. Over time, the child gets better at figuring out what he has in his hand, even though the objects in the box change.

As we work with our senses, they become sharper. And, as our senses become sharper, we obviously become more perceptive of our world. Over time, we discern more and more of its beautiful intricacies and miraculous harmonies.

Our spiritual senses are not unlike our physical senses, in this regard. As the mind of Christ grows within us, our faith grows. And, as our faith grows, so too does our ability to apply that faith to everyday life. Over time, we sharpen our ability to hear the voice of God, to see the work of God, and to feel the presence of God. And what our senses reveal to us is healing to our souls.

The next time you eat a meal, prepare your food slowly, noticing its every color and shape. Smell its aromas. Then eat, and celebrate its tastes, its textures. Thank God for giving you the ability to perceive such details. Finally, be aware that, just as your physical senses are sharpened by this kind of mindfulness, so too are your spiritual senses. Have the mind of Christ, and be healed!

My senses are sharpened.

Day 195　　　　　**My future is revealed.**

"When the Spirit of truth comes, he will guide you into all the truth; for he will not speak on his own, but will speak whatever he hears, and he will declare to you the things that are to come."

—John 16:13

A basic theme of this book is that, if we ask for guidance, we will not be left in confusion and uncertainty. God has promised to make the way known to us as we move forward in our spiritual journeys. We need only to ask God to show us what our next step should be. That is all we need to know. It is not important that we see what is around the corner or in the distant future.

Before beginning this meditative prayer, write on a piece of paper one area of your life where you would like some direction. Now, find a comfortable spot. Close out any distractions. Begin to relax every muscle of your body. Release any tension you feel. Breathe deeply and slowly, using the full capacity of your lungs.

Now, imagine that you are outdoors in a very beautiful setting, surrounded by plants and flowers. For a few minutes, you walk among them, enjoying their pleasant fragrances. Then you see a spot ahead of you where some soil has been prepared for planting. You go to it and discover that your name is on a little sign nearby. The spot is yours. There are some seeds waiting to be planted. You reach down and pick them up, knowing that these seeds are your future. As they grow, your potential will be realized. Carefully and lovingly, you plant the seeds and cover them gently with soil. Now you settle back in a lawn chair and wait to see what will happen.

The sun is shining warmly. After a short time, the soil slowly breaks open, and a sprout appears. A plant begins to grow. You watch in amazement as it continues to develop and reach maturity. What kind of plant is it?

Now, think awhile about the situation for which you are in need of guidance. If this plant were bringing you a message about the next step you should take, what would it be? Listen. Be still and know the answer to your question.

If a clear answer doesn't come to you, don't get frustrated. A message *will* come, in its own time, in its own way. Whether it comes today, tomorrow, or next week, be ready. And when you receive it, prepare to do as God has prompted.

My future is revealed.

Day 196　　　**I perceive the mystery of God's will.**

He has made known to us the mystery of his will, according to his good pleasure that he set forth in Christ.

—*Ephesians 1:9*

*D*o you have a favorite mystery program that you enjoy watching on TV? When you watch it, do you look for clues, trying to solve the mystery before the program concludes? If you are a devoted fan of such programs, you may have sharpened your detective skills. You may have become more astute in your observations and more accurate and quick in your solutions.

Discerning God's will for our life can be like solving a mystery. We can be certain that the mystery has an answer, and that we will know it by the end of the "program." But can we discover the answer before then? We can, if we look for the clues and make good sense of them. The greatest clue that we are given is the mind of Christ. When we examine the life, ministry, and teachings of Jesus, we receive insight into the will of God for our life. Most especially, we receive insight into the law of *agape*. Whatever else it is to be, our life is to be a *loving* life. We are to love God with all that we have and love our neighbor as we love ourselves.

Today, become one of God's detectives. Look everywhere for "evidence" that *agape* is alive and well in your world. Search for "suspects"—people who are loving God and loving others. Each time you discover a bit of *agape*, celebrate that you are solving the mystery of the will of God.

I perceive the mystery of God's will.

Day 197   **Signs of God's will are all around me.**

In the time of King Herod, after Jesus was born in Bethlehem of Judea, wise men from the East came to Jerusalem, asking, "Where is the child who has been born king of the Jews? For we observed his star at its rising, and have come to pay him homage."

—Matthew 2:1-2

*T*he wisemen were not the type to spend every free evening reclining in their easy chairs, watching a movie on cable. They were constantly out and about, studying their world. They weren't always sure what they were looking for, exactly, *but they always expected to discover something that had significance for their lives*. With great anticipation and even greater patience, they searched creation for signs of the divine at work. And, sure enough, one day a sign was there. A new star in the sky. And immediately they were on the move.

The star that the wisemen saw was an external sign from God. External signs come through your physical senses. Something outside yourself makes you feel that you are being guided. Examples of external signs would include God-incidences, important discoveries, eye-opening surprises, major obstacles, and new acquaintances.

Internal signs, on the other hand, come through your spiritual senses. Something inside you makes you feel that you are being led. Examples of internal signs would include intuitions, unusually strong emotions (whether positive or negative), significant changes in your health or energy level, and dreams.

Be alert in the next week or so, and keep a daily record of the signs you receive of God's will for your life. Expect to see them around you. Expect to feel them inside you. Whenever you suspect that you have perceived a sign—and you will—ask yourself what it might mean. And then, like the wisemen who discerned God's will, prepare at once to act.

Signs of God's will are all around me.

Day 198   Creation is happening all around me.

Then I saw a new heaven and a new earth; for the first heaven and the first earth had passed away, and the sea was no more.

—Revelation 21:1

As the scripture text says, "The sea was no more." In other words, in the perfect world chaos no longer exists. There is no place where monsters still lurk, where storms blow up, where winds whip waves into a frenzy. There are no more boats that sink, no more souls that drown. There is only God's peace, and God's peace is never disturbed.

God depends on us to help make this vision of the new earth a reality. God implores us to stop conquering and exploiting and destroying the earth. God asks us instead to deeply love and respect the earth, to regard every animal and individual, every forest and river as equally precious. God calls us to be co-creators of a new earth, where *agape* rules and *shalom* is real.

In answer to our calling, we swear to protect the earth's unfolding life. It is no wonder, then, that we begin to see creation happening all around us. We recognize that we are vital participants in the creative process. Whenever we do justice and show kindness, whenever we offer love, we bring the dream of the new earth a little closer to reality.

Write a letter to God in which you pledge your willingness to co-create the world. Make your pledge as specific as possible. For example, identify an instance of chaos in your life ("My days are too busy—I'm going crazy"). You could pledge to help God transform this chaos into peace by simplifying your daily schedule to allow for at least one half-hour of personal reflection. As another example, identify a way in which contempt for the earth is being shown in your neighborhood ("There's a lot of litter around here"). You could pledge to help God transform this contempt into respect by picking up the litter in a certain area on a regular basis. Whatever you pledge in your letter, express your desire to be God's partner in bringing about a new creation, celebrating the trust and hope that God has placed in you.

Creation is happening all around me.

Day 199 Creation speaks.

Some of the Pharisees in the crowd said to him, "Teacher, order your disciples to stop [proclaiming you the Messiah]." He answered, "I tell you, if these were silent, the stones would shout out."

—Luke 19:39-40

One morning Enrique was walking from the parking lot toward the building where he worked. His steps were heavy; he was already tired, and his day had not yet begun. Part of him really wanted to turn around, go back to his car, and go home. Suddenly, though, he heard something in the air above him. He looked up. A gaggle of seven Canadian geese was flying low in a V, almost directly above him. He stood and watched. For a moment, he forgot work. He forgot himself. And when finally the geese had become specks against the gray winter sky, he walked on to his workplace with a lighter step. As he said later, "The geese just let me know there was more to the world than my work. And somehow that made everything better."

Whenever there is truth to be told, creation will tell it. Sometimes the message comes through a gaggle of geese whose steady flight toward a distant horizon gives us a fresh perspective on where we are. Sometimes the message comes through a gigantic rock formation which, having stood against the weather for countless generations, teaches us that we can endure. Sometimes the message comes through huge, shape-shifting clouds which remind us that what we see often depends on what we are looking for. The voice of creation constantly speaks, telling us something we need to know, but only those of us who are listening will hear.

Listening to the voice of creation requires a ready heart and a quiet mind. And it takes time. So, make time today. Go outside and take a meditative walk, stopping every so often to sit or stand in silence. Then wait, watch, feel, listen, smell. The natural order will have one or more lessons for you. Perhaps you will be taught by a tree, or the sun, or a pair of birds singing to one another, or a breeze that is both fresh and cold. Let the teachers of creation speak to you, and be grateful for the wisdom you receive.

Creation speaks.

Day 200   Creation sings.

For you shall go out in joy, and be led back in peace; the mountains and the hills before you shall burst into song, and all the trees of the field shall clap their hands.

—Isaiah 55:12

*C*reation sings wonderful words of life. Apparently the music industry has finally caught on to this fact. More and more recordings are being made which feature the sounds of nature, either alone or in combination with instrumental and vocal music. Sales of this "new music" are booming. Those of us who are buying it find that the music can inspire, relax, and soothe us. We like what we hear, and we clamor for more.

If you are lucky, you do not always have to resort to "canned creation music" for refreshment. You can listen to the real thing. Take time today to go to a place where you know that creation will sing to you. Go expecting to hear beautiful music, just as you would when attending any other concert. Sit down in a comfortable spot and let the performance begin.

As creation serenades you, listen for high notes and low notes. Listen for different qualities or timbres in the voices—sweetness, harshness, gentleness, shrillness. Listen for rhythms, both steady and sporadic. Pick out sounds that are especially pleasing to you, as if they were your favorite instruments in an orchestra, or your favorite parts of a chorus. Above all, just let yourself be surrounded by the music. Allow the joy and peace of its songs to fill your soul.

Creation sings.

Day 201   Creation is endless.

You are the hope of all the ends of the earth and of the farthest seas. By your strength you established the mountains; you are girded with might. You silence the roaring of the seas, the roaring of their waves, the tumult of the peoples. Those who live at earth's farthest bounds are awed by your signs; you make the gateways of the morning and the evening shout for joy.

—*Psalm 65:5b-8*

*N*owhere does God's creation leave off and something else begin. Creation is not limited by geography, as is supposed by people who tell us that certain nations are cursed while others are blessed. Creation is not limited by time, as is supposed by people who tell us that the age of miracles and prophets and visions is past. Creation is not limited in form, as is supposed by people who tell us that the old ways are the only ways and the new ways will be our ruin. No, the transforming work of creation goes on and on, crossing all borders, stopping all clocks, and breaking all molds.

God's creation has no boundaries of any kind. Therefore, as co-creators with God, we must diligently un-create any boundaries that we have somehow created. One way to do this is to recognize instances of our own "divided thinking." For example, if we hear a voice within us say, "That war is happening far away. It has no effect on me," or, "Things were so much better back then than they are now," or, "This divorce has absolutely ruined my life," we must pay it no attention. That voice does not belong to the mind of Christ. If it did, it would be saying, in full honesty, "I am every soldier in that war, and every victim of it," and, "Things couldn't be better than they are right now," and, "Not even a divorce can ruin my life." This is the voice we must listen for. This is the voice we must follow.

Today, help to co-create God's endless creation. First, be aware of when you are becoming tense or upset, even mildly so. Recognize this emotional response as a symptom of divided thinking. Next, take a deep breath and ask yourself how you are seeing the situation in a "broken" way. What have you falsely set apart?

Suppose that you are running late. You are caught in a traffic jam, and someone pulls in front of you. You feel irritated. If you calm your thinking, you will recognize that your anger is the result of seeing yourself as separate from the other driver (and so somehow more deserving of your own place in the traffic). Your anger is also the result of regarding your time on the road as a waste of time. This, too, is divided thinking. If all time is God's time, no time can be wasted.

When you have identified your divided thinking, relax. Then mentally affirm the divine connectedness of what you were trying to separate. Say, for example, "The other driver and I are the same person—a child of God"; and, "My time here is the same as it would be anywhere else—God's time."

Doing this, you will gain a deeper appreciation for the endlessness of God's creation. Then you will know that morning and evening shout for joy—not because they are separate, but because they are inseparably joined!

Creation is endless.

Day 202 **Creation offers unlimited possibilities.**

About midnight Paul and Silas were praying and singing hymns to God, and the prisoners were listening to them. Suddenly there was an earthquake, so violent that the foundations of the prison were shaken; and immediately all the doors were opened and everyone's chains were unfastened.

—*Acts 16:25-26*

*B*ecause God's creation is endless, it offers unlimited possibilities. *Anything can happen.*

Paul and Silas had every reason to despair. They had been on a long missionary trip, over land and sea, and finally they had ended up in Philippi. They had been in the city for several days, spreading the gospel and resting their travel-weary bones. Then, on the Sabbath, as they were going to a place of prayer, Paul casually exorcised a slave girl's spirit of prophecy. Her owners—who, incidentally, had been making good money off her powers—promptly dragged Paul and Silas off to court. There, with no opportunity to defend themselves, the two were stripped naked, beaten with rods, and finally tossed in jail. Their feet were clamped in stocks. Sore and bleeding, tired, cold, hungry, uncomfortable in their shackles, uncertain of the future, locked up in the innermost part of a prison in a foreign country with no one to come to their aid, what did Paul and Silas do? Complain? Worry? Scream at the guards? Blame God? No. They prayed. They sang. They trusted.

And God heard. And when God heard, creation responded. News flash: "An earthquake of strong magnitude has just struck the city of Philippi in Macedonia. No damage estimates have been reported yet, but prisoners are rumored to have escaped from the penitentiary. . . ."

Anything can happen, this story suggests, unless you choose to keep your spirit in shackles. If your spirit is being prevented from moving ahead on its journey, it is only because you allow it to be. Whether you are tying down your spirit with old prejudices, old mind-sets, old grudges, or old wounds, you must allow God's power to break them.

Identify one "shackle" that currently prevents you from freely co-creating your life with God (for example, a lack of confidence or a sense of financial insecurity). Ask God to help you "create it away." Prayerfully strategize how you might help God to break its hold on your spirit. Listen for any ideas or insights that God may inspire, knowing that if they don't come at this moment, they will come at another. Remain attentive, and trust that one day the earth will quake, the prison door will open, and all your chains will fall away.

Creation offers unlimited possibilities.

Day 203   **The future is wide open.**

Then Jesus cried again with a loud voice and breathed his last. At that moment the curtain of the temple was torn in two from top to bottom. The earth shook, and the rocks were split.

—Matthew 27:50-51

The curtain spoken of in this passage concealed the most holy place in the Jewish temple. This was an entirely empty, totally dark sanctuary which was entered only once a year, on the Day of Atonement, and then only by one person, the high priest. When its curtain was torn from top to bottom at the moment of Jesus' death, the barrier between God and humanity was removed. This was a sign that all people now had equal access to the divine presence. Nothing stood between earth and heaven. And, just as the curtain of the temple was torn, the rocks of the ground were split. All of creation lay open to the presence of God. Good Friday was, indeed, a day that shook the world. The shock waves of that day continue. Along with the rest of creation, you stand in the fullness of God's presence, and the future lies open before you. Do you believe?

Yesterday you identified one shackle that has been holding your spirit down. Now, using a marker on a large piece of old cloth (or, if you have none, a sheet of newspaper), list additional ways that you have been limiting yourself, confining yourself, creating obstacles for yourself, and erecting barriers between yourself and God. Be thorough. When you are finished writing, stand up. Take hold of the cloth, and rip it through. Celebrate your freedom. Praise God for the power of Christ, which releases you from all the bonds of the past and opens you to all the possibilities of the future.

The future is wide open.

Day 204   Peace is with me.

When it was evening on that day, the first day of the week, and the doors of the house where the disciples had met were locked for fear of the Jews, Jesus came and stood among them and said, "Peace be with you."

—John 20:19

The disciples hid behind locked doors. Their master was dead. They were stricken with grief. They were ashamed that they had been unfaithful. They were afraid that they would be persecuted as coconspirators. But then, Jesus appeared, there in the room with them. "Peace be with you," he said. Just the right words. He knew their need for reassurance and for hope.

Their need is our need also. We, too, are afraid, and our fear makes peace impossible. It makes us stay indoors behind locked doors, to avoid whatever threats might await us, and to guard against whatever might intrude. Perhaps we are afraid of being hurt. Perhaps we are afraid of being changed. So, we close the doors and lock out the world. That is not peace. Peace comes to us when our hearts are courageous, when we stand out in the open, vulnerable to the realities of life, yet confident of God's protection.

Walk outside for a few minutes. If it is raining, consider going out without an umbrella. If it is cold, go out without a coat. Allow your body to feel the elements, if only for a short time. As you do, let go of any fears or anxieties that you may have. Feel the peace that comes when you stand vulnerable, yet safe, in the midst of the world God has given you. This peace is but a taste of the peace that God wants you to carry with you always.

Peace is with me.

I am not troubled.

"Do not let your hearts be troubled. Believe in God, believe also in me."

—John 14:1

*I*f you are honest, you will almost surely admit that your heart is troubled about something. You may be distressed about a particular relationship. You may be worried by your financial situation. You may be filled with uncertainty about your future. Whatever is troubling you, it is preventing you from experiencing perfect peace.

Today's passage of scripture reinforces the idea that a connection exists between what you believe and how troubled you are. What is it? Think back to the four-step interaction process that we discussed on Day 121. Every exchange you have with others includes a triggering event, a belief, a feeling, and a response. What you believe is of utmost importance. What you say to yourself in that step has a great influence on the rest of the interaction.

The same is true in your own "inner-action." When you are stewing and fussing over a particular dilemma in your life, one of the most helpful things you can do is identify the beliefs and assumptions that are operative in your thinking. Once you have clarified these, you can decide whether it would be best to hold onto them or let go. Your decision will significantly influence your feelings about the situation, as well as any response actions you might take.

Write down the details of a situation that has been bothering you lately. Now, state in one or two sentences what you believe about the situation that causes you to be anxious or fearful. Next, note how this belief negatively influences your feelings and responses. Finally, reframe your belief in a way that might positively influence your feelings and responses.

Here is an example. Perhaps you have a co-worker whose negative attitude is very frustrating to you. After describing this situation in detail, you would state your beliefs about it—beliefs that are probably contributing to your frustration, such as "That person shouldn't be so nasty. It makes it impossible for me to work. I can't enjoy what I'm doing." How do these beliefs negatively influence you? Perhaps you go to work expecting trouble. Perhaps you are so busy judging your co-worker that you never seek to understand the reasons for the bad attitude. Perhaps you focus so much on your co-worker's negativity that you don't notice the good things about your job. Perhaps you are ready to look in the help-wanted ads for another position, and so on. How might you reframe your beliefs about the situation in a more positive way? Perhaps you could say: "The person is doing the best that he (or she) is capable of right now. I don't have to let his (or her) negativity get me down. I enjoy this job very much, so I'm going to concentrate on feeling that joy and sense of accomplishment," and so on. As you clarify your beliefs and reframe them toward the positive, see your problem becoming more manageable. Feel your troubles melting away.

I am not troubled.

Day 206   **I do not fear death.**

For he was teaching his disciples, saying to them, "The Son of Man is to be betrayed into human hands, and they will kill him, and three days after being killed, he will rise again."

—*Mark 9:31*

*W*hat is death? Is it not the shedding of the physical body that has carried us through this life? In death we leave the "tent" that we have used awhile (2 Corinthians 5:1) and enter a "mansion" that was not made with human hands. There we experience a life of perfect unity with God. Why does this "change of residence" fill us with fear?

If we focus our attention upon the physical side of death, there can be great cause for fear. We can be anxious over the pain and suffering of our body during the dying process. We can be troubled by the idea of being separated from our loved ones. We can be frightened of entering the unknown.

However, if we look at the spiritual side of death, our fear begins to fade. Unlike our body, our spirit will last forever. God promises that it will never be destroyed. In fact, when our physical life is no more, our spiritual life will only be strengthened as we enter into complete union with God. For our spirits, then, death is a beautiful transformation. This is a cause for rejoicing!

On a sheet of paper, list any fears that you have about death. Be honest with yourself. When you have completed your list, go through it and check the fears that relate to the physical side of death. How much of your overall fear is related to the physical?

As the mind of Christ grows within you, your fears about the physical aspects of death will gradually diminish. You will come to celebrate death as a beautiful transformation from this life to the next.

I do not fear death.

Day 207   God will not fail me.

"It is the LORD who goes before you. He will be with you; he will not fail you or forsake you. Do not fear or be dismayed."

—Deuteronomy 31:8

A trusted friend has given you detailed directions to help you find a new restaurant that has just opened. For a time you drive along, following the directions, and everything seems to be going fine. Then you get to a place where the options before you do not seem to match the directions you were given. You pull over in confusion, wondering what might have gone wrong. Did you take a wrong turn? Did your friend make a mistake? You are uncertain as to what you should do next.

Anything human, anything physical, anything of this world will let you down sometime. Even the best directions can lead you astray. Even your most trusted friend can be wrong. But not God. God will not fail you. God will always be there for you, always listening to you, always understanding you, always giving you the guidance that you need. You can count on God, not just some of the time but *all* of the time.

Take time for a period of meditative prayer today. Find a comfortable spot away from any distractions. Relax your body and allow your breathing to become regular and deep. Feel all of your worry and anxiety disappear. Center yourself in the presence of God.

Now, imagine a path leading into a woods. You are walking on this path. It is smooth and straight. Somehow you know that it will take you to peaceful and beautiful places. As you continue on your way, you become aware of the presence of another person. This is God, who journeys with you. Suddenly, it begins to grow dark. You hear ominous noises up ahead, and sense danger. In that moment you feel an arm slip around your shoulders. It is God's arm. It reassures you that the way is safe. So, you continue on until you come to a spot where the path splits into two.

You are unsure which way to go. Then you feel a gentle tugging in one direction. You proceed with confidence, knowing that you are going the way God wants you to go. At last, you come to a clearing where the sun is shining brightly. A bench is there with your name on it. You sit down on it and rest. You know that God has guided you to this place. Here you will find great joy. Celebrate!

God will not fail me.

Day 208   I see with faith.

But when the disciples saw him walking on the sea, they were terrified, saying, "It is a ghost!" And they cried out in fear. But immediately Jesus spoke to them and said, "Take heart, it is I; do not be afraid."

—*Matthew 14:26-27*

*P*erhaps you have had the experience of being startled out of your sleep in the middle of the night. You try to orient yourself, wondering what might have awakened you. You listen intently but hear nothing. You may even get out of bed and search the house, only to find nothing out of place. When you return to bed, you are unable to get back to sleep. Fear has overtaken you. Were you awakened by a dream, or was something really wrong? You have no way of knowing. It is only when you have finally convinced yourself that there is nothing to fear that you are able to drift back to sleep.

The fear that we feel in an experience like this is not so unlike the fear that the disciples must have felt that long-ago night. Out on the lake in the early morning hours, in a boat being battered by wind and waves, they peered out into the pre-dawn gloom and thought they saw a shadowy figure coming toward them across the water. Exhausted, what else could they think? It must be a ghost! Or, was it just a bad dream?

It is precisely when we are seeing with fear that we must remind ourselves to see with faith. To begin today's exercise, identify a situation or problem that you have been viewing mainly out of fear. Write it down, briefly. Now, find a piece of cloth that can serve as a blindfold. Put it on securely, so that you are unable to see. Begin to walk around the room. What emotions do you feel? Whenever you feel afraid or uncertain, pause, breathe deeply, and relax before moving forward. The less anxious you are, the more you will be able to sense where things are. You will begin to "see" things in a different way. When you become relatively comfortable moving about the room, reflect on how your feelings and your perceptions have changed.

Now remove the blindfold. Reconsider the problem that you have been viewing out of fear. Could you somehow view it another way, just as you were able to find other ways of "viewing" the room? What would it mean to see this problem "with faith"? Take time to write down your thoughts.

The eyes of faith can see past fear. Trust what they reveal to you!

I see with faith.

Day 209   Faith brings power.

And they went and woke him up, saying, "Lord, save us! We are perishing!" And he said to them, "Why are you afraid, you of little faith?" Then he got up and rebuked the winds and the sea; and there was a dead calm. They were amazed, saying, "What sort of man is this, that even the winds and the sea obey him?"

—Matthew 8:25-27

On the way home from school each day, Timmy had to pass a very large factory filled with dirty, noisy machines. When the weather permitted, the huge doors of the factory would be opened so that the clean air from outside would come in. On those days the sound of the machines was even louder and more ominous than usual. It frightened Timmy. However, he soon discovered that if he whistled songs that he had learned in Bible school as he passed by the factory doors, he didn't feel so afraid. Whistling them seemed to give him the courage that he needed.

When Timmy began to whistle those Bible school songs, his mind was filled with the thought that he was not alone. God was with him, he knew, and this thought empowered him to pass by the factory despite his fear. Such is the power of faith, which says "yes" to life in even the most trying times.

For today's exercise, you will need a partner. As you stand face to face, lift one of your arms straight out to the side until your hand is at shoulder level. Ask your partner to grasp your outstretched wrist. Now, think of a place, person, or situation that is very intimidating to you. As you do, your partner should try to pull your arm down. Your partner will probably discover that it is fairly easy to do. Try the exercise again, only this time think of a place, person, or situation that is very inspiring to you. Your partner will probably find that it is now much more difficult to pull your arm down. You have more strength to resist. Such is the power of faith. **Faith brings power.**

Day 210   Love is powerful.

There is no fear in love, but perfect love casts out fear; for fear has to do with punishment, and whoever fears has not reached perfection in love.

—1 John 4:18

Sometimes, no matter how hard you try to explain, your child does not understand why he has to follow the rules you have established. Nevertheless, if those rules are important to his safety, you have to enforce them. To impress the importance of following the rules on your child's young mind, you may have to attach some appropriate form of punishment to their violation. Therefore, fear may be a factor in his choices to obey, especially when he is young. However, as he grows older and starts to understand "cause and effect," he will also begin to comprehend the reasons for the rules you establish. He will realize that you sometimes have to say "no" for his benefit, that you set limits on his behavior because you love him. Once he fully understands this, he will obey your rules not out of fear but respect.

Fear disappears as understanding grows. And understanding grows as love becomes a stronger force in the relationship. Ideally, your child will gradually come to understand that you love him unconditionally, that you will not stop loving him if he doesn't behave. His desire to obey your limits will grow along with his respect for your care. This love is much more powerful than the fear by which you earlier attempted to control his behavior. While one day he will grow strong enough that the threat of punishment will hold little meaning for him, he will never outgrow his need for love. That is something that lasts a lifetime. So, when *agape* is present, there is power—*real* power—to do what is right and good.

Think of someone of whom you are a little bit frightened, or who may be frightened of you. If you were to speak to this person in the spirit of *agape*, what might you say? Identify several statements that would be helpful to your relationship. Now, practice saying them aloud, pretending that the person is in the room with you. Repeat your loving words with confidence. Feel their power. **Love is powerful.**

Day 211   **Without love, I suffer.**

Then he began to teach them that the Son of Man must undergo great suffering, and be rejected by the elders, the chief priests, and the scribes, and be killed, and after three days rise again.

—Mark 8:31

*C*onflict exists to the degree that *agape* does not. And with conflict comes suffering. Jesus was rejected and finally killed because someone feared him, then sought to control and, ultimately, to silence him. But *agape* does not fear others. *Agape* does not try to silence others. *Agape does not cause another to suffer to protect itself.*

Write in response to these questions:

(1) Who have been the "elders, chief priests, and scribes" in your life—those who, at times, have made you feel rejected?
(2) In what ways, small and large, have these persons been "killing" your spirit?
(3) In what ways, small and large, has the love of God enabled you to overcome their rejection and "rise from the dead"?

Now, turn the questions around:

(1) Name one person for whom have you been "elder, chief priest, or scribe." Whom have you made to feel rejected?
(2) In what ways, small and large, have you "killed" this person's spirit?
(3) In what ways might you offer the love of God and help this person to "rise from the dead"?

Without love, I suffer.

Day 212   **Without love, I struggle.**

I do not understand my own actions. For I do not do what I want, but I do the very thing I hate.

—Romans 7:15

A married couple is canoeing down a river. Earlier, before their trek began, they had argued over something petty. Accusations were made. Feelings were hurt. And now they paddle without thought of each other, except to dwell on the offense. They cannot seem to keep a straight course. First the canoe veers off toward the left bank and begins to scrape bottom. Then it heads off to the right, where it snags on rocks and fallen trees. Back and forth on the river they go, and sometimes in between the canoe swings around and they are suddenly, somehow, headed back upstream. The trip downriver should be fast and easy, even for canoeists as inexperienced as they, but instead, every minute is a struggle. Finally, they put ashore for a lunch break. Over their sandwiches and soda, they begin to talk things out, and soon they are laughing at their own pettiness—and at their poor canoeing. When at last they resume their trip downstream, they are able to maintain their course, almost without trying.

Love is a unifying force. With it, you—and your relationships—feel intact. Without it, you feel that something essential is missing, something that holds everything together. Suddenly you can't seem to do what you want to do, and what you don't want to do is precisely what you choose to do. You fight yourself. You fight the world. Everything seems out of sync. Things start to fall apart. And maybe you do too.

Enter into prayer. Acknowledge to the Spirit the ways in which you are in conflict with yourself right now. What inner turmoil is making your journey downstream a struggle? What parts of you are fighting, making it difficult for you to maintain a straight course?

Ask for the love of God to well up within you and ease your mind. Feel its warmth; trust its presence. Allow it to bring your divided self together and make your spirit whole.

Without love, I struggle.

Day 213   **I need a new heart.**

He looked around at [the Pharisees] with anger; he was grieved at their hardness of heart and said to the man, "Stretch out your hand." He stretched it out, and his hand was restored.

—*Mark 3:5*

WOMAN RECEIVES NEW HEART ON SUNDAY

HOPE CITY, Oh. (United Peace International)—Ima Crabb, a well-known businesswoman recently found guilty of first-degree hardness of heart and second-degree self-righteousness, underwent a heart transplant yesterday at Hope General Hospital. The transplant was performed specifically on a Sunday in strict compliance with the sentence handed down by the high court. On strenuous advice of counsel, Ms. Crabb had not appealed the court's decision.

A spokesperson for the hospital reports that Ms. Crabb is resting quite comfortably and has even been heard to laugh, give compliments, and offer praise. Her condition has been upgraded from critical to heartwarming.

The high court had required that the operation be performed on a Sunday because Ms. Crabb had testified during her trial that she would never help anyone in need on "God's day." "People shouldn't work on Sunday," she had said. "She is now quite grateful," reported the hospital spokesperson, "that the court broke the law on her behalf."

The transplanted heart was harvested from a mystery donor.

It was the Sabbath. Jesus was in the synagogue when he was approached by a man with a crippled hand. "You shouldn't heal him today," the Pharisees protested. "Do you want to disobey God's laws?"

Jesus could have chosen to wait and heal the man when the sabbath was over. But he refused to put rules ahead of people—even if someone claimed that those rules had been established by God. Angered by the Pharisees' hardness of heart, he made the man whole again, right there on the spot.

Like the self-righteous Ima Crabb, the Pharisees needed a heart transplant. They needed a heart made of flesh rather than stone, a heart that was compassionate instead of critical. They needed a heart that was ready at all times and in all places to serve God's children.

On a piece of paper, draw two large hearts. In one of them, list ways in which you sometimes have a heart of stone; in the other, the ways in which you have a heart of flesh. Cut out the heart of flesh and carry it with you today. Let your heart be compassionate, even when you must be tough.

I need a new heart.

Day 214   **I need an open mind.**

And he said, "Truly I tell you, no prophet is accepted in the prophet's hometown."

—*Luke 4:24*

GOD OFWIS DOM
KEEP MYMIN DOP ENT OY OURTRUTH
ESPEC IAL LYSO I CANSE EIT
WHE REIL EASTEXPEC TTOF INDI TAM EN

*U*nless you are blessed with exceptional insight, the preceding lines probably look like a bunch of gobbledygook. But hold this page up to a mirror. Now what do you see? Yes, yes, yes, it still requires a little effort to make out the words, but don't you get it? This gobbledygook is really . . .

A prayer.

And that carpenter who lives down the street (you know, the one who runs with a bad crowd and whose mom was already pregnant when she got married), he is really . . .

A prophet.

Things are not always what they appear to be. God's world is full of surprises. It is infinitely bigger than what we think, and far more astonishing than what we expect! So, we have to keep an open mind. If we are to see a prayer in a bunch of gobbledygook, we have to read in a new way. If we are to see a prophet in a carpenter, we have to look at people in a new way. This is what the people of Nazareth never understood. They never knew exactly what to make of Jesus, but they did know he wasn't a prophet. A carpenter *couldn't* be a prophet. Everybody said so.

But you do not have the mind of the prophet's hometown. You have the mind of Christ. Keep it open. Keep it ready, willing, and able to be surprised—even changed.

I need an open mind.

Day 215   **I need a steadfast spirit.**

"Brother will betray brother to death, and a father his child, and children will rise against parents and have them put to death; and you will be hated by all because of my name. But the one who endures to the end will be saved."

—*Matthew 10:21-22*

*B*etrayal is a powerful word. We are not comfortable saying it. So, we have invented euphemisms for it. Rather than "being betrayed," we are stabbed in the back, double-crossed, sold out, thrown over, kissed by Judas, let down. . . .

Whichever words we use for it, though, the reality of betrayal is the same. Trust is broken. Faith is breached. And the pain of it is unbearable. Nevertheless, if we have a steadfast spirit, even the most painful betrayal cannot destroy us. Our life depends on no one but God. From God we draw our strength, and that strength never wavers. We endure to the end.

Make a list of the people who count on you. Identify the specific ways in which they have given you their trust. What promises have you made them, whether spoken or unspoken? What responsibilities have you assumed on their behalf? Now reflect on how you have been faithful to their trust. And where you are in need of a more steadfast spirit, ask God for help. God will faithfully provide all the strength and support you need.

I need a steadfast spirit.

Day 216 Even in conflict I am blessed.

"Blessed are you when people revile you and persecute you and utter all kinds of evil against you falsely on my account. Rejoice and be glad, for your reward is great in heaven, for in the same way they persecuted the prophets who were before you."

—Matthew 5:11-12

*I*t is difficult to believe that in every conflict we are blessed. "Surely," we protest, "there are times that are just plain horrible. There is nothing for us to learn from them, nothing for us to gain by them. We just have to trust God to get us through somehow."

Sometimes that is what it feels like. And sometimes that is what it looks like. But that is precisely when we have to find the prayer in the gobbledygook. Somewhere in every conflict there is a blessing. This is what God has promised us: not to bless us with conflict and suffering, but to bless us even in its midst.

Marj went out on a blind date with Phil, her best friend's friend. During dinner, their conversation somehow turned to the breakdown of the traditional family in American society. "It would help if getting a divorce wasn't so easy," Marj remarked.

"Married people ought to try harder to stay together. After all, divorce is against the will of God. Just because it's legal doesn't make it right." Phil stared at Marj for a moment, then laid his napkin down on the table. "You should know that I'm divorced," he declared, rising from his chair, "and you have no idea what you're talking about." Phil promptly walked out of the restaurant, and Marj never saw him again.

Marj never forgot this confrontation. For her, "divorce" had always been an abstract theological issue. But Phil's reaction had changed it into a "people issue." Never again did she speak of divorce in such sweeping—and harsh—generalities. Her clash with Phil had blessed her by increasing her awareness and sensitivity.

On a piece of paper, create two columns. Label one of them "Times of Conflict" and the other "Blessings Received." In the first column, list past or current conflicts that you have experienced. Then, in the second column, indicate how you benefitted from each of them. Write down discoveries that you made, insights that you gained, meaningful moments that you shared, and so on. Try to view each conflict from new angles. Can you see ways that you were blessed?

Even in conflict I am blessed.

Day 217   **Conflict ends in peace.**

For he shall judge between the nations, and shall arbitrate for many peoples; they shall beat their swords into plowshares, and their spears into pruning hooks; nation shall not lift up sword against nation, neither shall they learn war any more.

—Isaiah 2:4

*T*oday spend your meditation time in prayer. First, list all the conflicts of which you are aware on a piece of paper. Think of your own struggles and those of relatives and friends. Think of controversies in your town, your state, or your nation. Think of tensions that exist between certain groups of people, of wars being fought within or between other countries. List as many conflicts as you can. Then select one of them to focus on during a period of meditative prayer.

Center yourself in God's presence. Let your mind be calm and your body relaxed. Feel the fullness of the Spirit within you.

When you are ready, think about the specific conflict that you have chosen. Begin to envision its resolution. What, specifically, would "peace" look like in that situation? Do not force images to come. Be patient. Be full of hope. Allow a picture of peace to gradually emerge in your mind, then sustain it for as long as you can. See it becoming more vivid, more real. Know that this vision of peace is not only a hope of your heart but a prayer of your soul.

Be sensitive to the Spirit's promptings as you meditate. If you receive insight into a possible course of action, be prepared to follow up on it.

Conflict ends in peace.

Day 218 — Forgiveness brings life.

"Very truly, I tell you, anyone who hears my word and believes him who sent me has eternal life, and does not come under judgment, but has passed from death to life."

—John 5:24

*W*hen we harbor resentment and bitterness toward another person, we are building a wall that will divide us. As time goes along and we still do not forgive, that wall increases in size. And, as the wall gets higher and thicker, we lose track of what is happening with the person on the other side. The person doesn't seem to matter anymore. All that matters is our memory of the way that he or she hurt us and the hostility we feel. After awhile, we begin to believe that the wall is all there is. Even if the other person wanted to make amends, we would not be able to allow it.

Forgiveness removes the wall, sometimes all at once, sometimes piece by piece. We begin to see past our hurt to the other person again. And, as the wall shrinks, the possibility grows that the two of us can once again be in relationship.

God's forgiveness of us is the same. How often we build a wall of self-judgment, guilt, and shame that would close God out! But God has told us that we who believe are no longer under judgment. When we remember this, the wall comes tumbling down. Then we are free to pass from death to life, from denying our relationship with God to celebrating it.

Put your name on the left side of a piece of paper and the name of someone you are having a great deal of trouble relating to on the right side. Between the two names begin to draw blocks or bricks to represent the wall that divides you. In each block put a word or phrase that describes a feeling you have toward the person. You might also want to include some of the attitudes or behaviors of the other person that make it hard for you to be in relationship. Continue adding blocks until you can't think of any more resentments. Now, look at the barrier that has been created. Decide if you are ready for the wall to come down. If so, how, with God's help, will you begin to tear it down? Can you destroy it all at once, or do you need to select one or two blocks that you are ready to remove? Begin to break down the wall. Invite the other person into restored relationship. Know that as you do, you are beginning to experience life as it was meant to be.

Forgiveness brings life.

Day 219 Forgiveness brings abundant life.

"For God so loved the world that he gave his only Son, so that everyone who believes in him may not perish but may have eternal life."

—John 3:16

*F*orgiveness is letting go of the past and opening yourself to the possibility of reestablishing a relationship with the other person. But what if that person is unable or unwilling to be in relationship? Perhaps the individual is no longer living, or is living far away. Perhaps he or she still carries a grudge. Perhaps the person's behaviors are destructive, making it unsafe or unwise for you to be together. Whatever the case, if you cannot restore a meaningful relationship, you can still do yourself a great favor by forgiving him or her.

In today's passage of scripture, we are told that if we believe, we will have eternal life. Once again, it is important to remember that "eternal" refers to a quality, not a quantity, of life. We are being promised that, if we accept the fact that we are not under judgment but have been saved (made complete), then we will have a life that is worth living. God says that we are okay—what do we need to worry about? So, we are freed from the anxiety of our guilt and can enjoy life to its fullest.

Knowing the renewal of life that comes to us when we are forgiven by God, we can understand the renewal that comes when we forgive someone else—even when we can no longer be in relationship with that person. Now, however, we are freed not from a burden of anxiety and guilt, but from a burden of anger and bitterness.

Imagine that a person whom you have had trouble forgiving is in the room with you. Point your finger at the person in an accusatory fashion. As we have mentioned before, when you do this, three of your fingers curve back and point at you. This is the body's way of indicating that the hurt you are trying to direct toward the other person is more intensely felt in your own life. Think about the damage that your unresolved anger does to your body and your spirit.

Now, point again, but as you do, gradually unfold the other fingers of your hand. Open your hand completely. Realize that you are now ready to let go of any hostility and resentment that you were holding. You have opened up to new possibilities of living. **Forgiveness brings abundant life.**

Day 220 **Forgiveness brings wholeness.**

But Jesus said, "No more of this!" And he touched [the slave's] ear and healed him.

—*Luke 22:51*

*T*he authorities had come to arrest Jesus. Those who were with him were uncertain what to do. One of them pulled his sword in anger and struck the slave of the high priest, cutting off an ear. But Jesus would have no violence. He instantly healed the man, though soon he and the others would take him away, to his death. His healing act was one of forgiveness, restoring not only the body but also the spirit of one who was about to do wrong. It was also a plea for his followers to begin forgiving those who were going to harm him.

When we refuse to forgive, a dark spot begins to grow inside us. That dark spot lodges in our body and acts like a block to our natural flow of vitality and energy. It stays there, getting darker and harder, creating dis-ease, until we are finally ready to forgive and let go. Then, when we forgive, the dark spot begins to dissolve, and eventually we are whole again.

Find a comfortable spot. Eliminate any distractions. Settle in for a time of relaxation and rejuvenation. Let go of any stress that you may be feeling. Allow the worries that you carry with you to be left behind. Spend a few moments just breathing deeply. Now, begin a mental search of your body. Think about each muscle, beginning with your feet and moving up. Notice whether it feels tense, uncomfortable, or painful. If it is, think of the pain as a little ball. Imagine the ball getting smaller and smaller until it disappears. Feel the pain or tension disappear at the same time. Do this for any area of discomfort that you discover. When you are finished removing these "blocks," many of which may have been due to unresolved differences with other persons, feel the power of God moving freely through you. Know that you are whole.

Forgiveness brings wholeness.

Day 221   **Forgiveness removes sin.**

For as the heavens are high above the earth, so great is his steadfast love toward those who fear him; as far as the east is from the west, so far he removes our transgressions from us.

—Psalm 103:11-12

The psalmist tells us that when God forgives us, our mistakes are as far removed from us as the east is from the west. An empty blue sky lies between them and us. This is clearly an indication that God does not keep track of our sins. If God were keeping track, the psalmist would more likely have described a great scorecard in the heavens, where every sin we commit is written down. God might draw a line through any sin for which we asked forgiveness, but it would still remain on the card. God could always refer back to it. Thank goodness this isn't the picture the psalmist gives us!

God may not keep score, but do *you*? If you say to someone, with bitterness, "I'll forgive what you have done to me, but I'll never forget it," then you are really confessing your unwillingness to let go of the hurt. You cannot forgive if you are unwilling to forget. Carefully ponder this statement. It does not say that forgiveness *is* forgetting. It says that forgiveness is being *willing* to forget. When forgiving, you may remember well any lessons you have learned, but you will be ready to forget the pain of them. You will be willing to let go of the hurt so that both you and the other person will have the opportunity to live more abundantly.

Go outdoors, if possible. Think of a person who has hurt you in the past. Stand facing the west and imagine that all of the pain of your past is held there where the sun sets each day. Focus your attention on the one whom you find it difficult to forgive and the hurt that he has caused you. Now, turn to face the east, where the sun rises fresh each day. With your back turned on the past, focus your attention on the miracle of forgiveness and the joy that it can bring into your life. Notice that, from where you are standing, you cannot see the past at all. So long as you choose to look toward forgiveness and the new possibilities that it offers, you cannot continue to focus on the hurts of the past. You must decide whether you will see only the sin of other days or the renewal that can be yours today.

Forgiveness removes sin.

Day 222   Forgiveness removes shame.

I will establish my covenant with you, and you shall know that I am the LORD, in order that you may remember and be confounded, and never open your mouth again because of your shame, when I forgive you all that you have done, says the LORD GOD.

—Ezekiel 16:62-63

Guilt and shame are not the same. Guilt says, "I made a mistake." Shame says, "I am a mistake." We feel guilt when we do something that we know we should not have done. It is our guilt that says, "Here is what I should have done, here is what I did, and I know that I did the wrong thing." We feel shame, on the other hand, when we feel like we *are* our bad behavior, and therefore undeserving of love. It is our shame that says, "I can do nothing right because I *am* nothing."

Forgiveness removes both guilt and shame. It removes guilt because it sees beyond the bad behavior to the person. When God offers us forgiveness, our sins are not even remembered. Since they are forgotten, there can be no more guilt.

Forgiveness also removes shame, because in being willing to forget our sins, God affirms who we are. We are not "nothing." We are children of God. When we receive God's affirmation, no shame can remain in us.

God knows all your mistakes, your flaws, your weaknesses. And yet, God says:

My child, you are wonderfully created.
My child, my kingdom is within you.
My child, my angels guard you.
My child, I will be with you wherever you go.

Ponder these divine affirmations of your worth. Then write a response of gratitude to them. Give thanks that your need to feel guilt or shame is no more.

Forgiveness removes shame.

Day 223   I am cleansed.

I will sprinkle clean water upon you, and you shall be clean from all your uncleannesses, and from all your idols I will cleanse you.

—Ezekiel 36:25

Water is essential to all of life, including yours. It has a cleansing effect upon your body. For example, when you are ill, you are told to drink lots of water. Your body needs that water to rinse away cast-off cells as it fights its sickness. This allows your body to return to wholeness.

Just as water cleanses our bodies, God cleanses our spirits. The cleansing power of God merges with that of water in the celebration of baptism. By the imposition of water, we recall the life-changing role that water has played in our relationship with God from the very beginning of time. It was amidst the waters of chaos that creation happened. It was through the waters of the flood that the earth was purified in the time of Noah. It was because of the waters of the Red Sea that the Israelites were saved from the pursuing Egyptians. And it was with a baptism of repentance that John prepared the way for the arrival of Jesus. The water of baptism is a powerful reminder, indeed, of God's gracious acts on our behalf.

Today, in symbolic recognition of how water purifies our bodies and symbolically cleanses our spirits, eliminate the use of your dishwasher. With great deliberateness, wash your dishes by hand. Fill the sink with warm, sudsy water. Take time to examine each dish before you wash it. Notice the remains of food that cling to it. Then, as you wash it, think about the forgiveness of God that cleanses you. When you remove each dish from the water and rinse it, celebrate the fact that you too have been made pure. Allow your dishwashing to be a holy experience.

I am cleansed.

Day 224   **I always forgive.**

Then Peter came and said to him, "Lord, if another member of the church sins against me, how often should I forgive? As many as seven times?" Jesus said to him, "Not seven times, but, I tell you, seventy-seven times."

—Matthew 18:21-22

*P*eter asked Jesus how many times he should forgive someone who sins against him. Jesus' answer of seventy-seven times was a way of telling Peter that he should not be keeping track. Who could forgive someone seventy-seven times without losing count? Poor Peter. In suggesting to Jesus that he might forgive seven times, he had been generous. After all, he was required by the law of his religion to forgive only three times. Jesus' response must have floored him.

The point of all this is not how many times we must forgive. The point is that if we are keeping track, then we are not really forgiving at all. Remember, forgiving means being willing to forget. We cannot intentionally hold onto the memories of past offenses and forgive them at the same time.

Forgiveness is not a matter of the mind. It is a condition of the heart. The mind keeps track. The heart does not. When we forgive from the heart, our focus is not on the offense but on the person. We are inviting the person back into right relationship with us. When we do that, the past is over and done. We begin again.

On separate pieces of paper, write the names of persons you have a hard time forgiving, as well as the offenses you have a hard time forgetting. Now, find a way to burn all of these papers together. As you watch them being destroyed, know that you can let go of any hurt or resentment. After the fire is out, notice that you cannot sort out the individual pieces of paper. All the offenses are gone. Let them also be gone from your heart, and celebrate your freedom.

I always forgive.

Love binds soul to soul.

When David had finished speaking to Saul, the soul of Jonathan was bound to the soul of David, and Jonathan loved him as his own soul.

—1 Samuel 18:1

*J*onathan and David could not have been closer. It was as if the prince and the shepherd shared one heart and soul. They were inseparable, bound by a love that couldn't be broken. They didn't love each another because they could be useful to each other. They loved each other because God had made it so.

Unfortunately, a quick glance at yesterday's newspaper head-lines suggests that one-heartedness is not a common thing in our world: "Burundian official assassinated," "Frivolous lawsuits draw attention," "In 'tough guy' jobs, women still face discrimi-nation and harassment," "Man sentenced for raping two girls, 11 and 12. . . ."

The newspaper would read much differently if only more of us had the one-heartedness of Jonathan and David. If only none of us regarded another person's life as something to price-tag, dom-inate, violate, and even casually take away! If only all of us loved every other person on this planet as our own soul!

Write a letter to a child in which you try to explain what one-heartedness is. Consider carefully the examples or stories you might use to clearly illustrate it. Also, find a way to express how important it is for us to become more one-hearted in our rela-tionships. Finally, send the letter to a child you know.

Love binds soul to soul.

Day 226 **My love welcomes every person.**

Contribute to the needs of the saints; extend hospitality to strangers.

—Romans 12:13

*W*elcome the saint; welcome the stranger. In other words, do not let your love distinguish between persons, but let your love welcome every person unconditionally, as a child of God. Gra-ciously provide for his or her needs from the best that you have to offer, and expect nothing in return.

An old house was home to a family of ten, as well as to two elderly boarders—Mrs. March, who lived in an upstairs apartment, and Mrs. Pratt, who lived in the basement. The boarders kept to themselves, mostly; the family knew little about them except that they always paid their rent on time. But when Thanksgiving Day came, two extra places were set at the family's already crowded table. One child went upstairs and soon came down again with Mrs. March; another child went downstairs and soon came up again with Mrs. Pratt, and the family's feast began.

These people celebrated communion together, just as surely as if they had shared juice and bread in church. Their table was the Lord's table—the Round Table where every person has a seat, and that seat is a place of honor. No one was left out, or kept out. Everyone was welcomed in the spirit of *agape*.

Your table is the Lord's table, too. So, as a sign of your welcoming love, set an extra place at the table at least once every day in the coming week. Mark that place with a small card on which you have written a description of someone who you would find difficult to have at your table. Use a different card for every meal. As you eat, imagine what it would be like to actually have that person present. Imagine yourself overcoming your pre-judgments and accepting this child of God in the spirit of *agape*.

My love welcomes every person.

Day 227 **My love welcomes angels.**

Let mutual love continue. Do not neglect to show hospitality to strangers, for by doing that some have entertained angels without knowing it.

—Hebrews 13:1-2

An angel is a messenger of God, a spiritual being or person through whom a divine message comes to us. Whoever happens to bring it, an angelic message has a good chance of getting through only if our hearts are ready to receive it. So we must be vigilant, twenty-four hours a day. Sometimes the message will come through someone we would least expect.

For the next few days, pay especially close attention to strangers. Some of them will be appearing on your path for a reason. Welcome them. Reach out to them. Look into their eyes and smile instead of dropping your gaze. Strike up a conversation with them instead of putting up a wall of silence. Ask someone in pain if you might help instead of turning away. Take a risk instead of playing it safe. And, in the midst of these brief, unexpected interactions, watch and listen for unexpected messages from God.

Keep this thought running through your mind, and be ready: **My love welcomes angels.**

Day 228 My love welcomes God.

[And Jacob said to his brother Esau:] "For truly to see your face is like seeing the face of God—since you have received me with such favor."

—*Genesis 33:10*b

*T*hough Jacob had once betrayed him, Esau ran out to welcome him home as soon as he saw him coming. After long, bitter years of separation, he greeted his brother as if he were none other than God come to visit. Moved to tears by the welcome he received, Jacob exclaimed, "Esau, to see your face is like seeing the face of God!"

In this story Esau was the host and Jacob, the guest. And, standing in the presence of one another, each brother recognized God in the other's face. This is what happens in holy hospitality!

Interestingly, the English words "host" and "guest" were once the same Indo-European word, *ghosti*. This means that, at one time, people drew no clear distinction between them. They recognized that, in true hospitality, the host always received as much as the guest, and the guest always gave as much as the host.

On a further note, *ghosti* also meant "stranger." This reveals that, in ancient times, no one was to be excluded from the giving and receiving of hospitality. The outsider as well as the insider, the long-time foe as well as the long-lost brother was to be treated with utmost respect and generosity. You might say that everyone, whether host or guest, was to welcome the God seen in his or her brother or sister. So it was with Esau and Jacob.

Identify persons who have received you so graciously into their homes that you felt God's presence. Acknowledge the characteristics of God that you saw revealed in them.

Now reflect on how you received their hospitality. Were you as gracious in receiving as they were in giving? Note how they might have seen God revealed in you.

My love welcomes God.

Day 229 — I welcome my enemy.

"If you love those who love you, what credit is that to you? For even sinners love those who love them. But love your enemies, do good, and lend, expecting nothing in return. Your reward will be great, and you will be children of the Most High; for he is kind to the ungrateful and the wicked. Be merciful, just as your Father is merciful."

—*Luke 6:32, 35-36*

*T*he way of the world is to do good for a friend. The way of Christ is to do good for a friend and do the same for an enemy.

This is so easy to say—and so hard to practice.

Who is your enemy? Since "enemy" is another one of those words that make us uncomfortable, here are some descriptions that you could use instead:

A person toward whom you are hostile.
A person whom you resent.
A person whom you would rather not be around.
A person whom you would rather not talk to.
A person who has treated you badly.
A person whom you have not forgiven.
A person against whom you are holding a grudge.
A person who is a stranger or an outsider to you.
A person who does what you would not do, thinks as you
would not think, or says what you would not say.

Identify one of your "enemies." Now, decide on something kind that you might do for this person today. Extend God's presence in a very thoughtful way, with no regard for what you might receive in return.

I welcome my enemy.

Day 230 — I lift up the powerless.

Thus says the LORD of hosts: "Render true judgments, show kindness and mercy to one another; do not oppress the widow, the orphan, the alien, or the poor; and do not devise evil in your hearts against one another."

—*Zechariah 7:9-10*

$\mathcal{T}$he widow, the orphan, the alien, the poor—all terms for "the powerless." Consider the widow, for example. In Old Testament times a woman was dependent first on her father and then on her husband. If she survived them both, she had no status or money to speak of. She received no inheritance. In fact, as a widow she became part of the inheritance bestowed on her oldest son. If she had no son, she had to rely on charity and often had to scrounge for food; thankfully she could glean in the fields of her neighbors, but only *after* the harvest. She had few if any legal rights that might protect her, and when she was accused of a crime, she was not allowed to defend herself in court.

In our society, of course, widows are not so powerless. But there are still many powerless people among us. Brainstorm a list of those who appear to have no power today. Make your list as complete as possible.

As you consider the sheer numbers of people in our world who are in need of help, you may begin to feel overwhelmed. You may be tempted to despair—to believe that you can't really make a difference. But you can. Your every act of *agape* makes a difference. So, today, choose to do *one* thing for *one* person who is powerless.

I lift up the powerless.

Day 231   **I offer hospitality.**

"Very truly, I tell you, whoever receives one whom I send receives me; and whoever receives me receives him who sent me."

—*John 13:20*

$\mathcal{A}$fter he laid down his hammer and nails and walked out of his carpenter's shop, Jesus had no place to call home. To survive he had to depend upon the hospitality of friends and strangers. In receiving their welcome he blessed them, taught them, accepted them, loved them. Was he their guest, or was he their host? He was both. *Ghosti.* And so are you.

When you are hospitable to another person out of love rather than obligation, the distinctions between host and guest, giver and receiver, enemy and friend, powerful and powerless, quickly disappear. You simply welcome the other person into your space, the best way you can. Hospitality is, finally, not a matter of etiquette but attitude.

Quiet yourself now, and enter into meditative prayer. Let yourself relax into a deep awareness of the presence of God. When you are centered, let the following drama unfold.

At the Spirit's request you have set a round table for four. "You are about to share a meal with three other persons," the Spirit informs you, and at that moment you hear a knock at the door. "That will be one of your friends," the Spirit says. You open the door. Who is standing there?

As you seat your friend at the table, a second guest arrives. "One of your enemies," says the Spirit. After hesitating, you reluctantly let the person in. Who is it?

Your enemy sits down beside your friend. You are concerned about whether they will get along, but the Spirit tells you not to be afraid. "Your table is the table of God. There is no friend or enemy here." At that moment the last guest shows up. "A powerless person," the Spirit says. You usher this guest to the table. Who is it?

After all of you join hands and offer thanks for the meal, you begin to serve the guests. As you fill the plate of the powerless person, the person says to you, "I have brought you a message," and goes on to tell you what it is. What message are you given?

Now you serve your friend, who says, "I, too, have something to tell you." Listen carefully to your friend's words.

Finally you reach out to put food on your enemy's plate. "Even I have news for you," the person says. What is this final message?

You feel blessed by all your guests. It suddenly seems that they, not you, are hosting the meal. And, as if reading your mind, the person you once regarded as your enemy takes your plate and serves you a generous portion.

I offer hospitality.

Day 232   **Hospitality gives glory to God.**

Be hospitable to one another without complaining. Like good stewards of the manifold grace of God, serve one another with whatever gift each of you has received.

—*1 Peter 4:9-10*

*O*ffering hospitality is making room for one another. It means recognizing that each of us is a child of God, and that each of us has been placed here in this time and place in order to enrich the community. Each of us has a gift needed by the other, granted to us through the gracious wisdom of the Giver of all good gifts. Therefore, in offering hospitality to one another, we honor one another and our God.

Over the years, you have received many tangible and intangible gifts from people who love and care for you. Indicate one of them that you could now use in such a way that it would be a blessing to someone else. If it is an object of art or beauty, place it where your friend can enjoy it, too. If it is a gift of music, allow your friend to listen to it. If it is a special book, copy a passage that has inspired you and share it. Tell your friend about the person who originally gave you the gift and the emotions you felt in receiving it. Know that as you share your gift, you are offering hospitality. You are making room for your friend to enjoy something that has brought joy to you. You are also bringing glory to the original giver of the gift and to the Giver of all good gifts.

Hospitality gives glory to God.

Day 233 In community, I am blessed.

Finally, all of you, have unity of spirit, sympathy, love for one another, a tender heart, and a humble mind. Do not repay evil for evil or abuse for abuse; but, on the contrary, repay with a blessing. It is for this that you were called—that you might inherit a blessing.

—1 Peter 3:8-9

*E*ach of us has received good gifts from God. We are meant to share them openly with each other. This builds up the community by helping it to experience the fullness of God's love. When you withhold your gift, you hurt the community as well as yourself. When you offer your gift, you bless yourself as well as the community.

Reflect upon the blessings mentioned in today's scripture:

Unity of Spirit. When we all agree, we have unity of mind. But when we are all of one attitude, we have unity of spirit. In community, we celebrate that the uniting force is the Spirit of God. Though we may disagree on many things, we agree in the Spirit to live together in harmony, genuinely respecting one another.

Sympathy. Sympathy is more than feeling sorry for one another. It is the ability to feel with one another. The hurts of one of us are felt by all of us, and the joys of one are celebrated by all.

233

Love. In community, we have a deep appreciation for one another. We are willing to work toward what is best for one another. This is *agape*.

Tender Heart. How easy it is to lose patience with one another! But when we know that we belong together, we find it easier to be gentle with one another. We understand that, at times, each of us needs a little extra care and consideration. So, we freely give it, whenever it is needed.

Humble Mind. Pride destroys community, putting one person above another. Humility, on the other hand, respects all persons for the gifts and graces that they bring to the group.

Where in your experience of community have you found these blessings? Identify people who you can count on to bless you with unity of spirit, sympathy, love, a tender heart, and a humble mind. Celebrate your blessings, praising God for the persons who so enrich your life.

In community, I am blessed.

Day 234   **Community is more than the sum of its parts.**

Two are better than one, because they have a good reward for their toil. For if they fall, one will lift up the other; but woe to one who is alone and falls and does not have another to help. Again, if two lie together, they keep warm; but how can one keep warm alone? And though one might prevail against another, two will withstand one. A threefold cord is not quickly broken.

—*Ecclesiastes 4:9-12*

*A*s we have discussed before, synergy is that phenomenon in which the parts of something, when added together, equal more than just the sum of those parts (Day 50). Synergy is operative whenever a think tank gets together to solve a problem. Though each member of the group might have already determined several possible solutions, when the group gathers and the creative juices begin to flow, solutions will arise that no one had considered. There is a special kind of energy that takes over the meeting, helping to generate results that are much more exciting than those which could have been achieved by the individuals working alone.

Gather a group of friends. Share a problem or dilemma with them and invite them to spend some time quietly thinking about possible solutions. After awhile, ask them to begin sharing their ideas. Brainstorm together without evaluating any of the suggestions that are made. As the brainstorming continues, silently ask God for an openness to even more possible solutions to the problem. Observe how the ideas develop and especially how the group's excitement increases as its members unite to accomplish a common task.

Community is more than the sum of its parts.

Day 235 Community bears the burden.

[The Lord said to Moses,] "I will come down and talk with you there; and I will take some of the spirit that is on you and put it on them; and they shall bear the burden of the people along with you so that you will not bear it all by yourself."

—Numbers 11:17

*E*very channel on TV is covering the same story. A bomb has exploded. All official emergency response and law enforcement agencies have been called into action. But it is not only the official personnel who are responding. Across the nation, people are lining up at blood donor stations to assure that an adequate supply of blood will be available. Radio and TV stations are broadcasting different ways that their audiences can contribute money and donate supplies. The widespread outpouring of concern overshadows the evil of those who have caused the disaster. Around the world, we hope and we mourn, together. And when the time comes, we will rebuild shattered lives, together. And forever we will witness, together, against the cruelty and hatred that could have done this.

At any given moment in time, there are persons in the world whose problems are so overwhelming that they feel helpless to solve them, whose burdens are so heavy that they feel unable to carry them. We must never allow others to feel that they are alone. We must go to them and help them bear the unbearable.

Brainstorm a variety of issues or problems that are in the forefront of the news today. You may want to use these categories to stimulate your thinking:

International Conflicts
Medical and Health-Related Problems

Racial or Social Class Tensions
Crime, Terrorism, or Other Violence
Economic Conditions

Pick one of the problems that our world is facing. Think of a specific way that you as an individual might respond to it in the spirit of *agape*. Trust that you will make a difference. Trust also that if thousands of individuals around the world were to take this same action, it would make an even greater difference. Remember that you are not alone when you act. You act as a part of the community, and the community can carry any burden until, by the power of God, it can be cast off.
Community bears the burden.

Day 236   In community I am born anew.

Now that you have purified your souls by your obedience to the truth so that you have genuine mutual love, love one another deeply from the heart. You have been born anew, not of perishable but of imperishable seed, through the living and enduring word of God.

—1 Peter 1:22-23

*Y*ou cannot fully know yourself unless you put yourself in communication with others. Without such interaction, what you will know of yourself will be very limited. You will be aware only of your own self-perceptions, and even in the wisest of persons, these are never completely accurate. In community you can test your self-perceptions against the honest feedback of others. And what you learn about yourself can change your life.

Laurie, a young student in a professional leadership class, once found herself amazed at the feedback she received from her classmates. The professor had divided the class into small groups and given each group member a different resource. One person was given paper, another a ruler, another a pencil. Their assignment was to draw a picture of their ideal school. As her group prepared to begin, Laurie was surprised to find its members looking at her. When she asked them why they were, they responded that they were awaiting her direction. Amazed, she again asked why, and was told that she was a natural born leader, and the group would follow her lead. All her life, Laurie had thought of herself as a follower. But here was honest and open feedback from her community. It changed her way of thinking about herself.

Bob was asked to join the church choir. At first, being rather shy, he declined the invitation. But again and again, different people would say how his tenor voice could really help the choir. Often it was someone who, sitting in front of him during worship, happened to hear him singing the hymns. Finally, Bob decided to give singing with the choir a try. Not only did he stick with it, but eventually he become one of the congregation's favorite soloists. The community had changed the way he thought of himself.

Find a trusted friend who is not afraid to talk with you openly and honestly. Ask for feedback on how your friend sees you. Ask for your friend's perceptions of your gifts and abilities. Seek guidance on how you can better use them to serve the community. As you listen, be non-defensive. There is nothing to be afraid of. Listen not only to your friend's words but also to the feelings behind them. Know that your friend means well, and that you will be transformed by what you hear.

In community I am born anew.

Day 237   **I never give up.**

So let us not grow weary in doing what is right, for we will reap at harvest-time, if we do not give up.

—*Galatians 6:9*

*H*ave you ever heard of an angel wing begonia? It is an indoor plant that is very much like a vine. Its leaves are shaped like the traditional angel wing, and its white flowers are absolutely stunning. The only problem is, it takes fourteen years from the time you start your angel wing begonia plant until it finally blossoms! That is a long time to wait. If you were to get impatient, you might easily give up and assume that it will never bloom. But it *will* bloom, and it will be worth the wait. You will invite your friends in to see the first blossom. It may even become an excuse for a party! When the waiting is over, the celebration begins.

Gardening can be very much like waiting for that begonia to blossom. When you move into a new home and begin to prepare the grounds for your garden, you may discover that the soil is hopelessly depleted of many essential nutrients. At that point, you could give up, but then you would never have any beautiful vegetables and melons. Or, you could begin the long process of revitalizing the soil. The first year, you will be helped somewhat by fertilizers and soil conditioners. But what will help the most is your constant tending of the soil over time. As you turn it over and under, year after year, adding the compost created by the previous season's plants and gradually working in more natural nutrients, you will begin to see more productivity and beauty from the renewed soil.

Think of a skill or ability that took you some time to acquire. Indeed, it may have required years of practice to perfect. It might be playing a musical instrument, typing, drawing, baking pies, woodworking, or riding a bicycle. Perhaps you have not used this skill for some time. Decide today to use that ability again, as soon as you possibly can. When you do, celebrate that everything you put into learning this skill was not lost. And know that all the good you do for others is never lost, either. Even when your efforts seem to have no immediate positive effect, "keep on keeping on." Someday you will rejoice in the results.

I never give up.

Day 238   I believe in community. Therefore I see it.

The word of the LORD came to me: Mortal, take a stick and write on it, "For Judah, and the Israelites associated with it"; then take another stick and write on it, "For Joseph (the stick of Ephraim) and all the house of Israel associated with it"; and join them together into one stick, so that they may become one in your hand.

—Ezekiel 37:15-17

*H*ow easy it is to focus our attention upon our differences! When we compare ourselves to someone else, we are younger or older, more or less talented, more or less educated, taller or shorter. . . . The list could go on and on. Emphasizing these differences often drives a wedge between us, and prevents our effectively relating to one another and working together. But let a natural disaster hit and suddenly these "important" differences seem to disappear. As everyone pitches in to sandbag a house against floodwaters, no one seems to notice that some workers are teens and others are retired, that some have ponytails and others have crewcuts, that some attend church and others don't. All that matters is filling the bags with sand. Suddenly we are all one in the Spirit, joined together in God's hand.

As a terrible fire ravaged a church building in a small community, all kinds of people pitched in to save anything that could be pulled from it before it was too late. Some were members of the church; a great many were not. It didn't matter. No one asked. So long as they were able-bodied, their help was welcomed. In the months that followed the fire, fundraising events were held so that the church could be rebuilt. The entire community was invited to participate. People who had never been involved in the life of the church were asked for help, and their ideas were valued along with those of the congregation's members. Whatever anyone had to offer was gratefully accepted. A new church building was soon a reality, and so was the unity that the Spirit had created among very different individuals.

When we look for the common bonds among people, we can find them. It shouldn't take a disaster for us to see the community around us. It should only require that we look for it, and work toward it.

Take time to jot down the names of people who have helped you in the past week. They may have done little things or big things—it really doesn't matter. When you have listed as many people as you can, celebrate each way that they have blessed your life. Think of them as members of your community of support. Finally, take time to write a note of thanks to at least one of them. As you do so, know that you are always surrounded by people who are willing and able to help you.

I believe in community. Therefore I see it.

Day 239   **I see visions.**

"'In the last days it will be,' God declares, that I will pour out my Spirit upon all flesh, and your sons and your daughters shall prophesy, and your young men shall see visions, and your old men shall dream dreams. Even upon my slaves, both men and women, in those days I will pour out my Spirit; and they shall prophesy.'"

—*Acts 2:17-18*

*A*s we learn from the day of Pentecost, the Spirit does not play favorites. It dwells in everyone, near and far—men and

239

women, young and old, slaves and free—*everyone*. It dwells in *you*. And it gives you the power to have prophetic visions.

What does this mean? It is hard to say. Since every person has his or her own unique relationship with the Spirit, you must discover for yourself the particular nature of your own visionary power. But, in general, let us say that when you have a prophetic vision, you experience a profound enlarging of your mind. You gain new insight—new for you, anyway—into the reality of God and, at the same time, into the nature of humanity. It makes more clear who God is and who you are. The vision may sometimes come to you in an extraordinary way that you find difficult to describe to others. But however it comes, it is not the vision itself but the message it brings that is important.

Be sure of these things: First, to receive a vision requires only that you be open to the indwelling Spirit. Next, your vision need not be dramatic to be divine. Finally, your vision should not set you apart from others, but bring you together. Only when a vision's effect is to build up community rather than tear it down is it truly of God.

So, be open. Quietly sing or pray the words below from David Iverson's hymn *Spirit of the Living God* until your spirit is calm. Wait with expectancy, today and every day, knowing that visions will come to you in their own time and in their own way:

Spirit of the Living God, fall afresh on me.

I see visions.

Day 240   **I pray in the Spirit.**

Likewise the Spirit helps us in our weakness; for we do not know how to pray as we ought, but that very Spirit intercedes with sighs too deep for words. And God, who searches the heart, knows what is the mind of the Spirit.

—Romans 8:26-27a

*S*usan Polis Schutz once said, "There is no need for an outpouring of words to explain oneself to a friend. Friends understand each other's thoughts even before they are spoken." If you have ever had a true friend, no doubt you will agree.

But then at times, in the presence of that same person, you may have experienced the frustration of not being able "to find words." There was something that you wanted to say out loud, not because you *needed* to but because you *wanted* to—yet somehow you couldn't. Your feelings ran deeper than any words could express. Still, your friend seemed to understand; you could tell from the look in his eyes or the smile that brightened her face.

Prayer is your communication with the greatest Friend of all. And even when you can't find the right words, you can trust that the message will get through. The Spirit understands. In prayer as in friendship, the words you say aren't as important as the feelings you share. And those feelings may run far deeper than any words can express.

Today you will experience a form of prayer that uses no words. Kneel in a darkened room, and sit on the soles of your feet. (If you wish, use a pillow to cushion your knees.) Hold your arms out in front of you, palms upturned, as an expression of openness to the Spirit's presence. Quiet yourself. Soon you will feel completely calm and full of the divine presence.

When you are centered in the Spirit, bow. Turn your hands over, then let your chest, shoulders, and arms fall forward, slowly, until your forehead is touching the floor. Imagine the Spirit passing through you into the earth, *yet not leaving you empty.* Remain in this prayerful position as long as you would like.

I pray in the Spirit.

Day 241　　　　**The Spirit speaks to me.**

So we have the prophetic message more fully confirmed. You will do well to be attentive to this as to a lamp shining in a dark place, until the day dawns and the morning star rises in your hearts.

—*2 Peter 1:19*

*H*ank is a middle-aged man who loves to paint in his spare time. His work reveals considerable talent, one that has been developed without benefit of training beyond a few arts and crafts courses held at a local yard goods shop. Yet Hank will quickly admit that not one of his dozens and dozens of paintings is an original. "I always have to copy off something," he says. "I wish I could just draw 'out of my head,' but somehow I'm not able to."

Hank relies on the Spirit's inspiration to create his paintings. The Spirit points out beautiful photographs and magazine ads which he then reproduces on canvas. But Hank is not satisfied. He knows that if he could only trust himself enough, he would be able to hear the Spirit speaking inside his soul, inspiring original art.

Let us think about Hank for a moment in terms of the scripture passage. Right now it is as if Hank sits in a dark room waiting for the Spirit to turn on a lamp. When the lamp comes on, he paints whatever the light illumines. But Hank doesn't want to have to depend on the lamp anymore. He wants the light of the Spirit to shine inside him so that he can create inspired art from his own soul. He longs for the day when the "morning star will rise in his heart." In the meantime, though, he goes on painting by lamplight.

In the work of art that is your life, must you hear the Spirit's voice coming to you from outside—through other people, for instance—in order to feel confident? Or have you learned to trust the internal Voice?

Today's exercise is meant to better acquaint you with the interior Voice. After quieting yourself, write a sentence or two to the Spirit asking for counsel regarding a certain situation or issue. Wait prayerfully for a brief time. Then, when it feels right, place your pencil in your *non-writing* hand and begin to write again, this time in response to your request. Do not worry about how the writing looks or how the process feels. Remain open to the Voice of the Spirit, thinking as little as possible about what you are doing. Take as much time as you need. If you become frustrated, quiet yourself again. Sometimes this procedure takes practice. Using your nondominant hand in this way helps to free up the writing process from the control you usually exercise over it; this allows the Spirit to speak with less restraint. We are uncomfortable yielding control and unaccustomed to listening to a Voice that must be heard with the heart.

Conclude by reading what the Spirit has said to you and then writing a response with your dominant hand.

The Spirit speaks to me.

Day 242 The Spirit speaks through me.

"When they bring you before the synagogues, the rulers, and the authorities, do not worry about how you are to defend yourselves or what you are to say; for the Holy Spirit will teach you at that very hour what you ought to say."

—*Luke 12:11-12*

Mother Wove the Morning is a one-woman play imaginatively written and dramatically performed by Carol Lynn Pearson. As Pearson pulls her stage props one by one from her trunk, she portrays one character after another, sixteen women in all—women from different times and places who have something to teach us about how God is like a mother. Sitting in the audience or watching the video, you would believe that Pearson actually *becomes* each of the characters. Or more accurately, you would believe that each of the characters *becomes her*. Their laughter becomes her laughter; their tears, her tears; their struggles, her struggles; their words, her words. "That's what any good actor should do," you might observe. "She should make you believe." And, of course, you would be right.

You might say that all of us on the journey of the Spirit are a traveling drama troupe. We are actors for God. It is our calling to let God live and move in us, and speak through us, that all the world might see and believe. So, we must give ourselves over to our part, study it, become one with it, let it become one with us, that God's laughter might become our laughter; God's tears, our tears; God's struggles, our struggles; God's words, our words.

Choose something to read aloud. Let it be something that is meaningful to you: a favorite poem, a children's story, a scripture passage, an excerpt from Shakespeare, a letter from a friend. Before you read it, hold it in your hands, close your eyes, and feel the Spirit's presence. Then stand up, take a deep breath, and read. Read with confidence; read with expression; read with feeling; read with power. Unite yourself with the text, and the Spirit will speak through you. When you finish, you may want to read it again. The Spirit's presence will feel even stronger the second time, for then you will be able to focus less on reading and more on *being* the text.

Even as the Spirit speaks through you while you read, it speaks through you as you go about your daily life. That is, it does when you let it. So, be an actor for God. Let the Spirit live and move in you, and speak through you, that all the world might see and hear, and believe.

The Spirit speaks through me.

Day 243   I speak God's wisdom.

Yet among the mature we do speak wisdom, though it is not a wisdom of this age or of the rulers of this age, who are doomed to perish. But we speak God's wisdom, secret and hidden, which God decreed before the ages for our glory.

—1 Corinthians 2:6-7

*T*wo Jewish boys decide to take turns playing rabbi. One will be rabbi to the other for a week, then they will exchange roles. "I'll go first," the older boy volunteers. So the week goes by, and the younger boy comes to the older boy time and again, seeking advice for imaginary grown-up problems. Each time the "rabbi" sits back in his chair, folds his hands across his chest, listens thoughtfully to the question, and sighs deeply. Then he says what needs to be said, in a very solemn tone.

Finally it is the younger boy's turn to be rabbi. On the first day the older boy comes to him with a terrible "problem." The little rabbi leans back in his chair, folds his hands across his chest, listens thoughtfully, and finally speaks. "No, no, no!" the older boy exclaims, breaking out of character. "You're not doing it right! You forgot to sigh!"

This story teaches us that, in God's eyes, there is no wisdom without sympathy. When asked for advice, a truly wise person does not offer it unless he or she can "sigh" first. That sigh is one of deep understanding. It is a sign that the person remembers specific times when he or she felt the same feelings, or faced the same struggles, or experienced the same frailties as someone else. Recognizing his or her own life story in the story told by the other, the wise person sighs. That sigh entitles the person to speak. Then the person may offer any wisdom given by God on the subject. If in regard to a particular matter the person has not yet experienced enough to sigh, he or she remains silent, knowing that one cannot "play rabbi" having only the wisdom of the world.

Be careful today of what you say, especially when serious matters are being discussed. Offer counsel only if you can first "sigh" with recognition.

I speak God's wisdom.

Day 244   **I am becoming.**

And to be renewed in the spirit of your minds, and to clothe yourselves with the new self, created according to the likeness of God in true righteousness and holiness.

—Ephesians 4:23-24

$\mathcal{O}$n a sheet of paper, jot down the particular styles of clothing that you have worn during specific periods of your life, from your birth until the present. Think of everything, from the hats you wore on your head to the shoes you wore on your feet. Any accessories? Any "lucky clothes"? Any clothes you donned only on Sunday? Any that you wore only with certain groups of people? Did you tend to have more clothes of one color than another?

Next, for each time period, write down what kind of person you were. Use adjectives to describe yourself, such as proud, serious, happy-go-lucky, depressed, popular, lonely, carefree, rebellious, hard-working, and so on. When you finish, reflect on your notes. How have you changed over the years? How has your identity corresponded to the style or color of clothes that you have worn? To what extent have your clothes announced your identity to others? Concealed it from others?

If you are like many people, your "becoming" has revealed itself in your wardrobe. And now you are learning to "clothe yourself" with "the new self, created according to the likeness of God." The "style" of your spiritual existence and the "color" of your disposition are beginning to correspond to your identity as a child of God.

As our minds are transformed into the mind of Christ, we often have to clean out our spiritual clothes closets. Some of our spiritual clothes don't look good on us anymore, or don't give us as much pleasure as they used to. Some of them wear out, unable to take the wear-and-tear of life. Some no longer fit quite right; others we simply outgrow. So, our wardrobe continually changes, with one very important exception. We will always wear the armor of God—the belt of truth, the breastplate of love, the shoes of peace, the shield of faith, and the helmet of hope (Ephesians 6:14ff.; 1 Thessalonians 5:8).

I am becoming.

$\mathcal{D}ay$ 245   I am becoming Christ-like.

I say, "You are gods, children of the Most High, all of you."

—*Psalm 82:6*

$\mathcal{T}$o clothe yourself with the new self is to become godly.
To become godly is to become Christ-like.

Each day as you move ahead on your journey of faith, the mind of Christ continues to grow within you, transforming and deepening your spirit. Pause today to consider how your spiritual understandings have changed even during the last half-year or so. To begin to reflect on your growth, think about the following questions. (You may find it helpful to write your responses.)

(1) How is your faith like a journey?
(2) How would you describe your relationship with the rest of God's creation?
(3) What is the connection between your faith and your fears?
(4) What role does conflict play in your life?
(5) What does it mean for you to forgive others? To have compassion?
(6) How is your idea of "community" expanding?
(7) How are you becoming more aware of the indwelling Spirit? Of the presence of God in everyday life?
(8) What does "healing" mean to you?
(9) Define "peace."
(10) How has your concept of "miracles" changed?

Know that you are becoming more Christ-like, more godly, with each day of your spiritual journey. Continue to allow the mind of Christ to grow within you, and rejoice in your transformation!
I am becoming Christ-like.

Day 246   I am free.

And just then there appeared a woman with a spirit that had crippled her for eighteen years. She was bent over and was quite unable to stand up straight. When Jesus saw her, he called her over and said, "Woman, you are set free from your ailment." When he laid his hands on her, immediately she stood up straight and began praising God.

—*Luke 13:11-13*

*I*n today's scripture we find a woman who had a spirit that had held her down for eighteen years. Bent over with her burden, she was unable to stand up straight. But she was able to put herself in the right place to be healed. In finding Jesus, she found what she needed to be set free.

How often we carry with us a spirit that burdens us and weighs us down! We may be bent over with the heaviness of despair. We may have family problems, or feel misunderstood and unappreciated by those who are closest to us. We may be under financial stress, or feel that the problems of our society are somehow our fault. Sometimes it can seem like all the weight of the world is resting on us, holding us down, breaking our backs.

The woman in today's story receives her healing after she places herself near someone who can provide it. She puts herself in a healing environment where it is possible for her weight to be lifted from her. What is a "healing environment"? It is a place where you come to sense the presence of God. It is a place in which you feel peace and wholeness—a place where you find solace apart from the hurts and demands of everyday life. Filled with beauty, it comforts you and, at the same time, creates in you a sense of anticipation. In this kind of setting, the possibility of your being released from any burdens that are holding you down is much greater.

Do you have such a spot? If you do, spend time there on a regular basis to find release from the "spirit that is bending you over." If you do not have a healing spot, create one. It might be an entire room or just one corner of a room. If possible, include objects of beauty; some plants or flowers, or other natural elements; colors that are very comforting to you; a symbol for the presence of God (a candle works nicely); some type of music source (such as a boombox or stereo), so that you can play soothing music; and a comfortable chair. Let your healing environment be a place of retreat and release from all the worries of life.

I am free.

Day 247   **I never die.**

"'But we had to celebrate and rejoice, because this brother of yours was dead and has come to life; he was lost and has been found.'"

—*Luke 15:32*

There is more than one kind of death. There is physical death, in which we leave behind our bodies. There is also the death of a relationship, in which we leave behind our connection to another living person—a loss that can be as difficult to deal with as any physical death. The father in today's scripture, for example, had lost connection with his wayward son. Finally, there is spiritual death, in which we close ourselves to the possibilities of life that God has planned for us. Think for a moment about these three different kinds of personal death, each of which can be overcome by the miracle of resurrection.

Physical Death. When we finish the journey of this life, we leave behind our physical bodies. We are done with breathing, eating, and concern for our health. We no longer need to be concerned with our bodily weaknesses or limitations. As our spirits move on to union with God, we experience resurrection.

Relational Death. Sometimes our relationships come to an end, sometimes due to misunderstandings or offenses. For whatever reason, the chance for meaningful relationship seems no longer to exist. As in today's story, however, forgiveness has the power to either resurrect a broken relationship or heal our grief over the loss.

Spiritual Death. If you read the full story of the return of the prodigal son in Luke 15, you will notice that the older brother experiences both a relational and a spiritual death. He is both unwilling to be reconciled with his wayward brother and unwilling to follow the Spirit's lead and celebrate his brother's safe return. Whenever we harden our hearts against another person or the guidance of the Spirit, a part of our spirit dies. But God always offers us opportunities for a resurrection of our spirit.

Identify which of these kinds of death comes closest to your experience of life right now. Are you undergoing a physical, relational, or spiritual death in any way? Know that the mind of Christ offers you a new way of understanding your situation. You have the chance for resurrection. Whatever your circumstances, open yourself to receiving new life. Say to yourself:

I never die.

Day 248　　　　　　**Healing opens me.**

They brought to him a deaf man who had an impediment in his speech; and they begged him to lay his hand on him. He took him aside in private, away from the crowd, and put his fingers into his ears, and he spat and touched his tongue. Then looking up to heaven, he sighed and said to him, "Ephphatha," that is, "Be opened." And immediately his ears were opened, his tongue was released, and he spoke plainly.

—Mark 7:32-35

*I*n today's story of healing, Jesus opens the man's ears so that he can hear clearly and then releases his tongue so that he can speak plainly. This suggests that we first need to hear clearly before we will be able to speak clearly.

In what situations do you find yourself hesitant to speak? Is there a certain group of people or a specific person that seems to inhibit your speech? If so, what are you afraid of that is "tying up your tongue"? Perhaps you are afraid of being misunderstood or of not having your opinion valued. Perhaps you are afraid that you will sound foolish or that you will have to defend your opinions. Whatever you are afraid of, your fear causes you to be silent.

However, once you have clearly heard God say that you are whole, that you are valued, and that you do not need to fear anything, you will find the courage to speak. Look up to heaven. Hear the voice of Christ saying to you, "Be opened!" Let your ears and your tongue be healed.

Healing opens me.

Day 249   **Healing may take time.**

He took the blind man by the hand and led him out of the village; and when he had put saliva on his eyes and laid his hands on him, he asked him, "Can you see anything?" And the man looked up and said, "I can see people, but they look like trees, walking." Then Jesus laid his hands on his eyes again; and he looked intently and his sight was restored, and he saw everything clearly.

—Mark 8:23-25

*I*n today's scripture, Jesus healed the blind man gradually. When his sight was not immediately restored, the man stayed with Jesus and followed his direction until the healing was complete. This required patience.

As we have previously noted, healing does not always come on our time line. Furthermore, it does not always come in the form that we want or expect. In the scriptures healing means wholeness. Wholeness is not the same as the perfection of all the parts. You can be whole and still have some physical problems that will not go away. If you are deaf or lame, for example, you can be whole even though you may never be able to hear or walk. Although you have a physical challenge, you are not prohibited from experiencing the fullness of life as God intended it to be.

In the same way, you can be a whole person and still have some life challenges that will not go away. You can still celebrate wholeness even when parts of your life are less than perfect.

Find a person who experiences a chronic physical problem. Ask this person to share his or her story with you. You might ask several of the following questions:

(1) What has it been like to struggle with your pain, weakness, or limitation?
(2) In what ways have you experienced the power of God working in your situation?
(3) How have you been blessed because of the difficulty you experience?
(4) What transformations have happened in your attitudes, your faith, or your relationships as a result of the problem?

As you converse with this person, listen for his or her own sense of wholeness. And celebrate that you, too, can feel whole even when some parts of your body or your life are less than perfect.

Healing may take time.

Day 250   **Healing comes to everyone.**

And all in the crowd were trying to touch him, for power came out from him and healed all of them.

—Luke 6:19

*I*n our everyday lives, it is very hard for us to live beyond the principle of scarcity. We have trouble imagining that there is plenty of everything. We have trouble remembering that, although we have not yet learned to share its bounty, the earth produces enough for all of us to experience life to its fullest. So, we tend to think that there is not enough to go around.

Do you suppose that we carry over this "scarcity thinking" into our ideas about healing? Today's verse of scripture suggests that everyone who came to Jesus found healing. Can this be? Can we imagine that there is enough healing power to reach out to all persons in need and bring them to wholeness—and still have some left over?

The Spirit has enough power to heal all the pain in the world. And this power is available to everyone. Do you believe this? Do you feel joy in the way that the Spirit reaches out to all? Or are you afraid that the Spirit might not have enough healing power for everyone? Are you afraid that the power will not be there when you need it? Remember, there is no scarcity with God.

Identify one or two people who seem to be surrounded by a positive energy, a sense of healing power. They are bright with joy and hope. When you are around them, you feel your own energy increasing. You are uplifted just to be in their presence. The power of God moves through them to touch you.

Visit such a positive person as soon as possible. Tune in to his or her energies. Feel yourself being encouraged and strengthened. Rejoice in the sense of wholeness that fills you when you are with this person. Remember that, through the infinite power of the Spirit, this healing can come to everyone.

Healing comes to everyone.

Day 251   **Healing never ends.**

I am going to bring [this city and its people] recovery and healing; I will heal them and reveal to them abundance of prosperity and security.

—Jeremiah 33:6

*O*ur bodies have been wonderfully made. The transformation that they are undergoing each moment of every day is remarkable. Did you know that . . .

- every morning you have fifty million new skin cells?
- every five days you have a completely new stomach lining?
- every three weeks your fat tissue is completely changed?
- every five weeks your skin is replaced?
- every three months your skeletal cells are completely changed?
- every four months your red blood cells are replaced by new ones?
- in one year's time, 98 percent of all the atoms in your body are changed?

Our bodies undergo an endless process of renewal and healing. There is no way to stop it. God has designed our bodies in such a way that they always move in the direction of self-healing and wholeness. Even when they are invaded by germs or damaged by accidents, our cells work toward healing. In fact, the greater the invasion or injury, the greater the response of the protective mechanisms of the body.

Today, throw a "re-birthday party" for yourself. Give yourself a gift that reminds you of renewal, rebirth, and constant healing. It might be a fragrance oil that you could use for a rejuvenating bath at the end of the day. It might be a flowering plant that reminds you of the newness of life. Whatever it is, celebrate the constant transformation that is happening at the cellular level of your body. Give thanks that:

Healing never ends.

Day 252   My sorrow ends.

"He will wipe every tear from their eyes. Death will be no more; mourning and crying and pain will be no more, for the first things have passed away."

—*Revelation 21:4*

Joyce pushed her full grocery cart up behind her van. It was the day of her mother's funeral. In just a few hours, family and friends would be gathering to mourn their loss, to share their grief. Would she be able to handle it? Where would she ever find the strength that she needed to get through the rest of the day?

She sighed a tired sigh and opened the back door of the van, ready to load her groceries. But the back of the van was full of boxes. She had forgotten. Earlier, her sister had placed some of their mother's belongings in the van for her to take home. On top of the boxes lay her mother's Bible. Almost in shock, Joyce picked it up and began to leaf through it. It was filled with slips of paper—personal notes and favorite scriptures. And there was a yellow piece of paper on which her mother had written a personal statement of faith; it was dated shortly before her death. As Joyce read it for the first time, a deep sense of peace and calm flooded through her body.

Joyce arrived at the funeral home in time to share her discovery with the pastor. He included the affirmation in the service, which was quickly transformed from an occasion of despair and loss to a celebration of life and faith. Joyce's sorrow, like that of many others in attendance, was changed to a tender joy.

With God's help, we can always change our sorrow for what was to a celebration of what is. Even in times of deepest grief, we can choose either to see what has been and is no more or to see what was not and now is. We can focus upon the loss of physical life or we can focus upon the experience of eternal life.

Where are you currently feeling a sense of loss? For a moment, back up from your feeling of despair to the thought or belief that is feeding it. Are you thinking that there is no hope? Are you imagining that there are no new possibilities? Do you believe that all is lost? Change your negative belief to a positive affirmation. You might wish to use one of these affirming statements, or create one of your own:

God is making room for something new in my life.
When one door is closed, another one is opened.
What God has in store for me will be better than what was.

Whenever you are experiencing loss or despair, use your affirmation. Notice your feelings begin to change. Know that God is always working to bring wholeness out of your pain.

My sorrow ends.

Day 253   I am amazed.

The LORD said to Abraham, "Why did Sarah laugh, and say, 'Shall I indeed bear a child, now that I am old?' Is anything too wonderful for the LORD? At the set time I will return to you, in due season, and Sarah shall have a son."

—Genesis 18:13-14

Messengers came to Sarah from God to tell her that, at her advanced age and after many years of barrenness, she would soon bear a child. How did she choose to respond? Did she accept that what she was being told would indeed happen? Not exactly. Did she say "Yes!" to the amazing news? Hardly. Sarah chose to laugh in disbelief.

Learning to say "Yes!" to what life brings our way is not always easy. Sometimes our faith and hope must overcome a great deal of doubt and fear. Jane was a person who welcomed a challenge. Each January she would create a slogan that would direct her growth for the coming year. One year her slogan was "Just say yes!" She resolved to accept any reasonable request that was made of her. And the requests came! She was asked to do many things that, at first, she was afraid she would be unable to do. But then, remembering her slogan, she accepted the challenges. To her amazement, she found the necessary skills and abilities to fulfill them. Most important, she received many blessings as a result of the new ways that she used her time and talents.

Sam was another person who learned to be amazed at life. All his life he had been terrified of dying. But then he ended up in the hospital with pain in his chest—not once, but twice. Each time he experienced a cardiac arrest. Both times he was revived. During those moments of near-death, he experienced the common phenomenon of traveling through a tunnel toward a light. Both times, he sensed the presence of loved ones waiting for his arrival "on the other side." They were beckoning to him, ready to welcome him. He felt an overwhelming desire to go to them and leave this life behind. At last, however, he decided that it was not yet time. He chose to return. After these near-death experiences, his fear of dying disappeared. He was ready to say "Yes!" to the amazing new life that awaited him, and he was ready to accept his death when it finally came.

In the coming week, allow life to amaze you. Determine to say "Yes!" to any request that comes to you that you could possibly carry out. Know that some requests will stretch you and others will seem to be beyond your abilities. Accept them as challenges to put into action all the gifts that God has given you. For one week, just say "Yes!" Be prepared to be richly blessed.

I am amazed.

Day 254 **God sends angels to help me.**

I am going to send an angel in front of you, to guard you on the way and to bring you to the place that I have prepared.

—Exodus 23:20

*R*emember that angels are simply messengers from God. They appear in many different forms. They may come in visions, dreams, or unusual encounters. They may even come in printed form, as through someone's life story that inspires us to do our very best, or devotional materials that open us to new understandings of the scriptures. But most often they come to us in the form of other human beings—our best friend, perhaps, or the stranger we have just met. Whenever anyone is carrying a message to us from God (knowingly or not), we are encountering an angel. Seldom are wings required!

Think back over your life and remember all those people who guided and directed you on your journey. Recall the Sunday school teachers, family members, neighbors, school teachers, and friends who were there when you needed them most. Celebrate the ways in which their love touched you and the ways in which their encouragement led you in the right directions. Have you ever thought of them as angels? One way to watch for angel encounters is to be aware of the "Ah ha!" feeling that springs up within you. You may be talking with a trusted friend and, in the midst of receiving some helpful feedback, the lightbulb comes on. That is an angel encounter moment. You may be reading a good book and suddenly realize that God is speaking to you through the words of the author. That is an encounter with the divine. Whenever you realize that there is more going on than the obvious, open yourself as fully as possible to the presence of God and celebrate that you are in the company of angels.

Today, open yourself to an awareness of angels in your midst. Anticipate that God will send messengers to help you. Fully anticipate those "Ah ha!" moments that let you know that you have been visited by God.

God sends angels to help me.

Day 255 Angels come at just the right moment.

The very night before Herod was going to bring him out, Peter, bound with two chains, was sleeping between two soldiers, while guards in front of the door were keeping watch over the prison. Suddenly an angel of the Lord appeared and a light shone in the cell. He tapped Peter on the side and woke him, saying, "Get up quickly." And the chains fell off his wrists.

—Acts 12:6-7

*T*ony had been on vacation for a week. He felt refreshed as he returned to work. But as soon as he walked in the door, he knew that something was up. People were treating him differently, as though they knew something he didn't. Then his boss called him into the office. A lawyer was there to question him about his job performance. An accusation had been made, and they wanted to "get to the bottom of it." Stunned by this news, Tony snapped. Without thinking about the possible consequences for his family, he quit. Just like that. Before he realized what he had done, he had resigned and was out the door.

Now what? He couldn't go home. What would he say to his wife and children? That he had just quit his job without any concern for them? Of course not. He took off in the car, driving without a destination in mind. Finally, two days later, he found himself back in his hometown again. But he still couldn't bring himself to go home. He drove around in the dark of the night until he came to a deserted park. There, in despair, he wrote letters to his loved ones, trying to explain what had happened and why he had no other way out of the situation. Then he hooked up a hose to his exhaust pipe and ran it into the front seat.

Tony was beginning to lose consciousness when, all at once, he heard a sharp rapping on the car window. A child's voice cried out, "Hey, are you all right, mister?" Opening the car door, he stumbled out to see who was there. He fainted. When he regained consciousness, he searched the park but found no one.

Was it really a child that had startled him back into awareness? Could a child really have been there, alone in the park, in the middle of the night? Or had an angel come to rescue him in his moment of desperation? Whatever had happened, it happened at just the right moment. Tony immediately began to plan his return home. Coincidence? *God-incidence.*

Many books recount the experiences of people who have been visited by angels. Locate one of these and read at least one encounter story. Celebrate the active presence of divine messengers in our lives.

Angels come at just the right moment.

Day 256   **I am led by angels.**

But during the night an angel of the Lord opened the prison doors, brought them out, and said, "Go, stand in the temple and tell the people the whole message about this life."

—Acts 5:19-20

*T*he angel in today's passage gave the apostles very specific directions regarding where they were to go, what they were to do, and what they were to say. This messenger of God appeared in order to give guidance.

Do you believe that *you* have ever been led by an angel?

Steve had no idea why he was on the men's retreat. He was a very private person; he had never attended anything like it before. But for three Sundays in a row, when the pastor had announced that the retreat sign-up sheet was posted on the bulletin board, he had felt led to sign up. For two Sundays he had resisted the impulse. By the third Sunday, however, the voice inside him was just too strong. He went directly to the bulletin board after the service and signed his name, still not understanding why he should.

Now here he was, feeling like a fish out of water. *Why had he come?* he wondered. Maybe he should go home.

But just then one of the other men came around the corner and said, "Steve, do you need to talk?" And he did. He talked and talked, well into the night. His new friend seemed to understand the pain he was experiencing in his life. They promised to continue their conversation and friendship when the retreat was over. This was the beginning of a relationship that made all the difference in both of their lives. Now Steve began to understand why he had been led to sign up for the retreat. "Led"—by an angel, perhaps?

In what ways do you feel that you are being led? Do you hear the voice of God telling you something that you need to do? Enter a time of prayer. Listen carefully. And continue to listen prayerfully even when your time of prayer has ended. Let yourself be led throughout your day.

I am led by angels.

Day 257　　**I am strengthened by angels.**

Again one in human form touched me and strengthened me. He said, "Do not fear, greatly beloved, you are safe. Be strong and courageous!" When he spoke to me, I was strengthened and said, "Let my lord speak, for you have strengthened me."

—Daniel 10:18-19

*T*he right words can make all the difference in the world to us, and the angel in today's scripture text spoke just exactly what Daniel needed to hear. No words are more powerful than "You are safe." Each of us needs to know that we are free from danger, whether physical or emotional. Until this basic need is met, nothing else really matters.

Perhaps even more important than the power of words is the power of touch. When the angel touched Daniel, he was strengthened. When we have experienced the loving and tender touch of another person, we find the courage that we need to face whatever challenges may come our way.

Muriel and Ted left the courthouse, shocked by the sentence. They had expected the judge to let Ted off lightly. That was what the lawyer had promised would happen. Instead, Ted had been ordered to prison. Now he was on his way there on a prison bus, and Muriel was driving home in her car. As the miles between them increased, each sat in silence, unable to believe what was happening. In total despair, each of them felt that life no longer had any purpose or meaning.

Then it happened. Although Muriel and Ted did not talk about it until years later, they eventually discovered that each of them had experienced the same thing at about the same moment. When they were feeling at their absolute lowest, each of them felt an arm slip around their shoulder and hold them securely. That touch reassured them that everything would be all right. An arm around the shoulder—yet, they were alone!

Take a moment to reflect upon the power of touch. Remember those times when someone who loved you dared to hold you until the fear went away. Remember the handshakes, the pats on the back, the arms around the shoulder that made all the difference in the way that you felt. Give thanks to God for the strength that has come to you through the touch of others.

I am strengthened by angels.

Day 258   **I am protected by angels.**

For he will command his angels concerning you to guard you in all your ways.

—*Psalm 91:11*

*H*ave there been times in your life when you walked through danger unharmed? Do you remember an incident when you came out safe and wondered how you had made it? Could it be that you were protected by angels? There are countless stories of survivals and rescues that cannot be explained in simple human terms. They are, simply, miraculous.

Being protected by angels does not mean that we will never experience physical harm. Think of the martyrs of the faith who lost their lives. Where were the angels while they were suffering? Right there with them, certainly. How else could they have gone to their deaths singing praises to God? God's angels are always with us, protecting our spirits. Therefore, we can rejoice even while undergoing extreme physical difficulties. And who knows? In the fullness of joy, God's angels may even succeed in helping us overcome those difficulties.

Reflect upon the following questions. You might find it helpful to write a brief response to each.

(1) When have you walked away from danger unharmed?
(2) When have you felt that you were not alone in the midst of a very trying time or difficult situation?
(3) Have you ever experienced a sense of being protected?

Create or locate a symbol for the protection that God provides. For example, it might be an angel lapel pin or a cross necklace. Wear it, carry it with you, or place it in a spot where you will notice it throughout the day. Allow it to be a gentle reminder that you are not alone.

I am protected by angels.

Day 259　　　　**I am revived by angels.**

But [Elijah] himself went a day's journey into the wilderness, and came and sat down under a solitary broom tree. He asked that he might die: "It is enough; now, O LORD, take away my life, for I am no better than my ancestors." Then he lay down under the broom tree and fell asleep. Suddenly an angel touched him and said to him, "Get up and eat." He looked, and there at his head was a cake baked on hot stones, and a jar of water. . . . Then he went in the strength of that food forty days and forty nights to Horeb the mount of God.

—1 Kings 19:4-8

Elijah was ready to die. Life was not worth living any longer. He begged God to take his life. But instead God sent an angel who ministered to him in such a way that his strength was restored and his hope was renewed. The angel ministered to Elijah in three ways. First, the angel touched him. Once again, we are reminded of the power of touch. When one is as discouraged as Elijah was, words may not do the trick. But the loving touch of one who understands and cares can make all the difference in the world. So, being wise, as angels are, this messenger from God greeted Elijah with a loving touch.

The second thing the angel did was offer Elijah food. In other words, the angel knew that Elijah needed nourishment, that his physical body was depleted of energy. Messengers from God know what we need to be revived. Understanding even better than we do what will renew our strength, they offer it to us.

The third way that the angel ministered to Elijah was to speak words of encouragement to him. The angel pointed in the direction of a new journey, giving hope where there was none. Little did Elijah realize that this encounter with an angel was only a prelude to a direct encounter with God (which is retold in the next few verses of 1 Kings 19).

On a piece of paper, list specific ways in which God has renewed your strength. How have you found courage to continue on your journey when you were ready to give up? How have you been revived? After you have completed your list, take time to reflect. Ask yourself whether any messengers of God, seen or unseen, might have been at work on your behalf. Finally, offer a prayer of thanksgiving for all the times that renewal has come to you when you needed it most.

It has been said that angels can fly because they take themselves lightly. Ponder that thought. How lightly do you take yourself? Perhaps, like Elijah, you focus too much on the fearful, dangerous, and weighty things of life. Do you need to "lighten up"? If so, we suggest that you bake or buy an angel food cake sometime soon. As you eat a piece, notice how light it is. Sit back, forget your worries, and enjoy!

I am revived by angels.

Day 260　　　　**I see with the eyes of peace.**

He makes wars cease to the end of the earth; he breaks the bow, and shatters the spear; he burns the shields with fire.

—Psalm 46:9

*P*reschool teachers understand that when toy guns, swords, and power heroes are allowed in the classroom, they have a negative effect on the children's behavior. Their play becomes more violent and combative. The images of violence and war encourage rough and hostile interaction. However, when such toys are left outside the classroom, the play is more cooperative and peaceful.

When we adults see "the bow, the spear, and the shield"—or the bomber, the missile, and the tank—we know that war is in the making. As these implements of war proliferate, it is war that we expect and war for which we prepare. But if we were to destroy these tools of destruction, then the possibility of war would become more remote. Without them, we could not plan for war. We would not be equipped for battle.

If our eyes saw no weapons of war, our minds would focus more on peace. Without the symbols of war and destruction all around us, we could see the tools of peace in one another's hands and approach one another in hope rather than fear. We could see each person as a potential friend rather than a potential adversary. We could seek out symbols of commonality and unity. This would be seeing the world with the eyes of peace.

Take a trip to a department store or toy store, or browse through a catalog or advertisement circular that includes toys. Notice the kinds of toys that are available to children today. If you are able to locate a peace-teaching toy—one that teaches children how to be cooperative or live peacefully with one another—make plans to purchase it and give it to a child.

I see with the eyes of peace.

Day 261   I see only peace.

And I will grant peace in the land, and you shall lie down, and no one shall make you afraid; I will remove dangerous animals from the land, and no sword shall go through your land.

—*Leviticus 26:6*

What does it mean when you say that you "slept like a baby"?

It means that you slept peacefully and soundly. Why can a baby sleep soundly when we adults toss and turn? The baby has no worries, of course. When a baby goes to sleep, there is but one goal: to restore and refresh the body. But when we try to fall asleep, we are trying to shut out all that is crowding our minds—

the problems of yesterday, the mistakes of today, the concerns for tomorrow. Is it any wonder that we have trouble sleeping?

Imagine for a moment that you really could lie down and know beyond a shadow of a doubt that no one could hurt you, that you had absolutely nothing to fear. Imagine that all implements of war and destruction no longer existed in your land. Imagine that you lived in a world in which everyone (even the wild animals) thought only of peace. Now, wouldn't you sleep like a baby? Yet, this is what God intends for you, *now*. God wants you to set your eyes and your mind on the things that lead to peace.

Locate a safe place outdoors where you will not have any fear. This might be in your own yard, or in a quiet park nearby. Or, you might have to travel a distance to find it, or even go there in your imagination. Once you are there, lie down on the ground. Focus your eyes on the sky above you. Imagine that you are a part of the earth, one with it. Feel no separation between you and the ground upon which you rest. Know that there is only one Creator of all that surrounds you. Be aware of the unity of everything that God has created. Celebrate the goodness of the Creator, and sense the divine love that protects you and all that you see. Give thanks to God for the peace that rises up within you.

I see only peace.

Day 262   **I am learning the way of peace.**

"By the tender mercy of our God, the dawn from on high will break upon us, to give light to those who sit in darkness and in the shadow of death, to guide our feet into the way of peace."

—*Luke 1:78-79*

*W*hen foreign exchange students visit another country, they and their host families find that they have much to learn about each other. One way that the students and families teach each other is to tell stories about life in their culture—about the clothes people wear, the foods they eat, the education they receive, the holidays they celebrate, the religions they practice, the family life they share, the games they play, the jokes they tell, the work they do. As the students and host families tell their stories, light is shed on who they are and where they come from. Gradually they adjust to each other. More than that, they begin to experience life together in ways that will someday make for more good stories—and, they hope, for a more peaceful world. Finally, when the period of exchange is over, the students and host families reluctantly say goodbye, knowing that they have entrusted precious parts of themselves to one another.

Such people are travelers on the way of peace. They are followers of the light of God, which reveals the preciousness of all life. As their respect for God's family grows, they become bearers of God's light. The light makes clear their life paths; they are unafraid to take any path of peace, no matter how strange it may be, because they know beyond a shadow of a doubt that their way is secure.

Go to the children's book section in your library or bookstore. There you will discover a large variety of international folktales and legends retold for children. Read one or more of them from a culture outside your own. Then reflect on what it might have in common with a story that you remember from your childhood (a fairy tale, for instance, or one of Aesop's fables). Do you see similar characters or themes? Similar plot lines? Similar views of the world? After citing similarities, acknowledge any striking differences between the stories.

Allow yourself to be taught by the story that you are reading. Learn about the culture from which the story comes and the way it seems to look at the world. Does the story tell you something of that culture's values, of what it regards as important? In becoming acquainted with other members of God's family, you are following the light of God. You are learning the way of peace.

I am learning the way of peace.

Day 26:3   **The way of peace is sure.**

Great peace have those who love your law; nothing can make them stumble.

—Psalm 119:165

*N*otice, this verse says that great peace comes to those who *love* the law, not to those who only *obey* the law. There is quite a difference. You can obey laws out of fear or obligation, almost with resentment or hostility. Such obedience certainly brings you little peace. In fact, it brings quite the opposite. It brings fear. Like a child obeying parental rules, you might be obedient only to avoid punishment. However, if you fulfill the law out of love for the law itself or for the lawgiver, your experience is quite different. Instead of resentment toward the "authorities," you feel a sense of cooperation and peace.

Have you ever noticed that when you walk in fear, the very things that you dread are much more likely to happen than if you walked with courage? Suppose, for example, that you are carrying a piece of your good china through the house. At some point, you say to yourself, "Boy, I hope I don't drop this." The very next moment, you stub your toe, and the rest is history.

So it is when we journey through life obeying God's law out of fear of being punished. With our fear working against us, we are much more likely to break the law—to stumble. However, if we can appreciate both the law of *agape* and the Lawgiver, if we can love the benefits that come from following God's will for our lives, we will be much more likely to walk safely and peacefully—to keep from stumbling. Our way will be more sure.

Find a book or other object that you can balance on your head. Place it there, then try walking around without holding onto it. At first, walk while focusing on your fear that the object will fall. Notice how uncertain and shaky your movements are. Now, stop and fill yourself with confidence that you will be able to balance the object successfully. Try walking again. Notice the difference that your positive attitude makes. You can walk with greater assurance that you will not drop the object.

Walk throughout the day allowing your inner peace to make your path sure.

The way of peace is sure.

Day 264   The way of peace is life.

To set the mind on the flesh is death, but to set the mind on the Spirit is life and peace.

—*Romans 8:6*

*F*or a moment, focus on the physical body. Think about the process of growing older. Early in life, you feel like you are growing stronger. Then, at some point, you begin to feel that the aging process is taking its toll. Your body starts to have all sorts of problems—illnesses that come more often and stay longer, chronic conditions that keep it from functioning at its optimum potential. Your body weakens and tires. Gradually, it moves toward its own demise. This is the reality of the physical body and of the things of this world. To set your mind on "the flesh"—which does not last—leaves you troubled and afraid.

Now focus on your spiritual body. Here you have unlimited potential for growth. The more you develop the spiritual side of life, the more strength you come to have in God—no matter how old you are! As your path continues to unfold, your spirit moves into a deeper awareness of life and peace, and into a deeper relationship with the One who gives them. Your spiritual body does not die but, at the moment of physical death, is released into a complete experience of the divine. Therefore, to set your mind on "the spirit"—on the things which do last—brings you everlasting peace.

Locate an older saint—someone who has spent a great deal of time and energy developing the spiritual side of life. Ask for some of this person's time, and listen carefully to his or her faith story. Receive the wisdom that this person has acquired on the journey. Notice the ways in which concerns for the things of this world decreased as he or she began to focus more on the things of the spirit. Also, be sure to ask questions about the future, such as "What plans do you have?" and "Where are you headed?" and "What do you imagine it will be like after you leave your body behind?" This testimony will show you that, in faith, the way of peace is synonymous with life.

The way of peace is life.

Day 265   **The way of peace respects the earth.**

At destruction and famine you shall laugh, and shall not fear the wild animals of the earth. For you shall be in league with the stones of the field, and the wild animals shall be at peace with you.

—Job 5:22-23

An older couple decided in their retirement to build a new home on several acres of ground. As the hole was being dug for their basement, they noticed that the earth contained a large number of rocks. At first, they were quite dismayed at the discovery. Both of them enjoyed gardening, and they had hoped that they would find good soil for growing things at their new home. After awhile, though, they rolled up their sleeves and began to pile the rocks in several large piles around their property. Over the next several years, the couple transformed those rock piles into beautiful rock gardens. They planted creeping flox, hen and chicks, and dozens of other rock garden plants that they had never grown before. An apparently troublesome part of creation became a powerful display of the way in which the various parts of nature can interact and compliment each other!

The way of peace is one of harmony with all of the created order. It respects, as in this case, the connection between living creatures and the stones of the field. No one part of creation is more or less important than another. Each part belongs to the other.

Today, get in touch with the natural world around you and appreciate each of its parts. Here are some ideas for getting in touch with nature in a meaningful way.

If the weather permits, take off your shoes and socks and walk barefooted in the grass or sand. Take each step slowly and intentionally, feeling the textures of the ground on the soles of your feet. Give thanks for the good earth. Or, stand outdoors without a coat or jacket when the weather is cold or the wind is blowing. Stand still and feel the wind move around you. Imagine that it is passing right through your body. Celebrate the wind. Or, if the sun is shining, find a way to be in it and absorb its warmth. Rejoice in its healing power. Or, if it is raining, allow the raindrops to fall on your hair. If it is snowing, watch as the snowflakes melt on the back of your hand. Give thanks for the refreshing moisture.

Whatever the conditions of the natural world around you might be, enjoy them. And celebrate the One who has given you life on this great earth.

The way of peace respects the earth.

Day 266 **The way of peace protects the earth.**

I will make for you a covenant on that day with the wild animals, the birds of the air, and the creeping things of the ground; and I will abolish the bow, the sword, and war from the land; and I will make you lie down in safety.

—Hosea 2:18

$\mathcal{H}$ave you heard about the conversation between the hog and the chicken? They were discussing the upcoming Easter breakfast at the local church. The chicken seemed quite pleased that the Breakfast Committee had decided to serve bacon and eggs. She was particularly proud to know that her eggs would be part of the celebration. Noticing the rather gloomy look on the face of the hog, she inquired if he were not as happy as she was about the plans. He replied, "No, I am not. Please remember that for you the breakfast requires only a contribution. For me, it requires a total sacrifice."

Seldom do we realize what the other parts of nature must do in order for us to enjoy the lifestyle that we want. Have you thanked a plant for giving you food, lately? Have you acknowledged the sacrifice that animals make so that you might eat meat?

It is God's plan that all creatures work together with a deep appreciation for one another and with an understanding of the interrelatedness of all of life. This world is not here for us human beings to use and misuse however we wish. It is not hard to see the results of our indiscriminate demands on the earth's resources. The earth groans with them. We have lost our respect for creation, as a whole and in its parts.

A Native American teaching asks that we consider the effects of our actions upon the future, to the seventh generation. The seventh generation not only of our children, but of all living things. If we took this challenge seriously, we would be much more careful about how we treat this earth upon which we live.

What do you do that has a positive effect upon the future, even to the seventh generation? Identify one way that you protect and care for the earth. For example, do you recycle? Do you live a simple lifestyle that places few demands upon the earth? Do you regularly buy used goods, repair them, use them until they are worn out, and then recycle them in some way? Do you grow plants or plant trees? Do you look for ways to decrease your use of water and electricity?

Find one new way that you can celebrate your interrelatedness with all of nature and your desire to preserve the earth for future generations. Take another positive step forward in protecting the earth.

The way of peace protects the earth.

Day 267   **Nothing perishes.**

You have been born anew, not of perishable but of imperishable seed,
through the living and enduring word of God.

—1 Peter 1:23

*N*othing, no one in the world is lost: this is the living and
enduring gospel of God. Those of us who do not believe it are
waiting to die, and cannot be made to live. But those of us who
do believe it are being reborn, and cannot be made to die. For
now we know the truth. Nothing, finally, can defeat us. Nothing,
finally, can destroy us. Nothing can destroy anything, for everything is God's.

Do you believe that nothing perishes? Can you overcome your
fear, reassuring yourself that you have no reason to be afraid?
Can you overcome your grief, consoling yourself that you have
no reason to mourn, since nothing can be lost from God?

Think about times when you have felt like something or someone was being destroyed. Perhaps a family business went bank-
rupt. A house went up in flames. A marriage broke up. A friend
became an alcoholic. A favorite possession was lost. A loved one
died. A dear neighbor moved away. A spouse was forced to retire.
A natural disaster struck your town. Whatever might have happened, what emotions did you feel? Make a list.

Now, ask yourself whether in the midst of those losses—and all
the emotions that accompanied them—you were able to find ways
to affirm the gospel. Were you able to see anything life-affirming
in the apparent destruction?

Seeing with the eyes of faith means trying to discover affirmations of life where other eyes can only see its denials. Renew
your own faith today by writing a personal affirmation of life.
When you have finished composing your affirmation, declare it
aloud, rejoicing that life is truly and totally victorious.

Nothing perishes.

Day 268   **Everything is transformed.**

Six days later, Jesus took with him Peter and James and John, and led
them up a high mountain apart, by themselves. And he was transfigured
before them, and his clothes became dazzling white, such as no one on
earth could bleach them. And there appeared to them Elijah with
Moses, who were talking with Jesus. . . . Then a cloud overshadowed

them, and from the cloud there came a voice, "This is my Son, the Beloved; listen to him!" Suddenly when they looked around, they saw no one with them any more, but only Jesus.

—*Mark 9:2-4, 7-8*

A story is told of how once, after a long period of extremely gloomy weather, a businessman chartered a plane and flew all of his office employees up through the clouds until, finally, they were above them all, soaring in the glorious light of the sun.

Sometimes when you get up high enough, you see things differently. Just ask the people on that plane. Just ask Peter, James, and John.

Have *you* ever been on a mountaintop? Or at the top of a tower looking out over an amazing vista? You stand up there looking down on where you came from, and you are awed by what you see. The view lifts you out of your ordinary way of looking at things. You might say that you see the world more like God sees it. You see the big picture. And when at last you must leave the mountaintop and walk again on the plain, you don't look at the landscape like you used to. Now you look at it with the miracle-mind. The hills don't seem so steep. The valleys don't seem so deep. And everything seems radiant with the light of God's presence.

Write a description of a "mountaintop experience" that you have had, which somehow changed your perspective. You may have actually been on a mountaintop or in some other high place that gave you a distinctly different vantage point. Or you may have had a spiritual experience that did the same thing. Whatever the experience was, identify ways in which it transformed your way of looking at things. Know that such experiences help to strengthen your Christ-mind, which, seeing the big picture, can discover life in the midst of death and joy in the midst of sorrow.

Everything is transformed.

Day 269   **I am transformed.**

Jesus said to him, "Stand up, take your mat and walk." At once the man was made well, and he took up his mat and began to walk.

—*John 5:8-9*

*T*he man in this story had been ill for *thirty-eight* years. Day after day he had come and lain beside the pool of Bethzatha, waiting for the water to ripple—the sign that an angel of God had arrived to heal the sick. Unfortunately, as everyone knew, only the first person to step into the pool after it had been "troubled" would be made well. This man, unable to move quickly, was always crowded out by someone else. But did he ever give up? No. Did he *want* to be healed? When Jesus asked him that, the man must have wanted to laugh.

So on this fateful day the man finally got what he had been waiting for. But notice, Jesus did not heal him by helping him climb into the pool at just the right time. All Jesus did was tell him to get up. After thirty-eight years of hoping for the help of an angel, all the man had to do was "stand up, take his mat and walk." It was that simple.

This story teaches us several things about how we are transformed. First, we must believe in the possibility of our transformation, even if it takes a long period of time. Even if it takes a lifetime. Next, we must believe more in the *fact* that transformation will take place than in the specific *form* it may take. Otherwise, we may miss seeing the healer because we are staring at the pool. Finally, we must play an active role in our transformation. We must do more than lie beside the pool. We must get up and walk.

Identify one way in which you have been "waiting by the pool." What change have you been quietly wishing for in your life? Now, reflect on three questions:

(1) Do you believe that this change can actually occur?
(2) Do you expect this change to occur in a very specific way? By doing so, are you perhaps preventing its happening in some other way?
(3) Are you playing an active role in helping to bring this change about? Are you a partner of God in your own transformation?

I am transformed.

Day 270   **My hope is renewed.**

When he was at the table with them, he took bread, blessed and broke it, and gave it to them. Then their eyes were opened, and they recognized him; and he vanished from their sight.

—Luke 24:30-31

The author of Luke reports that the resurrected Jesus sat down and broke bread with his friends. He came to them in such a way that they would recognize him. He did something with them that they had often done together; in fact, breaking bread was what they had done together just before he died. So now, as he broke the bread, their eyes were opened. And though he vanished instantly, his brief appearance renewed their hope. The supper table was filled with talk of him, and immediately after the meal, the witnesses returned to Jerusalem to tell the grief-stricken inner circle of disciples.

Miracles renew our hope. They remind us that what we see and what we know is not all there is, by a long shot.

Some of the most common and most touching miracles are those mysterious reassurances that come after our loved ones have died. Despite our grief, we are somehow made to know that all is well with them and with us. These miracles take many forms. Our departed loved ones may actually appear to us, as spirits. Or, they may communicate with us less directly, through dreams; through mysterious occurrences that we somehow associate with them; through messages that arise, unbidden, in our minds; through strong feelings and scents that tell us they are near, and so on. Since these communications come to comfort and inspire us, it is strange, indeed, that so many of us hesitate to talk about them.

Ask some friends, neighbors, and family members if they have had such experiences or know of people who have. Be a safe presence for them. Don't pry, but reassure them that you will graciously receive their stories. Be prepared to share your own experiences, if you have had any. Understand that all miracle stories are precious; do not try to analyze them, but receive them into your safekeeping with gratitude and thanksgiving. Let them bless your heart with hope.

My hope is renewed.

Day 271   # I carry the miracle of life within me.

And the angel of the LORD appeared to the woman and said to her, "Although you are barren, having borne no children, you shall conceive and bear a son."

—Judges 13:3

271

$\mathcal{T}$hat which is barren can bear no fruit. A tired land that can support no crops, a would-be parent who can conceive no children, a frustrated artist who can receive no inspiration, a suicidal adolescent who can cling to no hope, a closed mind that can believe in no miracles . . . all barren.

If you have faith, however, your spirit is never barren. You receive life where once you had none, and as a result you give life to the world. You begin to bear fruit. This is the miracle of God.

Look for ways that your house or your work-place has begun to look barren. Do one thing to transform it. Symbolize your spiritual vitality in your external environment. Buy a plant to "spruce up" a "dead" room. Set out some new pictures on your desk. Change your furniture around to freshen things up. Paint the walls a different, perhaps brighter, color. Open the drapes and let more light in. Whatever you choose to do, let your surroundings express the joy you feel—the joy that comes with knowing, like the woman in today's scripture text, that you carry the miracle of life within you.

I carry the miracle of life within me.

Day 272   I am freed.

When [Jesus] had said this, he cried out with a loud voice, "Lazarus, come out!" The dead man came out, his hands and feet bound with strips of cloth, and his face wrapped in a cloth. Jesus said to them, "Unbind him, and let him go."

—John 11:43-44

$\mathcal{T}$hree young girls were skating alone on a river when the ice broke beneath them. Pedestrians on a nearby bridge heard the girls' screams and saw them thrashing in the water, but somehow no one moved to help. A motorist who was passing by happened to look out his window, took in the scene, and immediately pulled over. A few minutes later he was there in the frigid water with the girls, reassuring them, trying to keep them afloat until more help came. A crowd gathered on the bank, cheering him on. When a rescue squad finally arrived and the girls were pulled from the river, they were amazingly alert. They would suffer little more than frostbite. But the man who had saved them had disappeared under the ice. By the time the rescue team found him, he was dead, and though they were able to resuscitate his body, he remains to this day in a deep coma.

We have all heard such stories, in which heroic individuals take risks or endanger their lives for someone they may not even know. In that flash when they decide to dive into the water, or go into the burning building, or jump between the gun and its intended victim, they are liberated from fear. They give no thought to their own safety. They do not weigh the stranger's life against their own. In the spirit of *agape*, they are truly free.

If you overcome your fear of death, you will be afraid of nothing. If you are afraid of nothing, you will be released from everything. Nothing will be able to hold your spirit captive, not even the grave. All your bindings will fall off, and by the power of God you will have new life.

Go and spend some time in a cemetery. Take inventory of your feelings as you walk among the graves. How does this place make you feel? Do you have any fears? Quiet yourself. Reassure yourself that the power of God can liberate you from all your fears, including the fear of aging, the fear of dying, the fear of death, and the fear of the unknown that comes after death. Say to yourself, again and again:

I am freed.

Day 273   **I move mountains.**

"For truly I tell you, if you have faith the size of a mustard seed, you will say to this mountain, 'Move from here to there,' and it will move; and nothing will be impossible for you."

—*Matthew 17:20*b

*P*arents are often heard to say to their children, "Never say *'can't,'* or, "*Can't* isn't in our vocabulary," or, "*Can't* died in the poorhouse." They don't want their kids, when faced with a difficult task or a problem, to assume defeat even before they try. So they recite one of these proverbs, hoping that their expression of encouragement will bolster their kids' shaky confidence or correct their negative attitude.

So, too, does the Spirit tell you to move a mountain. "What?" you protest. "Don't you know that this mountain is *big*? Fourteen-thousand four-hundred and ten feet above sea level, to be exact. And it's *old*—it has been standing there for centuries. If nobody else has ever been able to move it, how can you expect me to?"

Your complaint is long and loud. But just then somebody comes along and says, "You know, I think there might just be a way to slide that mountain a little to the left. . . ."

Sometimes that is all it takes to change things: one voice that manages to introduce just a tiny glimmer of hope into an otherwise impossible situation. That one voice shifts your perspective, even if only slightly, and suddenly the mountain begins to move "from here to there."

Watch for at least one opportunity today to be that voice in the midst of a difficult situation. Commit yourself to introducing the word of hope and encouragement. Offer a possibility instead of pessimism. Make "can" part of your spiritual vocabulary, and with God's help you will move mountains.

I move mountains.

Day 274   **Victory is mine.**

I have taught you the way of wisdom; I have led you in the paths of uprightness. When you walk, your step will not be hampered; and if you run, you will not stumble.

—Proverbs 4:11

On the first day of the term, a college professor told the members of his class that they would all receive an "A" for the course. Now they would have to decide how they would respond to their gift. Some of the students never returned to class, figuring there was no need to do anything more. Others did a minimum of work so that they would seem somewhat respectable. But some students really dug into their studies and more than earned the grade they had already received. They accepted the success that was already guaranteed them and, free from worry, decided to use their time to learn as much as they could about the subject matter.

God has already guaranteed your spiritual success. Hear the Teacher say, "I have taught you well. Now journey forward without fear. You will not stumble." How will you respond to this free gift? Free from worry about your status in the eyes of God, you can walk in the way of wisdom and do what is right. Your willingness to walk in harmony with God's ways is your response to God's gift of guaranteed success.

We celebrate the victory God has given us by serving others in the spirit of *agape*. As we do so, we do not need to compare how we are doing with how someone else is doing. We are not in competition with anyone. Rather, we are in cooperation with our Creator. When we are doing our part to help God bring about a reign of mercy and justice for all, we are testifying to the fact that God has already declared us victors.

For a moment, remember a time when you felt worthless, unimportant, overwhelmed, or defeated. Translate that feeling into body language. Take on the posture of a "loser." Pull in your arms tightly against your body. Constrict your muscles. Droop your shoulders. Lower your head. Get a feel for what it would be like *never* to win.

Now, straighten yourself up. Walk tall. Throw your shoulders back. Stick our your chest. Sit or stand tall, as though you know that you can never be anything but a winner. Get a feel for the posture of success. Sense the positive energy that moves freely through your body.

You are living and working in cooperation with the Creator of the universe. This One has called you a success. This One has given you victory. Allow this knowledge to sink in. Let it create in you feelings of confidence and power. Approach the rest of your day from a winning stance. Repeat to yourself:

Victory is mine.

Day 275 **I have passed through the fire.**

But now thus says the LORD, he who created you, O Jacob, he who formed you, O Israel: Do not fear, for I have redeemed you; I have called you by name, you are mine. When you pass through the waters, I will be with you; and through the rivers, they shall not overwhelm you; when you walk through fire you shall not be burned, and the flame shall not consume you.

—Isaiah 43:1-2

*T*wo images in today's scripture text serve to remind us of the trials and tribulations of this life: water and fire. Water is often a symbol in the scriptures for the chaos and uncertainty of life. It is as if each of us is in a little boat on the ocean in the middle of a storm. The waves may be tossing us back and forth, the winds may be blowing against us, but here Isaiah tells us that we will not be overwhelmed. God will bring us safely to shore.

Fire in the scriptures is often a symbol of danger and destruction. But Isaiah reassures us that when we pass through the flames of life, we will not be burned or consumed. We will move safely through these dangers, and, at the same time, we will be purified and refined. We will be strengthened, transformed into something greater than we were.

So, Isaiah says, God does not promise that you will never pass through water and fire on your spiritual journey. But God does promise that neither water nor fire need overwhelm you. You are safe. You have nothing to fear.

Find a candle and light it. Watch it burn for a few moments. Think of the danger that the flame represents. Now, quickly pass your finger through the flame. You are not burned. Do it again. The fire does not hurt you. Let this be a reminder to you that because you walk with the Spirit, you walk unharmed through life. The chaos and danger around you will not hurt you.

I have passed through the fire.

Day 276 I go wherever God sends me.

Then I heard the voice of the Lord saying, "Whom shall I send, and who will go for us?" And I said, "Here am I; send me!"

—*Isaiah 6:8*

It was about 11:00 in the morning. Jane, a minister, was sitting at her desk, puzzling over the agenda for that evening's Administrative Board meeting. She was supposed to present several reports, and she did not yet have all the information she needed. Growing more anxious by the minute, she suddenly had the urge to go to a nearby shopping mall. At first, she resisted, knowing she had no real reason to go. But as she felt a growing sense of urgency, she finally left the church and drove to the mall. As she neared the entrance, something told her to pull into a nearby fast-food restaurant. She wasn't particularly hungry, but when she resisted, the urge grew stronger. So she followed her intuition, all the while wondering why she wasn't back at her desk preparing for her evening meeting.

Upon entering the restaurant, Jane spotted three widows from the congregation. She recalled that the women regularly lunched together, but noticed one was missing. She went over to their table and, before she could even say hello, one of the women said, "Oh, Jane, you're just the person we wanted to talk to! We were shopping at the mall, and got to talking about Bonnie [the woman who wasn't with them]. We're worried about her. After lunch we were planning to come to your office to talk with you, but it looks like you came to us instead!" Could it be that God directed Jane to these women? What would have happened if she had paid no attention to the Spirit's promptings?

Our identity and purpose are clear. We are messengers for God, and it is our privilege to carry God's blessings to every person that we encounter. When our path joins up with someone else's, it is not by accident. It is for a purpose. We must be ready at all times to share whatever we have received from God with whoever needs it.

Today, be aware of that still small voice within you that invites you to go to a person in need and to meet that need. Do not wait to know all the facts and details. Do not wait until you have all the day's tasks completed. When you sense God calling—when you hear that inner voice or feel that intuition—just go, and be ready to bless another member of God's family.

I go wherever God sends me.

Day 277 **I do whatever God tells me.**

So shall my word be that goes out from my mouth; it shall not return to me empty, but it shall accomplish that which I purpose and succeed in the thing for which I sent it.

—*Isaiah 55:11*

Mary came into the Worship Committee meeting bubbling with excitement. She could hardly wait to share what had happened to her. While ironing, "God had given" her the entire script for the upcoming Easter sunrise service. She began to describe it to the Committee. "It begins with a little lamb that is the pet of a child. Eventually this child's lamb is sacrificed to symbolize the crucifixion of Jesus. . . ." The excitement in Mary's voice was matched by the horror on the faces of the other Committee members. After much prayerful and careful discussion, the Committee voted not to use Mary's script on Easter morning. Mary stormed out of the meeting, outraged that the other Committee members would have dared to question what God had clearly directed her to do.

How do we know when we are really listening to the voice of God? How can we be certain that what we are feeling led to do is truly the will of God? These are vitally important questions. We must carefully test the content of what we are hearing. Here are three guidelines that you might use (you might call them "the three C's"):

Compassion. Whatever God asks you to do will be an expression of *agape.* God would never ask you to do anything else. If you feel that what you are being led to do will hurt others, seriously question whether you are hearing the voice of God.

Consistency. Whatever God asks you to do will be consistent with the whole of the gospel. It will reflect the mind of Christ. It will not contradict what you would find Jesus doing in a similar situation. If you feel that you are being led to do something that you can't imagine him doing, seriously question whether you are hearing the voice of God.

Community. Whatever God asks you to do usually will not cause serious disagreement in your spiritual community. God would not lead you to do something that the gathered community would find offensive. If you feel that you are being led in that direction, seriously question whether you are hearing the voice of God.

As you listen for the voice of God in your life, test what you hear against the three C's. If the three C's are met, be ready to act.

I do whatever God tells me.

Day 278   I carry the light of life.

Again Jesus spoke to them, saying, "I am the light of the world. Whoever follows me will never walk in darkness but will have the light of life."

—*John 8:12*

*H*ave you ever attended a Christmas Eve candlelighting ceremony? If so, you will remember the moment when the entire sanctuary is darkened. All the lights are turned off, and only the Christ candle is burning. Each person holds an unlighted candle and waits with anticipation. The magic begins when the light is passed among the people. Someone lights a candle from the Christ candle, then lights the candle of the next person, and so on. When your candle is lighted, its glow is matched by the joy on your face. This symbol of the coming of the light into a darkened world touches something deep within you. Something more is happening than just a passing of the light. Something is speaking to the very essence of your purpose for being on this earth. You realize that you are here to be a bearer of light. You are here to dispel the world's darkness.

Tonight, to celebrate your calling to be a carrier of the light, plan to serve dinner by candlelight. Begin the meal in darkness. Then light the candles one by one, noticing how the joy of the occasion becomes greater as the room becomes more radiant. Do this even if you are eating alone. It only takes one to celebrate. Rejoice in your calling and your mission!

I carry the light of life.

Day 279   My path is radiant.

But the path of the righteous is like the light of dawn, which shines brighter and brighter until full day.

—Proverbs 4:18

*T*hink back to that Christmas Eve candlelighting ceremony that we described yesterday. Perhaps you also remember a moment when everyone is invited to slowly lift his or her candle in the air. If so, you are deeply aware of the power of sharing your light with those around you. When all the lighted candles are lifted, shadowy forms become recognizable as the furniture in the room. Silhouettes turn into friends. The entire space takes on a radiance in the shared light. The transformation is truly dramatic.

This is how it is as we journey through life, faithfully following God's will for our lives. With each step of the way, we share a little more light. That light continues to grow until our very lives are radiant with the power and glory of God. People notice that we are somehow different, that we bring something to them that they need. That something is the light of the world.

Gather as many candles as you can find. Place them in holders around the room. Use candles of all sizes and shapes. Now, remember a good deed that you did recently and light a candle to celebrate it. Light a candle for each way that you have shown kindness to another person. Continue until all the candles are burning around you. Take time to enjoy the power of the light that surrounds you. Close your celebration by affirming aloud,

My path is radiant.

Day 280   **God's glory is revealed to me.**

"Then the glory of the LORD shall be revealed, and all people shall see it together, for the mouth of the LORD has spoken."

—*Isaiah 40:5*

*T*oday, we will review some of the ways that God's glory is made known to us. These will sound familiar. We have talked about each of them over the last 279 days.

Nature. Watch a sunset or a sunrise and see the awesome beauty of God. Explore a square yard of the earth and be amazed at what God has placed in such a small space. Nurture and tend a young animal and know that there is a power at work in its growth that is beyond your understanding. Plant a seed and puzzle over what makes it develop. The unlimited glory of God is made known to you through the natural world.

People. Remember the people who have come to you over the years, blessing you, challenging you, and leading you on your journey. Think of great people of faith whose life stories and gifts have helped you in so many ways. In the lives of all these saints, you see the glory of God.

Scripture. Recall favorite verses that speak to you of God's power. Think of all the times that you conquered fear and uncertainty by repeating or rereading moving passages. From cover to cover, the scriptures reveal to you the glory of God.

Mountaintop Experiences. Remember those moments when you knew beyond a shadow of a doubt that God was with you. You may have been made especially aware of God's presence during a mystical experience, a dream, a vision, an encounter with a stranger, a wonderful worship service, or private study. All of these show you the glory of God.

To celebrate the glory of God in your life, plan a simple candlelight dinner with friends. Ask each person to bring several candles for the occasion, and to be ready to share with the other guests some ways that he or she has come to know God better. That evening, as the guests arrive, set their candles on the table and in the areas where you will be entertaining. Then, when everyone is seated for the meal, ask each person to light a candle, one at a time, and tell about a way that his or her relationship with God has deepened over time. Continue the sharing until all the candles are burning. Enjoy your meal and the fellowship. Then, after your friends have gone, let candles continue to burn in the kitchen as you clean up. Extinguish them gradually, allowing the light to linger awhile. When you have put out the last candle and are ready to sleep, settle down peacefully, grateful that the glory of God is made known in your life.

God's glory is revealed to me.

Day 281　　I move from glory into glory.

And all of us, with unveiled faces, seeing the glory of the Lord as though reflected in a mirror, are being transformed into the same image from one degree of glory to another.

—2 Corinthians 3:18a

In Old Testament days the "glory" of God was quite often described as a brilliant light. In fact, this light was so powerful that it had to be veiled from humanity. It was often veiled by a cloud, which itself became radiant with the divine presence.

Writing to the church at Corinth, Paul put a twist on this Old Testament understanding of "glory." Now, he said, we no longer need to be veiled from the divine light, because that glory is seen in us as well. As we are gradually transformed into the brilliant image of God, glory shines through our lives.

As we move from one degree of glory to another, we will quite literally become radiant. Think about the light that you have seen in someone who is filled with joy. The greater the joy, the brighter the light in his or her eyes. Now, what greater joy exists than that found in the fullness of faith? The glorious light of this joy becomes the halo around the heads of saints. It shines forth from spiritual masters to illumine pitch-dark rooms. And this joyous light is being seen in you, more and more every day, as your Christ-mind continues to grow.

In recognition of this gradual growth of the divine glory within you, observe the phases of the moon over the next month. Watch its development as it journeys across the night skies. Its movement is always toward fullness, even when it is on the wane. Your movement in Christ is no different.

I move from glory into glory.

Day 282　　What I see amazes me.

I will lead the blind by a road they do not know, by paths they have not known I will guide them. I will turn the darkness before them into light, the rough places into level ground. These are the things I will do, and I will not forsake them.

A high school girls' basketball team is leaving for the state tournament in the state capital. Boarding the bus, its members are astounded to see that they will be accompanied on their journey by a long caravan of vehicles decorated with school colors and victory slogans. Then, as their bus passes through the community, they are amazed at all the blue and white ribbons that have been tied around trees, and all the blue and white banners suddenly flying from flagpoles, and all the people who are lining the streets, waving and shouting well-wishes. Finally, their bus heads down the highway. Surprises continue. Huge blue and white signs hang from the overpasses. An airplane circles overhead, trailing words from the school fight song. And, arriving at the tournament site, their bus is greeted by the boys' basketball team. Its members have dribbled a basketball all the way from the school to the capital to show their support. The women's team enters the arena with confidence, ready to face any opponent, knowing that they have not come here alone.

Like the journey of this team, your life is a trek into unknown territory. But God has gone ahead of you to prepare the way. The more you become aware of this, the more amazed you will be. Your confidence will increase, until you can strike out toward places you would never have gone before, to do what you would never have done before.

Take a drive or a walk through an unfamiliar area. Visit it with a sense of curiosity and wonderment. Be observant, as if you were in a foreign country. Ask yourself questions like these: What do its buildings or natural features look like? What kind of people or animals live here? What surprises me? What feelings do I have in this place, and why?

Let this unfamiliar place teach you, speak to you, move you. *Want to be amazed.* Remember, God has already been here.

What I see amazes me.

Day 283   **I see a whole new world.**

See, the former things have come to pass, and new things I now declare; before they spring forth, I tell you of them.

—Isaiah 42:9

$\mathcal{T}$he new creation is here. The promised land is all around you. Let the bandages fall from your eyes. See light coming out of the darkness. See peace coming out of the strife. Old things are passing away, new things are being declared. Look upon a world of miracles!

Go into a dark, quiet place with a lighted candle. Calm your mind. Relax your body. Then, in the stillness, celebrate the glory of God that renews the world. In a prayerful whisper, read and respond to each of the following affirmations:

As I view my life, I see light rising in the darkness. I can see the rising light most especially in . . .

As I view my life, I see love shining on peoples' faces. The love is shining most brightly on the faces of . . .

As I view my life, I see new possibilities. Those that I am most excited about are . . .

Conclude your period of reflection by reading this statement of faith aloud three times, more loudly each time:

I see a whole new world.

$\mathcal{D}$ay 284   I see God revealed in everyone.

He shall not judge by what his eyes see, or decide by what his ears hear; but with righteousness he shall judge the poor, and decide with equity for the meek of the earth.

—*Isaiah 11:3b-4a*

$\mathcal{Y}$ou may have noticed that when a Hindu person greets someone, he puts his hands together palm to palm, as if in prayer, and bows slightly. He does this in recognition of the divine presence within the other. We would do well to learn from our Hindu brothers and sisters. Recognition of God in the other is the beginning of *agape*.

Gandhi, the great Hindu leader of India who was, like Jesus, assassinated by his enemies, once said, "I know how difficult it is to follow [the] grand law of love. But are not all great and good things difficult to do? Love of the hater is the most difficult of all. But by the grace of God even this most difficult thing becomes easy to accomplish if we want to do it."

Christ is the ultimate example of *agape*. Christ taught by his example and by his word that we are to love our neighbors as ourselves—including even those neighbors who are our enemies: "Love your enemies, do good to those who hate you, bless those who curse you, pray for those who abuse you" (Luke 6:27-28).

As the mind of Christ grows within you and you become more and more aware of God's presence in the world, you recognize the divine in everyone—even in those who hate, those who are the most difficult of all to love. Your eyes may look on someone whose appearance or behavior is displeasing, and your ears may listen to someone whose words are offensive, but you do not judge with your eyes or your ears. If you did, you could easily dismiss this person. Instead, regarding the person with the mind of Christ, you offer *agape*. You *must* offer *agape*, because God is within this person. No matter how godless this person may seem, he or she is never without God, and it is always to the God in this person that you respond.

Go to a place where you can casually observe a large variety of people. For example, sit on a bench in a city park or mall. Watch. Who captures your attention? Why? Do not allow yourself to have judgmental thoughts about anyone you see. Instead, silently extend your blessing to each person. Say within your mind, "I see God in you, and I rejoice."

I see God revealed in everyone.

Day 285 I love the God I see in others.

Therefore prepare your minds for action; discipline yourselves; set all your hope on the grace that Jesus Christ will bring you when he is revealed.

—*1 Peter 1:13*

*P*repare your mind for action; discipline yourself." This is what you do every day as you continue your spiritual journey. You are a partner with the Spirit in the training of your Christ-mind. The Spirit "puts you through your paces," so to speak. Your fundamental exercise is offering *agape*. You learn, both in attitude and action, to more openly love the God you see in other people. Remember, God is revealed in everyone; you can place no restrictions on your loving. If you prepare yourself to love one, you must prepare yourself to love all, without hesitation, the best way you can. Your Trainer will ask for nothing less!

Below are five attributes that we frequently ascribe to God:

> Forgiving
> Loving (Unconditionally)
> Generous
> Faithful
> Creative

For each of these divine attributes, identify one person whom you appreciate for revealing it. Indicate how he or she does so. In whom, for example, do you see the forgiveness of God? In what way(s) has this person revealed this to you?

It is rare, indeed, that any one person embodies all of these traits to a remarkable degree (though, of course, that is exactly what all of us hope to do someday). Therefore, when we look for the divine in others, we must look past any of their less admirable traits, just as they must look past ours. Then, seeing the divine, we render *agape* more freely and openly with each passing day.

I love the God I see in others.

Day 286 In loving others I know Christ.

And this is my prayer, that your love may overflow more and more with knowledge and full insight to help you to determine what is best, so that in the day of Christ you may be pure and blameless.

—*Philippians 1:9-10*

$\mathcal{O}$n the day that her son Ted was married, Janet politely welcomed her new daughter-in-law, Pat, into the family. Then, in the years that followed, Janet experienced two things that she never would have expected. First, she came to love her son even more than she had before. She saw him with new eyes, as a responsible and creative adult. Then, as her appreciation for Ted deepened, she began to understand Pat better. More than just being mother-in-law and daughter-in-law, the two of them became close friends who could rely on one another for advice and support.

As Janet's love for Ted grew, she gained a greater understanding of Pat. In the same way, when our love for other people overflows from our hearts, we come to understand Christ better.

Write about ways in which your understanding of Christ has

grown as you have expressed *agape* to others. For each phrase below, think about someone to whom you have reached out, and reflect on what you learned about Christ in doing so. Complete as many of the phrases as you can.

Loving those who mourn, I have come to know Christ in this way. . . .
Loving those who have hurt me, I have come to know Christ in this way. . . .
Loving the poor, I have come to know Christ in this way. . . .
Loving the sick, I have come to know Christ in this way. . . .
Loving the outsider, I have come to know Christ in this way. . . .
Loving those whom others hate, I have come to know Christ in this way. . . .

In loving others I know Christ.

Day 287 The mystery of Christ unites.

I want their hearts to be encouraged and united in love, so that they may have all the riches of assured understanding and have the knowledge of God's mystery, that is, Christ himself, in whom are hidden all the treasures of wisdom and knowledge.

—Colossians 2:2-3

*Y*ou can picture the mystery of Christ as the glory—the light —that connects all of us, one to another. And as our awareness of Christ increases, this glory becomes ever more radiant.

With a piece of paper and pencil beside you, enter into prayerful meditation. When you feel centered in the Spirit, begin to let the names of individuals come into your mind. Immediately write each name down, no matter who it is. Continue so long as the names continue to come.

Now imagine that you and all the persons whose names were given you are seated together in a circle around an old treasure chest. Get a clear image of every person in your mind. When you have done so, picture yourself standing up and going to the chest. Open the lid just a crack. A ray of golden-white light escapes from it: this light is the glory of Christ. See it radiating out to your companions, one by one, until all of them are joined by beams of light to the chest, like spokes to the hub of a wheel.

Feel yourself being joined, too. Feel the warmth of the light filling you. Now open the lid all the way and return to your seat in the circle. See the light growing brighter and brighter, moving out to surround each person, gradually filling the entire room. Sense the energy, the presence of the light. Open your soul to it. Know that as you do, you are also opening your soul to the souls of everyone in this room. Continue in this way for as long as you wish, and conclude with a prayer of thanksgiving.

The mystery of Christ unites.

Day 288   **All of creation works together.**

We know that all things work together for good for those who love God, who are called according to his purpose.

—Romans 8:28

*T*oday you are going to create the "cat's cradle," which children all over the world (including you, perhaps?) have made for centuries. Begin by taking out approximately two yards of string or yarn and tying the ends together in a knot. Put both your hands inside the loop, so that one side of the string passes between the thumb and index finger of each. Hold your hands parallel and draw the string taut. Now move your hands closer together and, one at a time, pass them under the string, and draw the string back. Move your hands apart. The upper palm of each hand should now be encircled by string. Next, insert your right middle finger under the string on your left palm; draw your right hand back. Do the same with your left middle finger and the string on your right palm.

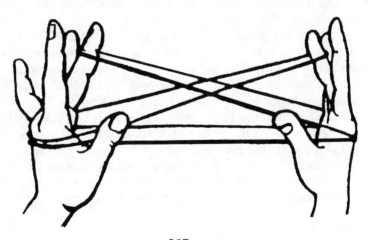

This is the cat's cradle. From this basic "string art" position, you can make an endless number of other designs, one right after another. In fact, if you have a youngster in the house, he or she may be able to show you a few string art tricks!

One piece of string. Endless designs. Every part of every design connected to every other part. Every inch of the entire string working with every other inch—and with your hands.

Now imagine that, in creating the world, God's hands are making string art. Every part of creation is connected to every other part, working with every other part, to produce one beautiful design after another. This is the way creation is meant to happen. And this is the way creation *does* happen, except when we humans interfere and cut the string.

Let's play along, shall we?

All of creation works together.

Day 289   Not all of creation is visible.

For in him all things in heaven and on earth were created, things visible and invisible, whether thrones or dominions or rulers or powers—all things have been created through him and for him. He himself is before all things, and in him all things hold together.

—Colossians 1:16-17

Most of us seem to be dominated by our sense of sight. As we are fond of saying, "Seeing is believing." If we can't lay our eyes on something, we have trouble wrapping our minds around it. Not so for things that we can't hear—they are simply "inaudible." But if things are "invisible," we are apt to doubt them, or to dismiss them altogether.

Or do we, really? Take a moment to jot down a list of all the things that you believe in that you never see. To get you started, what about the wind? Gravity? These are both powerful forces, yet we cannot see them. We can only see their effects. One moment you are wearing a hat, the next it is lying on the ground. When you reach down to retrieve it, it suddenly scoots away. Will you attribute all of this mischief to magic? Of course not. The wind and gravity are playing with you.

What are other invisible things in which you believe? Think of as many as you can. The number of items on your list might surprise you. Obviously you *can* believe in what you can't see.

Do you perhaps need to pay more attention to the unseen parts of creation? To be more sensitive to them, and respect them more?

Just think. How many *other* invisible things might there be, given the limitlessness of God's creation?

Not all of creation is visible.

Day 290   Nothing in creation happens by chance.

For thus says the LORD, who created the heavens (he is God!), who formed the earth and made it (he established it; he did not create it a chaos, he formed it to be inhabited!): I am the LORD, and there is no other. I did not speak in secret, in a land of darkness; I did not say to the offspring of Jacob, "Seek me in chaos." I the LORD speak the truth, I declare what is right.

—Isaiah 45:18-19

*N*othing in creation happens by chance *because everything is purposeful.* Some purposes are established by God, others by you, still others by other members of God's created order. Some purposes are good, some could be better, some could be better by far.

In a swirling universe of competing purposes, you may sometimes feel overwhelmed. Some of them will inevitably collide with each other. For example, your desire to further your education may bump up against your wish to be financially secure. Or, your need to buy groceries may get rear-ended by a car whose driver was intent on reading the newspaper before work.

Other purposes, however, will inevitably and happily coincide. Then you have God-incidences, as we have discussed before. For instance, your lifelong wish to explore the Rocky Mountains is satisfied when your boss sends you to a two-week conference in Boulder, Colorado. Or, your search for an inexpensive but dependable bicycle ends when your best friend announces that she no longer has need of her ten-speed.

The challenge before you is to align your purposes with God's, as often as you can, as best you can. This requires you to be prayerfully and constantly aware of the Spirit's guidance.

Pick an incident that occurred recently in your life to analyze in terms of its purposefulness. Look at it from many angles. What sequence of natural laws, intentions, desires, plans, and so on, led to its occurrence? How closely aligned were your purposes with God's, do you think?

Nothing in creation happens by chance.

Day 291 Creation provides all that is needed.

His divine power has given us everything needed for life and godliness, through the knowledge of him who called us by his own glory and goodness.

—2 Peter 1:3

In Jean Craighead George's *Julie of the Wolves,* Miyax, a young Eskimo girl, is lost and without food in an Alaskan wilderness. When she comes upon a pack of wolves, she works hard to be accepted by them. She depends upon them for her survival. Little by little, she learns their language. She is fed by their hunting and their companionship. She gives them names; she gives them love. Eventually, on the strength of caribou meat they have provided, she makes her way to her father. And what she discovers, living among humans once again, inspires her to sing a sad farewell song to the long-departed wolves.

Her song laments what is happening around her. Eskimo culture, along with the world of wolves, is passing away. The seals and whales and other animals that her people have traditionally and respectfully relied upon for their survival have been hunted almost to extinction by outsiders who know nothing of respect. And now the wolves, too, are threatened—the wolves who have been her family; the wolves who have taught her feet to dance, her eyes to see, her mind to think. And on this thundering night, her mind is thinking "that the hour of the wolf and the Eskimo is over."

Miyax knew this truth: While it is God's creation that provides, it is God's creatures who distribute. And Miyax was afraid that, unlike her family of wolves, we humans are taking much more than we need and sharing very little.

Like the wolves in this story, you have the power either to keep or share your "food," whether it be the food which feeds our bodies or that which feeds our spirits. God's law of *agape* asks you to share it. The more respect that you have for your food, the easier it is to share. When you know how much good it can provide, you do not want to hoard it all for yourself, but gladly distribute it at God's prompting.

In symbolic recognition of the preciousness of all "food," eat with deliberateness during at least one meal today. Overchew each bite of food. Savor its taste, whether sweet, bitter, sour, or salty. Bless the food to the nourishment of your body. Bless the food to the sustenance of your soul. Give thanks to God and creation for providing for your life.

Creation provides all that is needed.

Day 292   **Creation teaches me.**

"But ask the animals, and they will teach you; the birds of the air, and they will tell you; ask the plants of the earth, and they will teach you; and the fish of the sea will declare to you. Who among all these does not know that the hand of the Lord has done this? In his hand is the life of every living thing and the breath of every human being."

—*Job 12:7-10*

The Secret Life of Plants, by Peter Tompkins and Christopher Bird, reports that in 1966, Cleve Backster hooked up some electrodes to a leaf of one of his plants. The electrodes were connected to a galvanometer—which, for example, in a polygraph lie detector records changes in electrical charge due to fluctuating thoughts and emotions. Backster found that whenever he thought of doing harm to the plant, the galvanometer jumped dramatically. Hardly able to believe it, he and his fellow researchers tried a comparable experiment on twenty-five other varieties of plants and fruits, including lettuce, onions, oranges, and bananas. The results were astonishingly similar. These findings, along with other research that Backster went on to report, stimulated other scientists to investigate the possible communications that take place between human beings and plants. Extensive experimentation has since been conducted in respected universities in the United States, Europe, and Russia. Today it seems indisputable that plants have what we would have to call "awareness." They have taught us a valuable lesson about the interconnectedness of God's creation.

Its own interconnectedness is one of the greatest truths that

God's creation teaches us. A wonderful way to celebrate it is to make a terrarium. Locate a large glass jar, a fish bowl, or an aquarium. Put a layer of fine stone mixed with charcoal in the bottom of it and add about three inches of potting soil. Then plant some slow-growing, moisture-loving plants. After adding some moss, rocks, or other decorative materials, water the soil until it is barely damp. Seal the container with a tight lid or plastic wrap. Put your terrarium in a sunny window and enjoy watching it grow. If you have adequate water in the jar, you will see moisture collect on the insides of the glass from time to time. You should not have to add additional water.

You need not have a scientific mind nor specialized instruments to be taught by creation. All that is required is having the openness of the mind of Christ. So, allow yourself to be instructed by creation. Let the lessons present themselves in whatever ways they will. Be curious. Be receptive. And be grateful for the schoolroom that is the world.

Creation teaches me.

Day 293   **Creation teaches peace.**

The wolf shall live with the lamb, the leopard shall lie down with the kid, the calf and the lion and the fatling together, and a little child shall lead them. The cow and the bear shall graze, their young shall lie down together; and the lion shall eat straw like the ox. The nursing child shall play over the hole of the asp, and the weaned child shall put its hand on the adder's den. They will not hurt or destroy on all my holy mountain; for the earth will be full of the knowledge of the LORD as the waters cover the sea.

—*Isaiah 11:6-9*

*R*ead carefully through this scripture passage and discover as many poetic images of peace as you can. Imagine what the world would be like if all natural enemies were to peacefully coexist.

Then again, maybe you don't have to imagine it. Perhaps you have already seen glimpses of such a peace—as in a zoo, where lions lie in the sun just a few yards from where antelope graze, or even at home, where your pet dog and cat have become inseparable friends.

In Isaiah's vision of universal peace, all of the animals trust each other. They have overcome their fear. The elimination of fear is an essential step in the establishment of peace. So, if all of us are one day to "play over the hole of the asp" and co-exist peacefully with what has always frightened us, we must begin now to lose our fear. We must begin now to create the peace.

Visit a pet shop today or sometime in the near future. When you get there, browse among the animals. You will be less attracted to some than to others. Identify an animal that makes you uncomfortable. Watch it carefully. After a time, ask a clerk to give you information about the animal. Then, imagine yourself touching or holding it. (If you feel especially brave, actually touch or hold it.) Do not focus your thoughts on your fear of the animal. Instead, try to appreciate it as a unique creature of God. Make your peace with it. Let the "peaceable kingdom" begin with you.

Creation teaches peace.

Day 294   **Creation teaches truth.**

A voice cries out: "In the wilderness prepare the way of the LORD, make straight in the desert a highway for our God. Every valley shall be lifted up, and every mountain and hill be made low; the uneven ground shall become level, and the rough places a plain. Then the glory of the LORD shall be revealed, and all people shall see it together, for the mouth of the LORD has spoken."

—Isaiah 40:3-5

Al, a sixth grader, decided to clear a path through a small woods on his family's property. Then he and his friends would be able to ride bikes "in the wild," like the nature bikers did on TV. After receiving his parents' permission, he got started. First, he marked out a large looping trail, putting a splotch of red paint on the biggest trees along the route. Then, using a hatchet and a spade, he chopped and dug out dozens of young saplings growing in the pathway, which were so thick that few would have survived anyway. He smoothed one extremely bumpy place on the path by carrying in a few rocks and covering them with a thick layer of fill-dirt. He hopped on the riding lawn mower and repeatedly ran it over the trail, each time with the blades set a bit lower; this removed most of the remaining growth. Finally (and this was the most back-breaking part), he hoed the entire trail and packed it down with his shoes. At long last, the path was done. He proudly took his parents on a tour. "The funny thing is," he said when they had reached the end of it and were listening to a woodpecker off in the distance, "I'm not sure that I'll ever want to ride my bike back here." Al didn't know quite how to say it, but his relationship with the woods had changed as he made his path. Creation had become his quiet teacher, and it had taught him the true glory, the sacredness, of this place. For him, it was no longer a place to rip through on bikes with laughing, shouting friends.

What truths does creation teach you? Use your physical senses to receive some lessons today. Learn one truth from each of them: seeing, hearing, tasting, smelling, and touching. For example, as you are eating, you might begin to notice that different flavors are sensed by different areas of your tongue—that saltiness and sweetness are detected by the tip, bitterness by the base, and sourness along the sides. Perhaps you learn from this that each part of creation plays an important role. State the lesson you learn from each of your senses in a sentence. You will probably find that a couple of your senses are less sensitive than the others. Persevere, however, and allow creation to teach you about the glory of God.

Creation teaches truth.

Day 295   I speak the truth.

When the men of the place asked [Isaac] about his wife, he said, "She is my sister"; for he was afraid to say, "My wife," thinking, "or else the men of the place might kill me for the sake of Rebekah, because she is attractive in appearance." When Isaac had been there a long time, King Abimelech of the Philistines looked out of a window and saw him fondling his wife Rebekah. So Abimelech called for Isaac, and said, "So she is your wife! Why then did you say, 'She is my sister'?" Isaac said to him, "Because I thought I might die because of her."

—*Genesis 26:7-9*

How much easier life would have been for Isaac if he had always been up front about Rebekah being his wife! But instead he let his fear of the Philistines get the better of him, and he lied. This, of course, meant that he had to tell another lie, and then another, trying to make everyone believe that his wife was actually his sister. After awhile his head must have been spinning. It must have been hard to keep track of all the little lies he had to tell to support the big one. And all for what? In the end, his deceit was found out—and by the king, of all people. And, as King Abimelech went on to point out, his needless lies could have ended in tragedy.

Isaac was fortunate. Despite his foolishness, his story had a happy ending. Some of us aren't so lucky with our lies. Even if our lying is never discovered, its effects still spread. Sometimes we lie by misleading someone with what we say. Other times we lie by misleading someone with what we *don't* say. Either way, we are "keeping secrets." Take family secrets as an example. Say your family doesn't want outsiders to know about something— shaky finances, someone's addiction, spousal abuse, child abuse, marital troubles, troubles with a teenager, whatever—so no one in your family talks about it. Or, if you do, you lie. Everyone operates on the assumption that things will be better if no one knows "what's really going on." But the effects of the secret spread. . . .

Think about any secrets that your family has been keeping, little ones or big ones. Choose one to focus on. Do you see how you are running certain risks, either to yourself or to others, by helping to keep this secret? The effects of the secret may be hidden, at least at first, but they are still present, weakening the fabric of your family.

Do what Isaac was unable to do. Admit the truth *now*.

I speak the truth.

Day 296   **I speak the truth boldly.**

"So have no fear of them; for nothing is covered up that will not be uncovered, and nothing secret that will not become known. What I say to you in the dark, tell in the light; and what you hear whispered, proclaim from the housetops. Do not fear those who kill the body but cannot kill the soul."

—*Matthew 10:26-28a*

It is Christmas. Three sisters, two brothers, and their elderly mother are gathered around a kitchen table; their father, who suffers from Alzheimer's disease, is taking a nap in another room. The children express concern about their mother's obvious declining health. They suggest that she invite friends in to sit with their father so that she can get out of the house now and then. Or, maybe they should arrange for a home-care aide. Or, maybe their father should come and stay with one of them, briefly, though he doesn't travel well and they all live out of town. The discussion circles around and around, getting nowhere. Finally it ends. Things will remain as they are.

Later that evening, one of the sisters takes a brother aside and says, "Maybe it's time that we start checking out nursing homes." Her brother nods his head in agreement, then admits, "I've been thinking that for some time. But I didn't want to be the one to bring it up."

An elephant had been seated at this family's table, and, rather than acknowledge its presence, everybody had squeezed their chairs together to make room for it. But not talking about an elephant doesn't make it go away; in fact, over time it just seems to get bigger.

Yesterday you identified an "elephant" that has been seated at your family's table. Today you are invited to share that secret with someone. You might choose to discuss it with one of the other persons involved. However, this may be unwise. So, instead, you might decide to talk about it with a trusted friend. Take this friend into your confidence. Let it out. Whichever choice you make, you will find that speaking the truth boldly is very healing to your spirit.

I speak the truth boldly.

Day 297   **God gives me courage.**

So we can say with confidence, "The Lord is my helper; I will not be afraid. What can anyone do to me?"

—Hebrews 13:6

*S*usanna, a woman in her eighties, once told about her earliest childhood memory. Her father was carrying her across the yard. From his shoulder she looked down and spied a black snake slithering through the grass. "I wasn't at all afraid," she recalled. "I was up high, in my father's arms, and I just knew that I was safe. Nothing, not even that snake, could hurt me."

In the same way, we know that, upheld by the arms of God, nothing can ultimately harm us. Our spirits are untouchable, unconquerable. Having such knowledge, we need not fear anything.

One way that God upholds us is by giving us courage through other people. So, the next time that you must go somewhere that is intimidating or frightening to you, ask a friend or family member to accompany you, in order to give you moral support. Examples of such places would be a doctor's office or hospital, a funeral home, a police station, a lawyer's office or courthouse, or an intervention in someone's addiction. Let that person's strength be to you a divine source of courage. Let God's protective arms enfold you, and do not be afraid.

God gives me courage.

Day 298 My courage empowers others.

The officials shall continue to address the troops, saying, "Is anyone afraid or disheartened? He should go back to his house, or he might cause the heart of his comrades to melt like his own."

—*Deuteronomy 20:8*

Soldiers who have fought in wars, athletes who have played team sports, adults who have raised children, health care professionals who have treated patients and comforted their families—all of us, probably, have witnessed the power of courage. If we have seen how fear can spread from one person to another, producing a sense of helplessness and panic, we have also seen how courage can spread, inspiring confidence and strength. The officer commands, and the nervous soldiers become able troops. The team captain leads, and disheartened team members become an effective unit. The parent consoles, and the timid child becomes an eager playmate. The nurse encourages, and the anxious patient becomes a partner in her own healing.

When you have faith, you know that nothing can ultimately harm you. You have infinite courage. And by your infinite courage, others are empowered.

Yesterday you were encouraged to ask a friend to be a source of divine strength for you the next time that you must go somewhere that intimidates or frightens you. Today, the shoe is on the other foot. Look for an opportunity in the near future to accompany someone else to a place that *he or she* would rather not go. Make your friend's heart strong by allowing God's power to flow through you, giving reassurance.

My courage empowers others.

My courage grows with experience.

David said to Saul, "Let no one's heart fail because of [Goliath]; your servant will go and fight with this Philistine." Saul said to David, "You are not able to go against this Philistine to fight with him; for you are just a boy, and he has been a warrior from his youth." David said, "The LORD, who saved me from the paw of the lion and from the paw of the bear, will save me from the hand of this Philistine." So Saul said to David, "Go, and may the LORD be with you!"

—1 Samuel 17:32-33, 37a

The boy David says to the king, "Look, after wrestling with a lion and being tossed around by a bear, what's a little Philistine?"

You might think that David sounds not only fearless but a bit arrogant. However, he recognizes that it is God's strength, not his own, that has been the source of all his victories. God has supplied him with courage, and with each new struggle he has found that supply to be greater than he had supposed. And now he is ready to do battle even with a giant.

Write a response to the following questions:

(1) What have been the major "battles" of your life? Who or what have been the "giants"?
(2) Have you noticed that your spirit has grown most when fighting the biggest giants?
(3) During these battles, have you relied on your own strength only, or your own strength in combination with God's?
(4) What have these battles taught you about courage?
(5) In what way(s) has your courage grown with experience? In what way(s) are you still weak?

My courage grows with experience.

I courageously share.

And God is able to provide you with every blessing in abundance, so that by always having enough of everything, you may share abundantly in every good work.

—2 Corinthians 9:8

A long, long time ago, two neighbors owned adjoining wheat fields. And in a certain season both fields produced in abundance. On the day of harvest, each man piled his sheaves high, his heart grateful for the bounty. "I have been given plenty," each man thought to himself, "much more than I need." And that night, when the moon had risen high in the sky, the first man got up, went out to his field, picked up a sheaf of wheat, carried it over to his neighbor's pile, and returned to bed. His sandals had hardly grown cold before the second man arose, retrieved a sheaf of *his* wheat, and hurried over to add it to his neighbor's pile before the sun came up.

The next morning each man looked at his store of wheat and thought, "I still have more than I need. Tonight I will give my neighbor *two* sheaves." And so each neighbor did, and still their piles were stacked high. So the next night they carried three sheaves to their neighbor's pile, and then the next night four. Still their bounty was undiminished.

Finally, one night, in the midst of many trips toting many sheaves, the two men met beneath the moon. And it is said that in the place of their meeting, there appeared a holy shrine.

Choose today to do one act of courageous sharing from your bounty. Take a risk, and give abundantly. Perhaps the risk will be in the amount or quality of what you give. Perhaps the risk will be in not knowing how your giving will be received. But be bold. Share with others generously, as God has shared with you.

I courageously share.

Day 301   No act of love is ever lost.

"And now I am about to go the way of all the earth, and you know in your hearts and souls, all of you, that not one thing has failed of all the good things that the LORD your God promised concerning you."

—Joshua 23:14

*N*o act of love is ever lost. Today, as an illustration of this fundamental truth of *agape*, begin to make some delicious Friendship Bread, following the recipe below.

Begin by making a starter. In a plastic or glass bowl (*not* metal), dissolve 1 package of active dry yeast in 1 c. warm water.

Beat in 1 c. unsifted all-purpose flour and 1 T. sugar until smooth.* Cover and set aside at room temperature overnight. Then refrigerate until you use it, at least three more days, stirring once each day.

After the three days have passed, start the next phase. On Day 1, do nothing. On Days 2-5, mix the starter with a spoon. On Day 6, add 1 c. each of flour, sugar and milk. On Days 7-9, mix. On Day 10, combine in a large bowl all the batter with 1 c. each of flour, sugar and milk. Take out four 1 c. starters. Keep one of these, and give the others away (along with instructions).

Set aside your starter for the moment. Make the bread by adding these ingredients to the leftover batter in the bowl: 1 c. oil, 1 c. sugar, 1 t. vanilla, 3 large eggs, 1 t. baking powder, 1 t. salt, 2 c. flour, 1 c. milk, 1 t. baking soda, 1 large box instant vanilla pudding, and 2 t. cinnamon. Pour the batter into 2 large loaf pans and bake at 325° for one hour.

Finally, to replenish your 1 c. of starter, add 1 c. flour, 3 t. sugar, and 1 c. warm water. Return to the * and begin again.

No act of love is ever lost.

Day 302   **I am not afraid to love.**

Whoever says, "I am in the light," while hating a brother or sister, is still in the darkness.

—*1 John 2:9*

*I*f you say that you are in the light and yet you still have attitudes of darkness, it doesn't match up. God is light, and God is love. In God there is no darkness at all, and in God there is no hatred, anger, bitterness, or fear. So if we are living fully in the light, we will have let go of all negativity.

Kim and Jane attended the same high school, but they never spoke to each other. There had always seemed to be a wall of animosity between them. When they saw each other coming down the hall, they went out of their way to avoid each other. While they never had any "encounter," they just understood that they could not be friends. Then, on graduation night, they ended up at the same party. As luck would have it, they found themselves alone on the patio. Someone had to say something. Jane asked, "Why have you never liked me? What did I do?" Kim was shocked by the question. "I thought *you* didn't like *me!*" she declared. Each girl had mistakenly assumed that the other did not want to be friends. They had endured four years of darkness for no reason.

Identify a person whom you find difficult to love. It may be someone within your own family or someone at work. It may be someone who hurt you in the past. Whoever it is, write down his or her name. Then write a sentence that identifies a fear you have in loving this person. What harm might come to you if you dared to express *agape*? Now, imagine the light of God shining on the situation. See the darkness of fear melting away and being replaced with the radiance of love. Recall these loving thoughts whenever you think of the person you find difficult to love.

I am not afraid to love.

Day 303   **I am not afraid to care.**

Then the LORD said to Cain, "Where is your brother Abel?" He said, "I do not know, am I my brother's keeper?" And the LORD said, "What have you done? Listen; your brother's blood is crying out to me from the ground!"

—*Genesis 4:9-10*

In today's scripture, we discover that Cain was afraid to reach out and care for his brother. When jealousy arose between them, he chose to kill Abel instead of trying to work out their differences. In forgetting his connectedness to his brother, he revealed that he had also forgotten his connectedness to God. At that moment, he was lost.

Our sense of oneness with God is the solid foundation upon which we stand. The moment we step away from it, we begin to be afraid of expressing *agape*. The risks seem too great. What if other people misunderstand our caring? What if they do not appreciate what we are doing? In our fear we step away from others, just as we have stepped away from God. However, if we stand securely on the fact that we belong to God, we recognize that we all belong to one another. Then we are never unwilling to reach out and express *agape*, no matter what other people think.

Today you have only one mission: *Be caring.* Express *agape*. Make this your top priority and, so far as possible, allow nothing to take its place. If you get in too much of a hurry to care, slow down. If you get too preoccupied to care, remind yourself of what is most important. If you get too afraid to care, admit your fear and allow yourself to care anyway; your fear will begin to ease. Throughout the day, stand on the solid foundation of your connectedness to God and reach out.

I am not afraid to care.

Day 304   I am not afraid to let go of what I have.

Jesus, looking at him, loved him and said, "You lack one thing; go, sell what you own, and give the money to the poor, and you will have treasure in heaven; then come, follow me." When he heard this, he was shocked and went away grieving, for he had many possessions.

— Mark 10:21-22

*D*o you remember the old monkey trap? A banana is placed in a small jar that has been secured in place. Any monkey seeing the jar would want the fruit. He would reach inside and grasp the banana, but then discover that he couldn't pull it out. The jar's opening wasn't big enough for both his hand and the banana to pass through. Unwilling to let go of what he wanted, he would be easily captured.

We are not so different from this monkey. We spend a lot of our time and energy grasping bananas, fearful that if we let go, we will not have enough. However, as our Christ-mind grows, our need to hold onto the things of this earth diminishes. We begin to see that letting go of them is an act of faith.

People who have experienced being without the basic necessities of life often find it difficult to trust that their needs will be met, even when they have plenty. For example, some of those who lived through the Great Depression may have pantries and freezers stocked with more food than they will ever be able to eat, bank accounts and lock boxes filled with more money than they will ever be able to spend, and attics packed with more stuff than they will ever be able to use. Letting go of anything is a frightening experience for them. They are caught in the mind-set of their earlier poverty: What if there will not be enough tomorrow?

We approach life from either the principle of scarcity or the principle of plenty. If we live out of a sense of scarcity, we will always want to hold onto what we have for fear there may not be enough for us tomorrow. But if we live out of a sense of plenty, we will have little trouble letting go of what we have. Knowing that there will always be more available to us, we will share what we possess without worry. The principle that directs our thinking makes all the difference in our lives.

What ten possessions would you grab first if your house caught on fire? Write these "treasures" down. Now, select one of these items and give it to someone else. Observe this person's joy in receiving your gift. Take note of your feelings as you let go of it.

I am not afraid to let go of what I have.

Day 305   **I am not afraid of making a mistake.**

Let us therefore no longer pass judgment on one another, but resolve instead never to put a stumbling block or hindrance in the way of another.

—Romans 14:13

A mistake is simply a lesson in which you learn what will not work. It is one step you take down the path toward discovering what will work. So, instead of beating yourself up for making a mistake, it would be more appropriate to congratulate yourself. You have made a discovery. Now you can move on and try something else. Most great inventions come at the end of a long list of mistakes. Many trials and errors lead to the perfection of the final product. Just think of Thomas Edison and the light bulb. Edison made hundreds of errors before lighting it up. Aren't you glad that he never gave up?

When a mistake is made, many of us are quick to think that it is the end of the line. We easily lose our hope. But in fact that mistake may have been the last thing that didn't work before the one that will. The same holds true in our relationships with one another. When a wrong is done, we could easily give up. Or, we could decide that the mistake was just another part of learning what will and won't work in that particular relationship. If we regard our mistakes as stepping stones toward greater knowledge, we will keep on trying until we finally make our way through. Enjoy these trick questions. Remember that the first answer you think of may be a mistake. Do not give up. Keep going until you have the right answer.

(1) Some months have thirty days, and some thirty-one. How many have twenty-eight?

(2) If you had only one match and entered a room where there was an oil lamp, oil heater, and some kindling wood, which would you light first?

(3) A farmer had seventeen sheep. All but nine died. How many were left alive?

(4) How many animals of each kind did Moses take aboard the ark with him?

(5) A woman gave a beggar fifty cents. The woman is the beggar's sister, but the beggar is not the woman's brother. How come?

I am not afraid of making a mistake.

Answers:
(1) All months have twenty-eight days. (2) The match. (3) Nine. (4) None. *Noah* boarded the animals. (5) The beggar is a woman. She is the other woman's *sister.*

Day 306 # I am not afraid of knowing myself.

"Why do you see the speck in your neighbor's eye, but do not notice the log in your own eye? Or how can you say to your neighbor, 'Let me take the speck out of your eye,' while the log is in your own eye?"

—*Matthew 7:3-4*

When someone gives us a gift that is beautifully wrapped, we do not hesitate to open it. Even though we have no idea what is inside, we eagerly tear off the wrapping. Why? Because we know that the gift will be good. We trust the giver of the gift.

Why, then, are we reluctant to look at what is inside ourselves? We are beautiful gifts that God has given to the world. Yet many of us are afraid that if we remove our wrappings, we will discover something terrible inside us. Still, even discovering a "log" gives us the opportunity for greater self-awareness and spiritual growth. Acknowledging the flaws within ourselves helps us to become more accepting of the flaws in other people. So let us not be afraid to peel away the layers of wrapping that cover us over. We can trust God more than the giver of any good gift. Deep within ourselves we will find God-given beauty.

Take some time to do a personal inventory. Look within yourself, trusting that what you will find will be helpful to you. Do not be afraid of who you are. Begin by writing down one quality of your personality that you especially appreciate. Celebrate the good that you have accomplished by using this gift to help others. Now, identify one part of yourself (a behavior or attitude) of which you are not especially proud. Write it down next to the positive quality you named. Think about the ways in which you have allowed this attribute to hurt others. Offer a prayer of repentance and ask God to help you let go of this negative quality. Finally, list another positive quality. Celebrate the person that God has created you to be—the person you are becoming!

I am not afraid of knowing myself.

Day 307   I am not afraid of truth.

"Beware of false prophets, who come to you in sheep's clothing but inwardly are ravenous wolves. You will know them by their fruits. Are grapes gathered from thorns, or figs from thistles?"

—Matthew 7:15-16

When Betty was told she would need to have an operation, she was confident that her doctors knew what was best for her. But then her friends began to tell her that she should be worried. Many people had died, they said, from the very same surgery. Listening to them, Betty's fears began to mount. Finally, she scheduled an appointment with her doctors to discuss the risks. They reassured her that they had successfully performed the surgery hundreds of times. She had no reason to be concerned. She relaxed. In fact, her surgery did go well, and Betty recovered quickly and completely.

Many of us have a tendency to dwell on half-truths or imagined "truths"—our own inner "false prophets." We can see this even in our relationships. We can spend hours fretting over what we think another person meant by what he or she said or did, but until we ask and discover the truth of the person's feelings or intentions, we will be simply shadowboxing with our worst fears. A troubled situation can be resolved only when we ignore our inner false prophets and seek out the truth.

Think of a troublesome relationship that you are experiencing right now. On a piece of paper, make three columns entitled Past,

Present, and Future. In the Past column, list the events and words that you remember that have caused difficulty in the relationship. In the Future column, jot down any worries or concerns that you have about what the coming days might bring to the relationship. Finally, in the Present column, list only those conflicts that you are actually experiencing in the relationship at this moment.

Knowing that the past is over and gone, tear the Past column off the paper and throw it away. These past mistakes taught you much about what does and does not work in the relationship, but to continue to dwell on them would be to pay attention to false voices. Next, realizing that the future is only imagined and may never become a reality, tear the Future column off the paper. What you have written here are the words of other false voices. Now, you are down to the Present. Read over the list that remains and decide which of the conflicts you can do nothing about. Cross them off. You are left with what you can do something about. Here is the truth of the situation. How can you handle these conflicts? Doesn't the relationship look more manageable now?

I am not afraid of truth.

Day 308   I am not afraid of peace.

Too long have I had my dwelling among those who hate peace. I am for peace; but when I speak, they are for war.

—Psalm 120:6-7

*W*hy are so many of us afraid of peace? In the first place, we may have the mistaken notion that to have peace, we would all have to hold the same views and live the same way. Or, we may not trust other parties to truly coexist with us without attacking us in some way. Or, we may not want to give up the power we have in order to create peace. Or, we may be driven by our sense of scarcity, which says that, no matter who gets in the way, we must fight to get more than what we have.

Whenever we are afraid of peace, there will be conflict. But when we think with the mind of Christ, we do not need to fear. Nothing can threaten our security, for our security is God. However, sometimes we will find ourselves in the midst of conflict. How, then, do we create peace when others are afraid?

Conflict can be resolved in many different ways. One way is for one of the parties to give up or give in. This "You lose, I win" solution may bring an end to the external conflict, but an internal conflict will remain. Another approach is to compromise— each party gives up a little and gains a little of what it wants. This is a "You lose a little, I lose a little; you win a little, I win a little" solution to the problem. A better approach is to resolve the conflict through open and honest confrontation, done in a loving and caring way. This requires each party to put its agenda on the table and respect the desires of the other as equal to its own. After talking through the possibilities, the parties discover a solution can be found that meets the needs of both. This is a "You win, I win" solution. This is *shalom*, the just peace of God.

Prepare for a meditative prayer. Relax and breathe deeply. Think of a situation in which you do not have peace right now. Trust that God wants to show you a different way to deal with it. Imagine the worst case scenarios that could happen in the situation. Next, gradually eliminate each of them from your mind; they are products of your imagination. Since you have created them, you can also destroy them. Now, imagine several best case scenarios that might result from this troublesome situation. Review each positive possibility. Which one appears strongest? Trust that this is the outcome that God has in mind. Commit yourself to doing all that you can to resolve this conflict in a way that leads to peace. Do not be afraid.

I am not afraid of peace.

Day 309 **Peace comes through forgiveness.**

Joseph wept when they spoke to him. Then his brothers also wept, fell down before him, and said, "We are here as your slaves." But Joseph said to them, "Do not be afraid! Am I in the place of God? Even though you intended to do harm to me, God intended it for good, in order to preserve a numerous people, as he is doing today. So have no fear; I myself will provide for you and your little ones." In this way he reassured them, speaking kindly to them.

—*Genesis 50:17c-21*

*T*wo brothers are pallbearers at their sister's funeral. At the cemetery they stand next to each other behind the hearse, waiting. They have not spoken or seen each other in more than fifty years. Once, the younger brother had made the elder angry—no one can quite remember how. The elder brother's anger had, in turn, offended the younger. There has never been forgiveness. Now their families watch for any sign of reconciliation. Gray-haired, square-jawed, somewhat stooped, the two men closely resemble their long-dead father. They resemble each other. Will a shared grief finally bring them together? The brothers grip the handles of the casket. Their knuckles turn white. They keep their eyes lowered. They do not speak. Not as they carry her. Not as they lay her to rest. Not as they walk away from her grave.

There was never any forgiveness between these men. And so, there was no peace. Theirs is a story so unlike the story of Joseph and his brothers. As a boy, Joseph had been his brothers' victim; they had sold him into slavery. As a man, he had the chance to take revenge. In a time of crisis they cried out to him for help and declared they would be his slaves forever. But instead he offered them all the help he could. He and his brothers were set free from the burden of the past.

There was forgiveness among these men. And so, there was peace.

Reflect on these questions:

(1) If you had been Joseph, what thoughts would have run through your mind when you first saw your brothers again in Egypt?

(2) For what reason(s) would you have decided to forgive them?

(3) If you had been one of Joseph's brothers, how would you have felt when you realized that the man standing before you was actually the brother you had sold into slavery?

(4) What feelings would Joseph's response have aroused in you?

Peace comes through forgiveness.

Day 310   **Forgiveness is not earned.**

"Then his lord summoned him and said to him, 'You wicked slave! I forgave you all that debt because you pleaded with me. Should you not have had mercy on your fellow slave, as I had mercy on you?'"

—Matthew 18:32-33

$\mathcal{E}$arlier in this story, the lord had shown compassion for his servant by canceling his debt, the equivalent of *fifteen years'* wages. An incredible act of forgiveness. The servant's spirit of gratitude was not long-lasting, however. He walked out the door and immediately ran into a fellow slave who owed him *one day's* wage. He demanded his money, there on the spot. When the slave pleaded with him to be patient, saying that, given enough time, he would certainly be able to pay, the servant only sneered and had him hauled off to prison.

Two debts. One equivalent to fifteen years of labor, the other to one day's work. But the amount to be forgiven didn't really matter. Think about it. The equivalent of a day's wage probably meant as much to the poor servant as fifteen years' wages meant to the rich lord. What this story reveals, then, is that forgiveness is granted without regard for the size of an offense. It is not to be earned, so that some individuals deserve it more and others less. Forgiveness is, simply, *for free.*

Freely offer your forgiveness to the world. Purchase one helium balloon (or more, if you wish); tie to it a small piece of paper on which you have written a grudge that you have been carrying against someone. Then go to a favorite spot and release the balloon into the sky. Let forgiveness carry your grudge away on the winds of grace. In days to come, whenever you find yourself unable to forgive, remember the sight of that balloon rising into the sky, and *let go.*

Forgiveness is not earned.

Day 311   **Forgiveness brings unlimited joy.**

"Therefore, I tell you, her sins, which were many, have been forgiven; hence she has shown great love. But the one to whom little is forgiven, loves little." Then he said to her, "Your sins are forgiven."

—Luke 7:47-48

$\mathcal{Y}$esterday we discussed how, since forgiveness is unearned, the size of an offense does not matter to the one who forgives. But the size of an offense sometimes *does* matter to the one who is forgiven.

Suppose that you have acted wrongly toward another person. If you regard your offense as minor, you may hardly feel sorry, and may or may not apologize. Your reconciliation is effortless. It sends only the slightest of ripples across the waters of your relationship.

On the other hand, if you regard your offense as major, you may feel so ashamed that even to talk about it is immensely difficult. But when you finally do and are graciously received by the one you wronged, what joy you feel! An indescribable relief floods in when you are forgiven, as if high waters have just been released from a dam.

Return to Day 309 and reread the story about the two elderly brothers at their sister's funeral. Rewrite its ending so that the brothers somehow forgive each other and find great joy in their reconciliation. How do you imagine this reconciliation happening? What words do you imagine being spoken? Be a storyteller, and let the characters experience the joy of forgiveness.

Forgiveness brings unlimited joy.

Day 312   **Forgiveness is my mission.**

"If another member of the church sins against you, go and point out the fault when the two of you are alone. If the member listens to you, you have regained that one."

—*Matthew 18:15*

On my honor I will do my best to do my duty to God and my country and to obey the Scout Law; to help other people at all times; to keep myself physically strong, mentally awake, and morally straight." You may recognize this as the "Boy Scout's Oath or Promise." It is the faithful Scout's "mission statement," a declaration of the Scout's purpose and function in the world.

An essential part of your mission as a child of God is to forgive. This is your purpose, your function, your calling. What does that mean to you, exactly? How do you live out this calling?

Compose a "forgiveness mission statement." Write it with care and with prayer. Describe your responsibility to forgive and indicate some possible forms that your forgiveness might take. Let your forgiveness mission statement be a promise to God of what you intend to do and a challenge to yourself to actually do it.

Forgiveness is my mission.

Day 313 **I am faithful to my mission of forgiveness.**

Bear with one another and, if anyone has a complaint against another, forgive each other; just as the Lord has forgiven you, so you also must forgive.

—*Colossians 3:13*

*A*s anyone who has ever made a New Year's resolution knows, it is easier to make a vow than to keep it. So, declaring that forgiveness is your mission is much easier than actually forgiving people, day in and day out. You must keep your mission statement in the forefront of your mind; you must keep your intention to forgive in the center of your heart.

Look again at the words of the mission statement you composed yesterday. Now, ask yourself this: "How shall I measure my faithfulness to my mission?" List some specific things that you will try to do from now on to undertake the work of forgiveness, whenever you have been hurt. Include efforts to reconcile with the person who offended as well as efforts to resolve your own feelings.

After you have completed your list, write a letter to yourself in which you ask how well you are doing in fulfilling your mission. Ask specific questions of yourself, based on both your mission statement and the list of specific intentions you listed above. Finally, put the letter in a self-addressed stamped envelope and mail it. When it arrives a couple of days from now, answer its questions as honestly as you can.

I am faithful to my mission.

Day 314 **I speak forgiveness.**

Do not speak evil against one another, brothers and sisters. Whoever speaks evil against another or judges another, speaks evil against the law and judges the law; but if you judge the law, you are not a doer of the law but a judge. There is one lawgiver and judge who is able to save and to destroy. So who, then, are you to judge your neighbor?

—*James 4:11-12*

*A*ccording to the scripture text, evil speech is judgmental speech. It builds up one person (the judge) by putting down another (the one being judged). Brainstorm on paper as many kinds of evil speech as you can (gossip, accusations, and so on). Good speech, on the other hand, is nonjudgmental. It is compassionate, full of *agape*. It is forgiving. It is spoken to build up everyone and put down no one. Brainstorm as many kinds of good speech as you can (compliments, reassurances, and so on).

Whether our words are evil or good, they help to shape reality. Words are very powerful, as we learn in the very beginning of Genesis. In Genesis 1, God declares, "Let there be a universe," and, behold, a universe appears! This is the creative power of the divine word. Then, in Genesis 2, Adam gives a name to every living thing that God has made. In other words, he gives it an identity, thereby helping to determine its nature. This is the co-creative power of human words. Unfortunately, however, human words also have destructive power. So, we must be careful, indeed, of what we say.

Speaking words of forgiveness is one of the most creative things we can do. But before we can become consistent in speaking them, we must become more aware of what they sound like. We must learn to more clearly distinguish between nonjudgmental and judgmental kinds of speech. Today's exercise is therefore an awareness exercise.

Watch a TV program. Identify the different kinds of speech that you hear. Try especially to develop an ear for forgiving speech, which builds up everyone and puts down no one. Prepare yourself to speak more consistently words that create rather than destroy.

I speak forgiveness.

Day 315   **I forgive *now*.**

"So when you are offering your gift at the altar, if you remember that your brother or sister has something against you, leave your gift there before the altar and go; first be reconciled to your brother or sister, and then come and offer your gift."

—*Matthew 5:23-24*

*T*he message of today's scripture passage is clear. *Nothing* is more important than seeking to reconcile with someone from whom we are estranged. Forgiveness is not to be put off. Forgiveness starts *now*.

So far we have spoken of forgiveness mainly in terms of our reaching out to pardon others. But this scripture passage suggests that forgiveness also involves our reaching out to be pardoned *by* others. Since we are to undertake the work of forgiveness earlier rather than later, we do not sit back waiting for the one whom we have hurt to come to us and make the peace. Instead, we risk going to him or her, as soon as possible. We go for both our sakes, presenting an opportunity for reconciliation. We make no demands, but only hope and pray that this person, too, wishes to repair the relationship.

Reach out today to someone you have injured. Perhaps your relationship will be restored. If that is not possible at this time, at least your spirit will begin to heal. Then, having set forgiveness in motion, you can offer heaven the pure-hearted worship that God desires.

I forgive *now*.

Day 316   **My love has no limits.**

Do not withhold good from those to whom it is due, when it is in your power to do it.

—*Proverbs 3:27*

*W*endy was checking out of the grocery store on a busy day. The bag boy asked her if she preferred plastic or paper bags. When she replied that she preferred paper, he turned to a co-worker and made an unkind comment about people who don't understand that it is easier to put groceries in plastic bags. Wendy heard him, and he knew it. On their way to her car, they both walked in silence. Whatever the bag boy was feeling, Wendy was angry. As they neared her car, however, she allowed her anger to give way to forgiveness. Instead of giving the bag boy her usual $1 tip, she handed him a $5 bill. Nothing was said, but the look on his face assured her that they both had experienced the power of forgiving love.

Agape is not concerned with the worthiness of the other person. It has no limits. If we begin to express our love based upon the behavior of the other person, we will have stopped loving. Love reaches out to the other simply as a gesture of giving, without concern for getting.

When we stop being concerned about the worthiness of the

other person, we can begin to love without hesitation and without discrimination. We love because we ourselves have felt the love of God in our lives—both when we deserved it and when we did not. So we reach out to each person with a love that cares about that individual, just as he or she is. Our only concern is to express the unconditional love that God has placed in our hearts.

Make or purchase a supply of little gifts that can serve as tokens of your love. Have plenty of them available to you. For just one day, offer one to as many people as possible. Do not make any judgment about who should or should not receive the gift. Let each person know that the gift is simply an expression of love. Be observant of the responses that you get, but know that they are not to determine your willingness to share your love. Let this experience be an inspiration to share *agape* more openly each day. **My love has no limits.**

Day 317 My love meets the needs of others.

If there is among you anyone in need, a member of your community in any of your towns within the land that the Lord your God is giving you, do not be hard-hearted or tight-fisted toward your needy neighbor. You should rather open your hand, willingly lending enough to meet the need, whatever it may be.

—Deuteronomy 15:7-8

Life is really meant to be fairly simple. We complicate it with our judgments about one another. We muddle it up when we ask if someone is worthy of our generosity. Keep it simple. Tell yourself that if something needs to be done for another and you can do it, you will go ahead and get it done.

One Sunday after worship, a young minister was notified that the toilet in the nursery was running continuously. Taking off his robe and rolling up his sleeves, he quickly discovered the problem and began correcting it. Just then, a member of the church board walked in and found him with his hands in the toilet tank. Quite alarmed, she objected that a minister should do such a menial task. It was certainly "beneath him."

When we make valuative judgments about what is "beneath" (or "above") us, we complicate life. If something is to be done and you can do it. . . . If your neighbor has need of something and you have extra. . . . No need to ask why the other person is in need. No reason to analyze his or her work ethic. You have what is needed to meet the lack in the other. Share it.

Find a relaxing spot and prepare for a time of prayerful focusing. Allow the stress of the day to leave you. Think only of the generous hand of God reaching out to you. Know that all that you need will be supplied. As you celebrate the good gifts that God gives you, imagine your hands reaching out to meet the needs of others. See people coming to you, trusting that you will help them. Notice that you ask no questions about their worthiness to receive. You simply offer them what you have. Celebrate the joy that you feel in helping them in the spirit of *agape*.

My love meets the needs of others.

Day 318   My love does not grow weary.

Since there will never cease to be some in need on the earth, I therefore command you, "Open your hand to the poor and needy neighbor in your land."

—Deuteronomy 15:11

Early one morning, John found his friend Nick on the beach picking up starfish and throwing them back into the ocean. "Why are you doing that?" John asked. Nick replied, "To save them from dying on the dry beach." Looking around at the thousands of starfish that had washed ashore in the night, John asked Nick if his work was really making a difference. "It does to the ones I throw back," Nick declared.

Sometimes, when confronted by an immense need, we feel overwhelmed, almost paralyzed and unable to respond. But if we focus not on the crowd but on the individual, not on the whole problem but on a manageable part of it, we will find the strength to respond. When we love in order to see the results, we can easily become weary. If the results aren't up to our expectations, it may seem as though our love makes no difference in the big picture. But when we love only in order to love, then we do not lose heart, even when we can't do all that we would like to do. Our loving is a gift that is joined to the gifts of thousands of others who dare to love. All of these gifts combine to make this world a better place. The welfare of the world does not all depend upon you, but what you do *does* make a difference.

Think of someone whom you have been trying to love but to whom it seems to make no difference. For today, simply love this person with no thought of what will come back to you. Allow *agape* to flow freely. In response to the person's apparent non-response, increase your willingness to express your care and concern. Keep it up, knowing that when your love is shared it is never wasted. It *will* make a difference.

My love does not grow weary.

Day 319   My love takes risks.

"The next day he took out two denarii, gave them to the innkeeper, and said, 'Take care of him; and when I come back, I will repay you whatever more you spend.' Which of these three, do you think, was a neighbor to the man who fell into the hands of the robbers?" [The lawyer] said, "The one who showed him mercy." Jesus said to him, "Go and do likewise."

—Luke 10:35-37

Thomas was dying of AIDS. He refused to allow any of his friends to visit him. He didn't want them to see him in his condition. But he wasn't alone. His landlady, Mildred, was there for him. She cared for him, day in and day out, as if he were her own child. Her loving care continued until he died in her home. At his memorial service, Mildred was asked over and over if she had not been afraid to take care of him since he had such a dreaded disease. Her answer was always the same. She hadn't given it much thought. All that had been on her mind was the care of a young man who was dying. In his story of the Good Samaritan, Jesus tells about one who put himself at great risk in helping the man who was beaten. The Samaritan would not have been welcomed by the innkeeper or anyone else who was a part of the injured man's circle of friends. Samaritans were a despised people. They were not to mix with Jews. Yet this Samaritan responded to a Jewish man's cry for help with no thought of the risks to himself. Like Mildred, he was only concerned about helping someone in need.

Agape takes risks. There is the uncertainty about how the other person will respond. There is the danger of being misunderstood. There is the possibility of being hurt. But *agape* reaches out anyway.

Do you remember the excitement and fear that you felt when you tried something risky for the first time? Maybe you rode on the biggest roller coaster in the amusement park, or gave a speech in front of a roomful of people. Remember that feeling of success when you did "the impossible"? Hang onto that feeling. That is how you will feel when you dare to share your love even in risky situations.

Today, find someone who might least expect a kind word from you and share an expression of appreciation with them. Know that the apprehension you feel is normal, but move beyond it. Dare to express *agape*. Do not worry about the response you get. Share your love, and know that it is good.

My love takes risks.

Day 320   My love expects nothing in return.

[Jesus] said also to the one who had invited him, "When you give a luncheon or a dinner, do not invite your friends or your brothers or your relatives or rich neighbors, in case they may invite you in return, and you would be repaid. But when you give a banquet, invite the poor, the crippled, the lame and the blind. And you will be blessed, because they cannot repay you."

—*Luke 14:12-14*a

When it is time to send out your Christmas cards, how do you decide who will get one? Do you use last year's list of the cards you received as your guide? Or, do you simply address cards to those people with whom you would like to share a Christmas greeting? Are you concerned that you might send a card to someone who won't send one to you?

Love doesn't worry about keeping everything equal.

After you invite someone to your home for a meal, do you wait to see if the person will reciprocate? Do you hold off extending another invitation, even when you would welcome having this person over again? Love does not keep track of whose turn it is to issue the invitation.

The apple tree gives its apples because that is the purpose of the tree. The sun shares its warmth because that is the purpose of the sun. Why do we love? The answer is the same. We love because it is our purpose—our nature—to do so. We were created to offer *agape* to one another. It doesn't matter whether it comes back to us or not. When we truly love, we reach out and give without strings attached.

Make or purchase a small gift and wrap it. Now, take some time to think about how often the gifts you give have "strings attached." What kinds of strings are they? For example, you may give a gift in order to gain the favor of the recipient, or to put the recipient in your debt.

Anonymously give this small gift to someone who will appreciate it, and who will never find out that you were the giver. In other words, give it without any strings attached. This is loving without worrying about what happens in response.

My love expects nothing in return.

Day 321   My love is light.

If you offer your food to the hungry and satisfy the needs of the afflicted, then your light shall rise in the darkness and your gloom be like the noonday.

—Isaiah 58:10

Larry stopped by a friend's office one day. He was distraught. It seemed that life was passing him by. He had always wanted to go to college and study to be an engineer. But the circumstances of life had not allowed him to do so. For years he had been stuck in a factory job. Now life had little meaning, and even less joy. After listening for several minutes, his friend asked him to share some times when he remembered feeling happy. Larry thought awhile, then recounted several occasions. A common theme emerged. In each of those happier times, Larry was helping someone.

As they discussed the situation, Larry decided that he really couldn't change jobs at this time in his life. However, he could bring more joy into his life by regularly and intentionally involving himself in some form of service to others. Larry went on to find ways to help other people, and the joy he experienced carried over into the rest of his life. Even his job became more enjoyable. By reaching out in service to others, he found the meaning and happiness that his life had lacked.

Yesterday, you gave away a gift without allowing the person to discover that you were the giver. Today, increase your expressions of love. Give three little gifts anonymously to others. Sense the sheer joy of giving. Know that you can claim this joy at any time. The love you share will not only brighten the lives of those who receive it, but will return to brighten your life as well.

My love is light.

Day 322 My love does more than I know.

"Then the righteous will answer him, 'Lord, when was it that we saw you hungry and gave you food, or thirsty and gave you something to drink? And when was it that we saw you a stranger and welcomed you, or naked and gave you clothing? And when was it that we saw you sick or in prison and visited you?' And the king will answer them, 'Truly I tell you, just as you did it to one of the least of these who are members of my family, you did it to me.'"

—Matthew 25:37-40

At her farewell party, Paula encountered a man whose name she did not know. He came up to her and said, "Thank you, pastor, for saving my life. Without you, I would not be here today." Then he disappeared into the crowd. Paula stood there puzzling over what she had just heard. She couldn't even remember having seen the man before. Her mind traced back through her years of ministry in that place, but came up empty. She simply had to accept the fact that her love had touched him in a way that she hadn't been aware of.

When expressed without reservation, *agape* does far more than we will ever know. It has a ripple effect, very much like throwing a stone into a lake. The stone enters the water at a specific spot, but the ripples circle out until they reach the shores. This is what happens when we express our love. We may be able to identify a particular act of love, but its effects may ripple out to touch the lives of dozens of people. So, never despair of expressing your love. You cannot know how much good it will do.

Take a moment to give thanks to the Source of all love for the effect that your love has had on other people. Realize that you cannot know all that your love has done. Simply express your gratitude for the fact that your love makes a difference.

My love does more than I know.

Day 323   **Love reveals the way to community.**

Whoever loves a brother or sister lives in the light, and in such a person there is no cause for stumbling.

—1 John 2:10

*I*f you have ever been in Kentucky, you may have visited Mammoth Cave, one of the largest cave systems in the world, with more than 300 miles of passageways. Early in this century, long before it became a major tourist attraction, this cave was the site of worship services. Lantern-carrying guides led worshippers down into one of the cave's gigantic rooms. There a preacher would stand atop a rock formation and warn the assembled host of sinners to repent lest they be forever removed from the love of God. His voice would swell to a fevered pitch until, having struck terror deep into the people's hearts, he would signal his assistants to snuff out all the lanterns. Imagine the utter darkness, the sudden sense of total isolation, the dreadful echo of the preacher's words against the stone. And imagine the utter helplessness of the congregants when the preacher refused to relight the lamps until all of them had been "saved!"

For these worshippers, this could have hardly been an experience of community! With the lanterns extinguished, each person might as well have been alone in the cave, lost in the dark. What could each person do? He or she either could stay put, afraid to move, waiting for the lanterns to be relit, or stumble around, trying to find the way, with no chance at all of making it back up to the surface without help. There was nothing else that could be done, unless . . .

Unless someone happened to have a match and a candle and, getting tired of being alone and afraid and of knowing that everyone else was feeling alone and afraid, too, decided to make a little light so that everyone would feel better. Imagine what effect this one lit candle would have had! Especially when this person turned away from that preacher and started back to the light of day. Think anybody would have followed?

Love lights the candle and lets us know that someone is near. Love lights the candle and shows us the way out of fear. Love lights the candle and makes our way clear.

For today's exercise you will need a partner and a blindfold.

320

Put on the blindfold yourself. Ask your partner to be your eyes—the equivalent of the person carrying the candle in the cave. Have your partner guide you through a ten to fifteen-minute walk, taking you anywhere she or he wants. Your partner should stay at your side, gently holding your hand or elbow, and tell you how to proceed. Your partner's job is to keep you from stumbling. Your job is to trust and let your partner be a "light" for you "in the dark." Feel the connection between you grow as the minutes pass by.

Love reveals the way to community.

Day 324　　　**Humility is the way to community.**

In the same way, you who are younger must accept the authority of the elders. And all of you must clothe yourselves with humility in your dealings with one another, for "God opposes the proud, but gives grace to the humble."

—1 Peter 5:5

*I*magine that you are sitting in a worship service. The minister has just stood up behind the pulpit to begin her sermon. The man next to you picks up his tattered Bible. As the minister speaks, he thumbs through its pages, stopping every so often to thump his index finger down on a passage and mutter something under his breath. Then he cranes his neck to make eye-contact with another worshipper a couple of rows back and to the left. He rolls his eyes. As this behavior continues, you become quite uncomfortable. Obviously the man disagrees with what the minister is saying and is hunting for scripture passages to prove her wrong. You wish that you were sitting somewhere else. You have lost your enthusiasm for worship and can't wait for the service to be over.

This man's spirit was arrogant, puffed up with its own self-importance. In his own mind, he had already learned everything he needed to know. His way to interpret scripture was the only way. He was always right. And his arrogance divided the community.

Humility is understanding that you are here in this life as a seeker among seekers, as a journeyer among journeyers. Whatever age you are, you still have a lifetime of learning ahead of you, and a lifetime of sharing what you have learned. You will never have learned everything. In other words, you don't know it all. Your way isn't the only way. You aren't always right. Therefore, you listen with appreciation to those who know what you don't, and respect those whose ways are different, and willingly admit when you are wrong. To understand these things is the beginning of humility.

One of the most humble things you can do is to admit when you don't know something. Many of us try to cover up any lack of knowledge. We subtly change the subject, or make something up, or answer vaguely, or turn the question back on the one who asked it, or simply attack what we don't understand. All of these strategies hurt the community. Simply saying "I don't know," on the other hand, can be another step toward deeper community. At the very least, in saying it you will be answering honestly, and others will realize that they can trust you.

Get used to saying these three words: "I don't know." Your assignment today is to admit at least once when you don't know something. Feel the freedom and joy that comes to you when you walk in humility.

Humility is the way to community.

Day 325   The community holds all things in common.

Now the whole group of those who believed were of one heart and soul, and no one claimed private ownership of any possessions, but everything they owned was held in common.

—*Acts 4:32*

*T*he most fundamental values of a culture are quite often revealed by its language. The Chinese language is quite notable in that it has no word for "privacy" or "personal ownership." This fact is not a by-product of China's twentieth-century communism. Rather, it is an indication of China's five thousand-year-old belief that the family, not the individual, holds the key to survival and happiness. Society at large is simply the family on a grander scale.

Ideally, the Chinese family holds all things in common, gives all things in common, and receives all things in common. Consider the gift-giving between Chinese households, for example, which is a very important cultural ritual. No matter the occasion, gift-giving is always an exchange between families, not individuals. When you exchange gifts, the ages, genders, tastes, needs, and desires of individual family members are basically irrelevant. The gifts are not personalized, distributed by one member to another; they are collective, presented by all members to all.

In many ways, the ideal Chinese family resembles on a smaller scale the ideal community described in Acts. Can you, like the early Christian community, learn to give less emphasis to private ownership? Can your community come to express its growing "one-heartedness" by increasing its "one-handedness"?

A good way to practice one-handedness is to share your resources with members of your community whenever possible. For example, a man was in need of a power saw to do some remodeling on his house. He heard that his neighbor, who happened to have such a saw, was planning to buy a rototiller to work up her garden. He suggested that she borrow his rototiller and lend him her saw. Everyone was happy!

Think about something that you or someone in your family may need. Do you know someone who might be able to fill that need? What might you be able to do or provide in exchange? Try to arrange the exchange. View it less as a swapping of individual possessions or abilities than as a sharing of community resources.

The community holds all things in common.

Day 326 Nothing I own defines me.

All who believed were together and had all things in common; they would sell their possessions and goods and distribute the proceeds to all, as any had need.

—Acts 2:44-45

*E*verything you have is God's. Without exception. What you have, God has entrusted to your care. You are its steward. You are responsible for wisely giving from your portion of God's "storehouse" to meet the needs of others. You are to do so without possessiveness, and without prejudice.

It is hard to be a faithful steward while living in a consumer society. It is hard to see our possessions as God's instead of ours. In fact, it is hard to separate our possessions from our selves.

323

From early on, we are taught to work hard. Work hard to get. Not just to get *by*, but to get *more*. And more is never enough, when we measure ourselves by the prestige of our jobs, the amount of our salaries, the size of our houses, the quality of our clothes, the price-tag on our cars. . . .

Throw the measuring tape away. Realize that who you are depends on none of these things. Who you are is a child of God. Who you are is a member of God's family. Who you are is a care-taker of God's world. Learn to dis-own your possessions by own-ing your true identity. Allow your "consumer mentality" to be transformed into the mind of Christ.

Today's exercise is meant to help you better understand who you are apart from your possessions. If you were asked to write down ten responses to the phrase, "I have _____," you would probably find it easy to do. But what you have is not who you are. So, instead, write down ten responses to the phrase, "I am _____." Let your responses be descriptive of your inner qualities—of your personality and spirituality. (Do not, for example, write, "I am a doctor," or "I am a grandfather.") How difficult is it to identify your inner qualities?

As the mind of Christ grows within you, you will no longer feel compelled to substitute one materialistic desire for another. Gradually you will recognize the joy and freedom that comes when you allow God, not your possessions, to define you.

Nothing I own defines me.

Day 327 **Community nurtures me to maturity.**

The gifts he gave were that some would be apostles, some prophets, some evangelists, some pastors and teachers, to equip the saints for the work of ministry, for building up the body of Christ, until all of us come to the unity of the faith and of the knowledge of the Son of God, to maturity, to the measure of the full stature of Christ.

—Ephesians 4:11-13

$\mathcal{D}$orothea Matthews Dooling, writing about "The Inner Fami-ly," suggests that you have an inner "community" that is not unlike your outer community. Your inner community is made up of your different roles and abilities, whether actual or potential, just as your outer community is made up of people with different gifts and graces. As you relate to members of your outer community, your inner members receive the nurturing they need. Then, as your inner members grow and mature, your entire spirit thrives like never before.

Let's think about the scripture passage in this light. Just as your community's "apostles, prophets, evangelists, pastors, and teachers" serve God, they also serve your spirit. They help to nurture your own inner capacities. From the apostles you learn to venture out in mission and service; from the prophets, to receive divine inspiration; from the evangelists, to bear good news; from the pastors, to give comfort and counsel; from the teachers, to guide and instruct, and so on. And, to the extent that these members of your community work together for the common good, your own inner members become coordinated. Gradually, then, your spirit matures into the "measure of the full stature of Christ."

Think about how some of your inner capacities have been cultivated through the years as you have watched and worked with others. Also, identify which of your abilities are currently being nurtured, and by whom. Then ask yourself how open you are to being taught by members of your outer community. Do you ever assume that you can't do something, simply because you have never tried it? Allow members of your outer community to help you tap into your own inner potentials. Let them help to nurture your spirit toward maturity.

Community nurtures me to maturity.

Day 328 I celebrate uniqueness as part of community.

What should be done then, my friends? When you come together, each one has a hymn, a lesson, a revelation, a tongue, or an interpretation. Let all things be done for building up.

—1 Corinthians 14:26

*I*nstead of trying to make everyone like everybody else, true community celebrates "uniqueness." It honors whatever it is that makes a person who he is instead of somebody else. The community *must* celebrate uniqueness, for at least two reasons. First, by doing so the community creates a safe environment in which people can open up and begin to share their lives. Its members aren't so afraid to express themselves when they know that their personalities, abilities, backgrounds, beliefs, and so on, will be genuinely welcomed and appreciated. And then, in celebrating uniqueness the community can mature. The many different people in its midst challenge its mind to be more open, its heart to be more tender, and its spirit to be more whole.

To sum up, then, true community sees uniqueness as *essential* to the well-being of its members and to the development of its own spirit.

Make a list of your unique qualities, abilities, beliefs, and so on, as many as you can think of. Recognize even those parts of yourself that you have been afraid to reveal to others, because you thought that no one would understand. Celebrate that these are part of who God has created you to be.

Now identify a community to which you belong, and list the differences among its members. Think in terms of obvious dissimilarities, such as age, race, class, and lifestyle. Then think in terms of more subtle differences, in terms of people's skills, talents, temperaments, and interests. A community must appreciate the uniqueness of its members in order to grow spiritually. Commit yourself to celebrating the differences that enrich your community's life!

I celebrate uniqueness as part of community.

Day 329   Uniqueness is of the Spirit.

To each is given the manifestation of the Spirit for the common good.

—1 Corinthians 12:7

*T*here is a third reason why the community must celebrate uniqueness. This is the most fundamental reason of all: Uniqueness exists because God creates it.

We have been rather slow to catch on to this fact. If you were to look up "unique" in a book of synonyms, you would find that the English language regards it as a very *lonely* thing to be. To be a unique person is to be solitary, alone, peerless, matchless, and in a class by yourself. Furthermore, "unique" is a *next-to-impossible* thing to be. To qualify, you have to be unequaled, unparalleled, unheard of, unrivaled, unsurpassed, and second to none (which may also have something to do with the loneliness part). Finally, "unique" is a very *strange* thing to be. People might otherwise describe you as peculiar, odd, far-out, and weird.

Perhaps now it is obvious why a book of synonyms is not regarded as scripture (and why English is not the official language of the Spirit)! You might say that, in scripture, the only synonym for unique is "Spirit-filled." And when you are unique in true community, you are never alone; you are forever honored for being second to none; and, you can always be just as strange as the Spirit inspires you to be.

Choose at least one way that you can celebrate your uniqueness in the coming week. For example, you might do something that you really like to do even though others might not understand. In addition, find a way this week to honor the uniqueness of someone else, such as buying a card that somehow reflects who that person is, writing a note inside, and sending it.

Remember: true community celebrates uniqueness. In this way it creates an environment in which people from all walks of life can feel safe, it challenges itself to grow spiritually, and it rejoices in the amazing diversity of God's creation.

Uniqueness is of the Spirit.

Day 330   # I am of the Spirit.

When he had said this, he breathed on [the disciples] and said to them, "Receive the Holy Spirit."

—*John 20:22*

*H*ave you ever seen a little child holding his breath in the midst of a temper tantrum? He may do it for a little while in an attempt to get his way or to scare his parents. But soon he is gasping for air. If he were able to hold his breath long enough, he would pass out, and the first reflex of his body would be to begin breathing again. We cannot live without the gift of breath.

In the same way, we cannot live in the spiritual sense without the gift of the Spirit. But we do not need to worry, because the Spirit of God is always available to us. In fact, it is a part of us, and we are a part of it. It has been breathed into us from the very beginning of creation. Filled with the breath of life, we are truly of the Spirit.

Even as the Spirit gives us the breath of life, we can offer this gift to others. We have been placed in this particular time and space just so that we can pass on the Spirit's breath to the people we meet on our journeys. We can let them know that they, too, are alive in the Spirit. Because breath and wind are very much alike, the wind has become a traditional symbol for the Spirit. So find a way today to celebrate the power of the wind. Fly a kite. Observe a flag or banner blowing in the breeze. Locate some bubble-blowing solution and watch the wind take your bubbles up and away. Listen to a windchime. However you choose to experience the power of the wind, be reminded that the Spirit comes to you continually, giving you the breath of life.

I am of the Spirit.

Day 331   **The Spirit is with me forever.**

"If you love me, you will keep my commandments. And I will ask the Father, and he will give you another Advocate, to be with you forever. This is the Spirit of truth, whom the world cannot receive, because it neither sees him nor knows him. You know him, because he abides with you, and he will be in you."

—John 14:15-17

*A*ccording to today's scripture passage, the Spirit of truth will never leave us. It is with us forever. It abides with us. It is *in* us.

The Spirit joins us to one another. It joins our individual spirits so powerfully that our relationships can survive separation by long distances or periods of time. In fact, our relationships can even survive our dying. The Spirit, which is with us always, makes it possible for us to be together forever. It allows us to abide with one another for as long as love endures.

There was a lady named Sarah whose life was the epitome of generosity. She would often invite many of her friends to join her for dinner at a nearby restaurant after Sunday morning worship, and she would delight in picking up the bill. She would also predict her income and expenses for the year, then give away the always substantial difference. She died in the same way that she had lived, bequeathing her home to the church as a new parsonage. Today, years after her death, her friends still associate her with the word "generous." Whenever they see someone being especially big-hearted and open-handed, they think of her. Because the Holy Spirit abides, Sarah's spirit is still very much alive and well among those who knew her.

Do you have a friend who is no longer with you—perhaps

someone who has moved away or died? Find two chairs and place them near each other. Sit down in one of them and relax. Close your eyes and refresh your memory of the friend that you miss. What would you say were the person's most unique character traits? What did you appreciate most about your relationship? Now imagine that your friend is sitting in the chair beside you. Allow time for your friend's image to become strong in your mind. When it is, begin to talk with your friend. Keep your eyes closed, if that is helpful. If there are things that you wanted to say but never had the chance, say them now. If there are things that you need to explain or clear up, speak the truth, knowing that, through the Spirit, your friend hears and understands.

If you need to hear from your friend, you might want to ask a question and then get up and sit in the other chair. Reflect a moment on how your friend might think or feel; then create an answer to your question. Continue this process until you feel satisfied that you have touched base with one that you loved. Give thanks to God that the spirit of your loved one is always available to you. Give thanks to God that the Holy Spirit is always with you, joining you to others. Remember that all of us are united in one spirit—the Spirit of God.

The Spirit is with me forever.

Day 332   The Spirit is always at work in me.

For it is God who is at work in you, enabling you both to will and to work for his good pleasure.

—*Philippians 2:13*

The force of gravity is always at work in our lives. We may not be able to see gravity, but we can certainly see its effects. Just try to defy it. Do your best to jump off the surface of this earth. (If you come back down again, give it another try!) See if you can throw something so high into the air that it will not return to the earth. Try to place an object out in the empty space in front of you without it crashing to the ground.

Gravity is a powerful force. Without it, life as we know it would not be possible. The same is true for the Spirit of God. It is ever-present and ever hard at work in our lives. And, even as gravity pulls us back to the earth, the Spirit draws us back to our center. In fact, the Spirit *is* our center. When we move away from it, its power begins to work on us, drawing us back into right relationship with God. As we allow the Spirit to work in our lives, we begin to see evidences or "fruits" of the Spirit.

Use the following chart to indicate where you are in your experience of the nine fruits of the Spirit (see Galatians 5:22-23a). Mark on each line where you find yourself right now. Let the center represent a full expression of the fruit. The further you are from the center, the less you are expressing the fruit in your life.

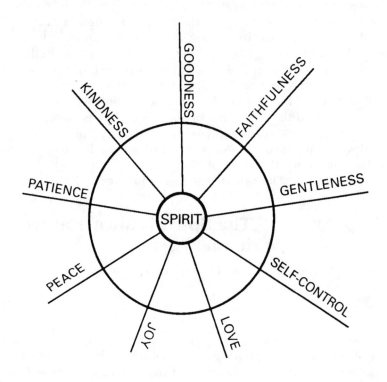

Conclude this exercise with a prayer of thanksgiving for the power of the Spirit at work in your life.

The Spirit is always at work in me.

     # The Spirit corrects me.

All who obey his commandments abide in him, and he abides in them. And by this we know that he abides in us, by the Spirit that he has given us.

—1 John 3:24

*T*o keep a car on the road you must continuously adjust the steering wheel. Curves, turns, bumps, obstacles in the road, other vehicles—all require you to adjust the wheel so that your car remains headed in the right direction.

The Spirit of God is constantly adjusting us, too, to keep us headed where we are supposed to go. Sometimes the Spirit sends a friend with a challenge that will strengthen us, or with an affirmation that will encourage us. Sometimes it tries to redirect our journey if we have gotten off track. Sometimes it stops us dead in our tracks when we need to evaluate where we are or reflect on where we have been. Constantly the Spirit works to keep us moving on our journeys and to help us maintain a healthy balance in our lives as we go.

Take a moment to examine the progress that you have made recently on your spiritual journey. Notice those ways in which the Spirit has corrected your path. For example, at some point you may have been stopped long enough to ask some important question about your life. Could this have been a time when the Spirit was asking you to make a correction in your path? When you have reviewed your progress, enter an attitude of prayer. Ask where you might need to make some adjustments in your schedule, your attitude, or your behavior right now in order to live more consistently with the will of God for your life. Make at least one of these necessary "corrections" as soon as possible.

The Spirit corrects me.

     # The Spirit prompts me.

The Spirit of the Lord GOD is upon me, because the LORD has anointed me; he has sent me to bring good news to the oppressed, to bind up the brokenhearted, to proclaim liberty to the captives, and release to the prisoners.

—Isaiah 61:1

$\mathscr{A}$bby was walking past the telephone when the name "Steve" popped into her mind. Having experienced these kinds of promptings many times before, she knew enough to pay attention to them. She picked up the phone and dialed his work number. He answered on the first ring. As "luck" would have it, she had caught him in the few moments that he had free between two high-powered, stressful meetings. He was sitting at his desk, feeling entirely overwhelmed by the demands of his job. Then the phone rang. After a brief conversation with Abby, he had regained the courage that he needed for the next meeting. What if Abby had not followed the prompting of the Spirit?

A young minister was on his way to visit some folks in the hospital. His mind was preoccupied with what might happen there. But as he drove past the farmhouse of an elderly couple who were members of his parish, something told him to stop. At first he resisted. He had just visited them the previous week. But he pulled his car into their driveway anyway, almost without realizing what he was doing. During his visit with the couple, it became apparent that they were quite discouraged about the health of the husband, who had recently been dismissed from the hospital. Closing their time together with a prayer for courage, the minister knew why he had stopped. And the reason became even more clear later in the day, when he got the phone call informing him that the elderly man had died. What if this minister had not followed the prompting of the Spirit?

In each of these stories and in today's scripture, the Spirit prompted someone to be in service to others. What does the Spirit have in mind for you today?

Take time for a meditation. Allow yourself to completely relax. Let go of anything that is preoccupying your mind. Center all your thoughts on the Spirit of God. Now, think of yourself as an empty vessel being gradually filled with the power of God. Feel yourself becoming more and more in tune with God's will for your life. Now, ask God what it is that you need to do next. God may want you to take a little step or a big leap of faith. You will know when the answer comes. Wait until you understand what God wants you to do. Be reassured that the Spirit will equip you to do anything that is asked of you.

The Spirit prompts me.

Day 335 The Spirit expands my world.

"But you will receive power when the Holy Spirit has come upon you; and you will be my witnesses in Jerusalem, in all Judea and Samaria, and to the ends of the earth."

—Acts 1:8

*M*ike and Betty were caught up in the endless acquisition of the things of this earth. And they had done a pretty good job of it! Mike had his own company and had built it up to a point that the return on his investment was substantial. Betty had established herself as one of the city's most successful dealers of fine ladies' wear. They both had it made, and they had all the trappings to prove it. But life somehow seemed empty.

Ernesto, one of their friends, was active in a volunteer mission organization that was ready to respond at a moment's notice to any disaster that might happen anywhere in the world. After a flood caused considerable damage in a neighboring state, Ernesto invited Mike and Betty to accompany him on a weekend clean-up mission. They reluctantly agreed to go. However, upon their return a few days later, they noticed that their thoughts kept going back to the site where they had been helping others recover from the devastation that had hit them. The next weekend, they went back to help again. Gradually, they found themselves spending more and more weekends going wherever they were needed. Then the weekends turned into weeks. They found increasing opportunities to use their God-given gifts and skills to help others. Their world expanded far beyond their businesses and their life of material acquisition. And, as their concern shifted from their own desires to the needs of others, their emptiness was filled.

Find a balloon that has not been inflated and a permanent magic marker. Write "agape" on the balloon. Carefully note the size of the word. Now, inflate the balloon as much as possible without it breaking. Look at the word again. The love that you have received from God has grown. So, too, will the world with which you share it.

The Spirit expands my world.

Day 336 The Spirit transforms my world.

I will give them one heart, and put a new spirit within them; I will remove the heart of stone from their flesh and give them a heart of flesh.

—Ezekiel 11:19

$\mathcal{V}$incent was the most difficult man in the community. He never had a good word to say about anyone. It seemed that, at one time or another, everyone had done something to anger him—even the church, which he had flatly refused to attend for many years. The only person who ever spent time with Vincent was his soft-spoken wife. And, when he finally died, a bitter and angry old man, his funeral was attended only by his wife, the minister, and the funeral director. Vincent lived and died with a heart of stone.

Pete, on the other hand, experienced a change of heart before it was too late. He had spent all of his working days as a hard-nosed businessman. No one pulled anything over on him. He demanded perfection from his workers and when he didn't get it, he fired them. Then a heart attack landed him flat on his back in the hospital. Though he insisted on getting "back at it" as soon as possible, his doctors had other plans. They prescribed days of quiet, weeks of rest, and months of taking it easy. Pete was beside himself. But, as his days of confinement stretched into weeks and months, the Spirit began to transform him. His attitude began to change. He softened. He made fewer and fewer demands on the nurses. He stopped trying to run his business from a distance. His family noticed a gentler and kinder person during their visits. When he finally returned to work, his employees were shocked. Their boss was treating them like human beings. In fact, he seemed more like a friend than a boss. His heart of stone had been turned into a heart of flesh.

On a sheet of paper, write down ways in which your heart is hard right now. Is there, for example, someone toward whom you feel resentment, or an issue about which you can feel only anger? Is there a "gripe" that you have? Is there a situation in which you are feeling stubborn or defeated? Take your time. Be honest. Be specific. In what ways is your heart like a stone?

Now, how might your heart of stone be transformed into a heart of flesh? Identify specific things that you might do to soften your hardness of heart; jot these down. To soften does not mean to become weak. It means to become authentically powerful. Authentic power is the power of *agape*. It is power by which you bring together instead of set apart, by which you create new possibilities instead of destroying all hope.

Once you have set your intention to change, begin to do what you can to create change. Choose one thing from your list that you can do today to soften your hardness of heart. Open your heart to the Spirit, that both you and your world may be transformed.

The Spirit transforms my world.

Day 337 The Spirit heals my world.

Then the eyes of the blind shall be opened, and the ears of the deaf unstopped; then the lame shall leap like a deer, and the tongue of the speechless sing for joy. For waters shall break forth in the wilderness, and streams in the desert.

—Isaiah 35:5-6

*W*hat a glorious, hopeful vision Isaiah gives us of a world healed by God! It is a world that we catch glimpses of daily. It is a world that, with each passing hour, we help to bring into existence.

Quiet yourself, preparing to enter meditative prayer. Take time to relax your body. When you are fully centered in God, allow this scene to unfold:

You are standing in a high place looking down on a desert wilderness. Everywhere there is sand, rock formations, boulders, and sun-bleached animal bones. There appears to be no life at all in the barren scene, not even a small cactus or armadillo. What does it feel like to be here?

Now your ears begin to detect a distant sound. You listen closely. Soon you recognize it as the sound of ocean surf rolling into shore. "That's not possible," you think, "not here in this desert!" But there, far off on the eastern horizon, you can see movement. Beautiful waves of water are slowly rolling in. Standing in your high place, you are not afraid. Rather, you are amazed. You watch the waters move quietly across the land, gently rising and falling. What do you hear? What do you feel through the soles of your feet?

Finally the waters have covered the land. The rich blue "sea" shimmers brilliantly in the sunlight, for as far as your eye can see. It is not deep; it is not overwhelming. Somehow you know that these are the waters of rebirth, come to heal the dead land. They have been sent by the Spirit. Give thanks to God.

After some time has passed, the waters begin to recede. Their

335

healing work is done. Look out over the landscape. How have the healing waters transformed the wilderness? Carry this vision with you as a gift, and remember:

The Spirit heals my world.

Day 338 **Healing surprises me.**

Three times I appealed to the Lord about this, that it would leave me, but he said to me, "My grace is sufficient for you, for power is made perfect in weakness."

—*2 Corinthians 12:8-9a*

*H*ow many times have you said, aloud or to yourself, "I wish this problem would just go away"? Well, then, you know exactly how Paul felt. No one is sure what Paul's "thorn in the flesh" (12:7) actually was. But whether it was a physical problem or a controversy in the church, he had finally had enough of it. He wanted to be rid of it. He said as much to God, over and over again. And, surprise! He never did get rid of it, so far as we know. But he *was* healed. The Spirit transformed his mind. He came to accept rather than resent that thorn in his flesh. He even began to learn from it.

One spring Cathy decided that, for the first time ever, she would put out a garden. The problem was, she knew absolutely nothing about preparing soil, planting seeds, tending plants, or harvesting produce. In other words, as a gardener she was more "green" than "green-thumbed." She was at a loss as to how to begin. Then one morning Jeanette, an elderly neighbor, stopped by. "A friend just gave me some tomato plants," Jeanette told Cathy, "but I don't think I'm up to gardening this year. Could you use them?" Cathy gratefully accepted Jeanette's offer, then confessed that she didn't know the first thing about raising tomatoes. Could Jeanette give her some tips? The eighty-eight-year-old laughed, and there began their unexpected but beautiful partnership. All during that growing season Jeanette taught Cathy everything she knew about gardening. At the same time, Cathy helped Jeanette realize that, despite the frailty of her body, she still had something to offer. Both women became more whole as a result of their sharing.

As soon as possible, have an older person teach you something that he or she knows how to do but perhaps can no longer do. Or, if *you* are that older person, volunteer to teach someone else something you know. Whichever the case, let the passing on of knowledge be a surprising form of healing. Let the grace of the elder bless the younger, that both of you might become stronger, even in your weaknesses.

Healing surprises me.

Day 339   I am a healer.

"Cure the sick, raise the dead, cleanse the lepers, cast out demons. You received without payment; give without payment."

—*Matthew 10:8*

*W*hen you have the mind of Christ, healing is not something you opt to do. It is something you exist to do. It becomes a vital part of your identity. It becomes who you are. Can an apple not be an apple? Can the sea not be the sea? Of course not. Can a child of God not be a child of God? No way. And to be a child of God is to be a healer. So, be who you are, just as naturally as an apple is an apple and the sea is the sea.

To heal is to promote wellness and restore wholeness. As the scripture text implies, healing takes a variety of forms. "Cure the sick" points to physical healing. "Raise the dead" indicates spiritual healing. "Cleanse the lepers" relates to social healing (lepers, as you may recall, were social outcasts). Finally, "cast out demons" suggests emotional or psychological healing.

God has not left all the work of healing to the specialists (doctors, ministers, social workers, psychologists, and so on). Far from it. That task has been given to us all. You have probably already been working as a healer, without giving it that name. For example, you may have helped nurse a child through an illness (physical healing). You may have taken a recently widowed parent on a trip to the mountains, to reconnect with nature and God (spiritual healing). You may have challenged an unjust policy in your workplace (social healing). Or, you may have prayed regularly for a woman trapped in a cycle of domestic abuse (psychological healing), and so on.

List a number of ways that you have served as a healer, whether in the physical, spiritual, social, or emotional/psychological sense. You may be surprised at just how much healing work you have done. What kind(s) of healing do you think you are especially good at? How might you improve your healing abilities?

I am a healer.

I offer the gift of healing.

And a man lame from birth was being carried in. People would lay him daily at the gate of the temple called the Beautiful Gate so that he could ask for alms from those entering the temple. . . . But Peter said, "I have no silver or gold, but what I have I give you; in the name of Jesus Christ of Nazareth, stand up and walk."

—*Acts 3:2, 6*

This story of healing is notable in at least two ways. First of all, Peter healed the man's lameness instead of giving him money like everybody else did. In other words, Peter addressed the root cause of the man's suffering instead of the secondary cause, which was the poverty resulting from his disability. And second, by choosing to heal the man, Peter did far more than anyone would have expected. Having no money, he could have walked right on by, and no one, not even the lame man himself, would have bothered to notice. Almsgiving was optional. But Peter didn't use that excuse. Instead, he gave to the man all that he had—the healing power of Christ.

You might say that the crowd was in something of a charity rut. It happens all the time. We get used to only tossing some money at a problem, just enough to keep things as they are. Or, we get used to only giving away the clothes and toys that we don't want anymore. Or, we get used to only feeding the homeless only during the holidays. Or, we get used to only sending a card when someone is sick, or to only fixing a casserole when somebody dies.

It isn't that doing any of these things is wrong. Sometimes we can do nothing more. But when we do these things just because they are customary for us, and convenient, and safe, and because they are what we *assume* someone needs, then chances are, we are in a charity rut. The Spirit is capable of doing far more through us, if we will let it. Like Peter, then, we must watch for opportunities to heal. We must be ready to tap into the power of Christ in any way necessary. Whenever possible, we must address the root causes rather than the secondary causes of suffering. And, most importantly, we must be prepared to do more than what others may expect of us—more than what we may expect of ourselves.

Identify one charity rut that you are in right now. Specify one or two ways that you might get out of it. For example, if you and other members of your community are in the habit of collecting food for Thanksgiving baskets for low-income families, you might consider starting an ongoing food pantry. Or, if you send regular checks to the Cancer Society, you might think about volunteering to work with cancer patients at a local hospice. Push yourself to offer God's healing in a new way.

I offer the gift of healing.

Day 341   **I offer healing to all.**

Then Jesus called the twelve together and gave them power and authority over all demons and to cure diseases, and he sent them out to proclaim the kingdom of God and to heal.

—*Luke 9:1-2*

We are sent into the world to heal, just as we are sent into the world to forgive. This is our divinely appointed mission. This is who we are. We offer healing to everyone, for their sake and for God's.

Take some time to scan the lessons of the last few days. Think about what these have taught you about healing. Also reflect on what you have learned from your own life experience and observations. Now, on the basis of your current understandings and beliefs, write a healing mission statement for yourself. God is sending you forth into the world to heal. Express your commitment to this divinely-appointed mission. In what ways are you ready to heal? Be as direct or as poetic as you would like, but let the statement you create serve as both a promise to God and a challenge to yourself. Put it somewhere that you will see it often.

I offer healing to all.

Day 342   **There are no limits on my healing.**

When he entered Capernaum, a centurion came to him, appealing to him and saying, "Lord, my servant is lying at home paralyzed, in terrible distress." And he said to him, "I will come and cure him." The centurion answered, "Lord, I am not worthy to have you come under my roof; but only speak the word, and my servant will be healed." And to the centurion Jesus said, "Go; let it be done for you according to your faith." And the servant was healed in that hour.

—Matthew 8:5-8, 13

*J*ust think how this story might have gone if the centurion had said, "So, my servant is sick. Too bad. If he dies, I'll buy another." Or, suppose that, deciding to save his servant's life, he had refused to go to Jesus, saying, "Why should I ask a homeless, dirty, Jewish magician for help?" Or, suppose that when he came to Jesus, Jesus had laughed and said, "Forget it! Why would I want to help *you*, a Roman soldier, an enemy of my people?"

Healing brings wholeness to what is broken, whether that brokenness is physical, spiritual, social, or psychological. If we allow our prejudices and assumptions to limit either our belief in healing or our willingness to heal, it will be hard for healing to happen. The healing power of God can be limited only by ourselves. Nothing else can stand in the way of it—not race, religion, nationality, class or gender, not even distance between the healer and the person needing healing—unless, by the smallness of our faith, we let something get in the way.

One of the most common limits on our belief in healing and our willingness to heal is our lack of respect for our own healing knowledge. You yourself probably have considerable healing experience, as you discovered on Day 339. What if each of us shared our best advice for different kinds of healing? What a magnificent wealth of healing knowledge the world would have!

Identify one of your favorite healing tips. For example, it may be a remedy for cold symptoms (physical). It may be an uplifting place to visit when life seems meaningless (spiritual). It may be a strategy to feed the hungry children in your neighborhood (social). It may be a way to ward off depression (psychological). Once you have your specific healing tip in mind, write it down and send it to at least five people of your acquaintance who are as different as possible from one another. Both you and they will benefit from your sharing.

There are no limits on my healing.

I am healed in community.

Therefore confess your sins to one another, and pray for one another, so that you may be healed. The prayer of the righteous is powerful and effective.

—James 5:16

*I*nmates in prisons around the world are punished by being placed in solitary confinement. How strange it is that so many of us who are perfectly free would volunteer for the same punishment, choosing to be completely solitary when we are in pain. Maybe we are too proud or too afraid, too embarrassed or too private to share our problems with at least one trusted friend or relative. Yet sharing may sometimes be exactly what we need in order to experience healing.

How open are you to being healed in community? Check the situations below in which you would seek support from at least one trusted friend:

_____ When deciding whether or not to commit to a relationship

_____ When concerned about the direction your career is taking

_____ When you have urgent questions about a moral issue

_____ When facing a problem with your mental health (e.g., depression)

_____ When someone close to you has a mental health problem

_____ When you are struggling with an addictive behavior, such as eating, drinking, spending, or gambling too much

_____ When someone close to you is struggling with addiction

_____ When concerned about your aging parents

_____ When confronting a health problem

_____ When someone close to you is facing a health problem

_____ When worrying about your education or training

_____ When doubting God or questioning your faith

_____ When dealing with a problem in your workplace

_____ When faced with a parenting issue

_____ When beset by legal difficulties
_____ When someone close to you has legal difficulties
_____ When your relationship with your "significant other"
is suffering
_____ When dealing with financial difficulties

Now reflect on what you have marked. How did you decide what you would and wouldn't share? Remember, talking to just one other person might sometimes help to alleviate your loneliness and pain during a period of struggle. Try to hold this possibility open, even though you may not always choose to act on it.
I am healed in community.

Day 344 The community is radiant.

Arise, shine; for your light has come, and the glory of the LORD has risen upon you. For darkness shall cover the earth, and thick darkness the peoples; but the LORD will arise upon you, and his glory will appear over you. Nations shall come to your light, and kings to the brightness of your dawn.

—Isaiah 60:1-3

*D*ave had not been in worship for a long time. In fact, he had not found a new church home since moving to the city several months before. Now he had received word that his aging mother was in the hospital and not doing well. Just now, he needed the comfort and encouragement of a caring community. He had noticed a church a mile from his home that he thought was of his denomination. He would go there. As he pulled into the parking lot that Sunday morning, he observed that it was full of cars. A good sign. This must be an alive and active congregation. He was met at the front door by greeters who welcomed him and oriented him to the building. Then, at the door of the sanctuary he was met by an usher, who showed him to a vacant seat. Dave glanced at the order of worship in the bulletin. Much to his surprise, this congregation belonged to a different denomination than he had thought.

Early in the service, there was a time of informal sharing of joys and concerns. Dave found himself on his feet sharing his worries about his mother. The pastor led the congregation in prayer for her. After the service, several people promised Dave that they would continue to remember his mother in their prayers. Dave felt like he had found his church home. He hadn't ended up where he had expected, but this was definitely the right church for him.

When the community genuinely cares for its members, it becomes a radiant and attractive community. When each person can bring his or her own needs and joys and hurts and be genuinely understood and accepted, then the community is being what God wants and needs it to be. It becomes a light that draws people in.

You are part of a community where you feel like you really belong. It might be a church, a support group, a Sunday school class, or a friendship circle. Wherever it is, celebrate that you are part of a caring community that is a light in your life. Have you recently invited another person, who desperately needs support, to join your group? If not, do so today.

The community is radiant.

Day 345 **The community is more that it knows.**

Then Amos answered Amaziah, "I am no prophet, nor a prophet's son; but I am a herdsman, and a dresser of sycamore trees, and the LORD took me from following the flock, and the LORD said to me, 'Go prophesy to my people Israel.'"

—*Amos 7:14-15*

*T*he adult Sunday school class had been together for years. Its members were very clear about its priorities. Number One was donuts and coffee. Number Two was fellowship, catching up on what was happening in everyone's life. Number Three was support, a willingness to be there for one another when needed. And Number Four was study, if any time remained after Numbers One through Three were accomplished. The class was a fairly light-hearted bunch of people—until Kim's cancer was diagnosed.

Kim, a long-term member of the class, had three young children and an adoring husband. When she found out that she had cancer and had only a short time to live, she turned to the group for support. They didn't let her down. They were there for her each step of the way, cleaning her house, planting a garden, offering child care, and providing meals.

The group was transformed as its members struggled together to understand Kim's illness. They began to ask deep and probing questions about life and its purpose, about death and its meaning. They felt an urgent need to learn all that they could in order to be more supportive of Kim. Through the months of her dying, their faith grew in ways that they could never have imagined possible. They also grew closer to one another and more committed to their shared spiritual journey.

Take time to write a purpose statement for one of the groups to which you belong. In it, state what you see to be the primary goal of the group. Why are its members together? Now, think about your own reasons for being a part of the group. Ask what God might have in mind for it. What additional needs might the group be able to meet? Finally, revise your purpose statement. Expand it in line with your reflections. In your mind and heart, challenge your community to be more than it knows.

The community is more than it knows.

Day 346 The community can do more than it knows.

Every generous act of giving, with every perfect gift, is from above, coming down from the Father of lights, with whom there is no variation or shadow due to change.

—*James 1:17*

*H*ave you ever witnessed an Amish barn-raising? It is a sight to behold. Entire families arrive in horse-drawn buggies from many miles in every direction. Then, almost by instinct, each person begins to perform a needed task. The women gather in the kitchen of the farmhouse to prepare the food that will be required for the day. The children gather in the yard and play their simple games, staying out of the way. The men pick up their hammers and saws and begin to assemble the walls that are soon lifted into place to become the framework for the barn. With dozens of people working efficiently and joyfully together, the barn is completed—in one day.

A local congregation had an annual operating budget of $500,000. It was always struggling to meet the budget. One day the stewardship chairperson decided to estimate the congregation's "giving potential." She guessed at the average income per household. Then she took ten percent of that figure and multiplied it by the total number of households in the congregation. The result of her calculations showed that, if each household tithed 10 percent of its income (the biblical standard for giving), the church's annual budget would be $5,000,000—ten times the current budget! She could hardly begin to imagine what the congregation could accomplish if every household faithfully tithed.

Go to a group to which you belong and really challenge them. Ask them to accept a new goal that would stretch the potential of the group. You might want to have several suggestions ready for the group. Allow others to offer ideas as well. Be sure that the goal would move the group beyond where it is presently. Believe that God will give the group all that it needs to accomplish the new goal. Step out in faith, because . . .

The community can do more than it knows.

Day 347 God knows the community's potential.

Now the word of the LORD came to me saying, "Before I formed you in the womb I knew you, and before you were born I consecrated you; I appointed you a prophet to the nations." Then I said, "Ah, Lord GOD! Truly I do not know how to speak, for I am only a boy." But the LORD said to me, "Do not say, 'I am only a boy'; for you shall go to all to whom I send you, and you shall speak whatever I command you, Do not be afraid of them, for I am with you to deliver you, says the LORD."

—*Jeremiah 1:4-8*

"We have always done it this way!" These are the seven last words of a community. When a group gets locked into thinking that things can only be done in the same ways as they have been done in the past, it is ensuring its own demise.

Think about the word "potential" for a moment. Believing in potential involves faith. It is seeing what is not yet there, trusting in what can one day be. Perhaps the seven everlasting words of a community should be, "Shall we try this a new way?"

In today's scripture passage Jeremiah is being called by God to be a prophet. He objects, pointing out that he is only a boy. Besides, he is not a good speaker. How could he ever speak for

God? God's reply indicates that there is much more to Jeremiah than is apparent. God sees his potential and knows that he will be able to do more than he could possibly imagine. When Jeremiah consents to becoming a messenger for God, mighty things happen. In fact, he eventually becomes one of the greatest Old Testament prophets.

Jeremiah had to get past his excuses. He had to get past his usual way of looking at things, his usual way of doing things. The same is true of our community. If we say that we are too small, do not have enough resources, or are unwilling to change in order to handle the challenges that come our way, then we will live down to our expectations. But if we understand that God will supply every need as we attempt to meet the challenges that come to us, we will begin to live up to our potential.

The following meditation can be done individually or in a group. In a comfortable posture, allow yourself to completely relax. Think of a community to which you belong. See it conducting its usual activities. Now, fast-forward five years into the future, imagining that all its limitations are falling away. Now pause the picture. See what the group is like and what it might be doing. Pretend that you are describing these activities to a friend. What would they be? What is your community's potential?

God knows the community's potential.

Day 348 The community's potential is unlimited.

And God heard the voice of [Ishmael]; and the angel of God called to Hagar from heaven, and said to her, "What troubles you, Hagar? Do not be afraid; for God has heard the voice of the boy where he is. Come, lift up the boy and hold him fast with your hand, for I will make a great nation of him."

—*Genesis 21:17-18*

*C*orrita had been teaching the preschool Sunday school class for over twenty years. It was obvious that she loved the children and that they loved her. Once, when asked how she began as a teacher, she recalled that one Sunday the regular teacher had not shown up, and she was asked to "stay with the children" for just that morning.

She enjoyed it so much that she never left. When the church wanted to recognize her for the important work that she was doing, she discounted it as "no big thing." But it *was* a big thing. If on the average twenty different children had been in her class each year, that would mean that over 400 children had benefitted from her years of teaching. And this number only represents the children with whom she had direct contact. Add to that number all the people touched by those children whom she inspired to reach out. And add to that number all the adults she inspired to take leadership in working with little children. One person's willingness to share her time and her love was unlimited in its potential.

Sometimes our potential is limited only by our thinking. Where Hagar saw only the boy of a servant, God saw the father of a great nation. Where Corrita saw only a Sunday school teacher, God saw a wonder-worker. Perhaps we need to see with God's vision rather than our own. If we faithfully follow the leadership of the Spirit, our individual and community potential will be realized in endless ways.

The following exercise would be especially fun as an outdoor group activity. Locate some drinking straws, string, dishwashing liquid, and a flat pan. Cut one straw into four equal pieces. Throw two pieces away, then thread a piece of string about eight inches long through the remaining two. Tie the ends of the string together. After mixing some soap and water in the pan, place the string-and-straw device in the solution. Stretch it into a rectangle. Then grasp a piece of the straw in each hand and gently lift the rectangle out of the water. Move it slowly through the air, creating a beautiful bubble. Watch it float in the wind. If you would like, make more bubble devices using larger pieces of straw and string. You will be amazed at how large a bubble you can create. Experienced bubble blowers are able to produce bubbles large enough for a person to step inside. The possibilities are unlimited.

The community's potential is unlimited.

Day 349   God works miracles.

Then the angel of the LORD appeared to him in a flame of fire out of a bush; he looked, and the bush was blazing, yet it was not consumed.

—Exodus 3:2

*W*hat a story! A bush that burns but is not consumed! And the voice of God coming from the bush! These things don't happen just every day. Or do they?

Nell was terrified. She had awakened to find a tablet of writing at her bedside. It was filled with inspiring poetry. She could not understand how it could have gotten there. She recognized the tablet—she had placed it on her nightstand to record her dreams—but she didn't recognize the penmanship. For days, she was troubled by this mysterious writing. Then, three weeks later, it happened again. Unable to keep her mind on other things, she went to talk to her pastor. He did not seem to be upset by her story. He asked if she had heard of automatic writing. She had not. Then he shared with her the stories of saints of the church, and of personal friends of his, who had experienced this same phenomenon. It was a divine communication. When Nell became aware that she was not alone in this experience and that it was nothing to be feared, she relaxed. She began to read the poetry for the sake of its message, and was surprised to find great comfort in it. Gradually she shared the poetry with others. Eventually she published it in an inspirational book.

Don was distraught over the death of his wife. They had shared fifty-three years together, the last thirty-eight of them in the same house. He wondered how he could go on living without her. One day, he was sitting in his favorite chair by the patio door. Seeing his wife's empty chair beside him, he felt overcome with loneliness and grief. Nearly every evening, the two of them had sat together and watched the birds come to the birdfeeder on the patio. Nothing had seemed to please his wife more. Now, as he sat there filled with despair, Don noticed a large yellow bird come and perch on the feeder. He knew a lot about birds, but he had never seen a bird like this one before. It seemed to be staring at him, almost as if it had a message for him. Suddenly, he felt a deep sense of peace well up in him. He felt as if his wife were with him again. It amazed him, this transformation of feeling. He looked closer at the strange bird. With a nod of its head, it flew straight up into the air. The bird never again returned, but the sense of peace stayed with him always.

Are you open to regarding Nell and Don's experiences as miracles from God? Are you open to God coming to you in miraculous ways?

God works miracles.

Day 350   **God wins.**

What then are we to say about these things? If God is for us, who is
against us?

—Romans 8:31

*D*o you recall those childhood days in gym class when teams
were being selected? If you were athletic, you would be picked
early in the process. If you were not, you would probably try to
disappear from the scene. The team that got the fastest runners
or highest jumpers would inevitably win. The other team had little hope. Often one terrific player made all the difference. Whatever team that player ended up on would surely win.

Sometimes we approach life as if we were still in gym class.
We think that if we can just get God to play on our team, we will
surely win. But this is just the opposite of what it takes to assure
our spiritual success. Rather than trying to convince God to join
our team, we need to join God's team. When we do that, we are
assured of success, because we are offering our talents, time, and
abilities to the One who always wins. Playing on an invincible
team, who can stand against us?

Where are you struggling just now? Identify a situation in
which it seems like you will never win. Now, instead of asking
God to be on your team—to be available to do anything you
want—offer yourself as a member of God's team, to be used in
whichever way the Spirit deems best. Do so knowing that your
team will never lose.

God wins.

Day 351   **God makes peace possible.**

If it is possible, so far as it depends on you, live peaceably with all.

—Romans 12:18

*W*hat war would have ever been waged—between nations, cultures, families, or individuals—if each party, before shouldering
its weapon, had stopped and declared, "I will not participate in
this. So far as it depends on me, there will be peace today."

"That's an idealist's view of the world," you might observe.

No, it is the Spirit's view.

The Spirit asks that, in any conflict, we do three things. First, by our own actions and attitudes, we are to do the things that make for *shalom*, a just peace. Second, we are to give up our need to control the actions and attitudes of the other party. And third, we are to give up our need to control the outcome of the situation. We are responsible only for controlling ourselves and expressing *agape*. God will be working on the rest.

And God really does work wonders! For example, today in Vietnam there is a factory owned by a former officer in the South Vietnamese army. This man employs veterans of both the South and the North Vietnamese military forces in his assembly line. Together the veterans make scissors from old military scrap. The war years apparently forgotten, they work side by side to "turn swords into plowshares."

With God and humanity in partnership, peace *is* possible.

Write in response to these questions:

(1) You may remember a time when many of us labeled the former Soviet Union "the Evil Empire." Such labels dehumanize—even *demonize*—entire groups of people. They also encourage an "us vs. them" mentality, which is not the mind of Christ. Now, what group(s) of people do you, personally, consider "evil"?

(2) How does your viewing these people in this way take away their humanity?

(3) God makes peace possible by inspiring us to see one another with *agape*. When you look at your "evil empire" with the eyes of God's love, do you see something different from before?

God makes peace possible.

Day 352   **Peace sees the good in others.**

But we appeal to you, brothers and sisters, to respect those who labor among you, and have charge of you in the Lord and admonish you; esteem them very highly in love because of their work. Be at peace among yourselves.

—1 Thessalonians 5:12-13

*T*aking a sheet of paper with you, go and stand in front of a mirror. Hold the paper in front of the left half of your face. Study the right half of your face carefully. Now cover it and examine the left side. Do you notice any difference? Move the paper back and forth, comparing the impressions the two sides seem to give. Do you have different reactions to them?

If you are like most people, one side of your face will seem to be "lighter." It will communicate more warmth, openness, and joy. The other side will appear more serious, and maybe even a little foreboding. The two sides combine to create the total picture which others see.

Often when we are in conflict with other persons, we aren't seeing them clearly. We may be seeing only one side of them—their less attractive side. As today's scripture text implies, this is often the case when we enter into conflict with our leaders. Focusing only on their power, we may not see their vulnerability, for example. We may not see how their feelings are hurt by criticism. If we stop trying to look for their other side, we may behave toward them as if it doesn't exist. If our intention is peace, however, we work to perceive the good in others. Even if it is hard to find, we find it. We recognize the presence of God in our brothers and sisters. Therefore, even while we are aware of their flaws, we regard them with *agape*.

Identify one person of whom you have been seeing only "the bad side" lately. It could be anyone, from a national politician to a co-worker to a member of your friendship circle—even yourself. Spend some time trying to look at that person from the other side. See the good. May God grant you the total vision of a peacemaker.

Peace sees the good in others.

Day 353   **Peace is contagious.**

"Salt is good; but if salt has lost its saltiness, how can you season it? Have salt in yourselves, and be at peace with one another."

—*Mark 9:50*

*T*hink about salt for a minute:

- You need to have it to survive.
- It has the power to preserve.
- It makes you thirsty.
- It melts ice.
- It changes the flavor of food.
- Its flavor is strong; a little bit of it goes a long way.

Salt sounds suspiciously like peace, doesn't it? You need peace in order to survive. Peace has the power to preserve. Peace makes you thirsty—for the waters of righteousness. Peace melts icy hearts. Peace changes the flavor of things. And a little bit of peace can go a long way, because its flavor is strong. You put a little bit here, and pretty soon it has spread over there.

Rachel was really hurting. She sat at her desk, trying hard to work, but she couldn't keep her mind on the papers in front of her. All she could think of was her mother, who had died the week before after an extended illness. Rachel had stayed with her mother around the clock during those last days, and when death finally came, she had been relieved that her mother's suffering was over. But now the anger and grief were setting in. Her emotions were raging within her. She decided to go home and try to get some rest.

When she parked in her garage, she felt an urge to go out and get the mail. At first, she resisted. What she really wanted, she told herself, was to crawl into bed. But when the feeling persisted, she went out to the curb and opened the box. Inside were nearly two dozen cards sent by members of her church! Rachel spent the rest of her afternoon reading through them. Their tender expressions of sympathy gave her heart the peace it needed—for that day, anyway, and that was enough.

Begin today to circulate the address of someone you think needs a calming, comforting word. Ask friends and family members to join you in spreading the peace by sending this person notes of encouragement.

Peace is contagious.

Day 354   **Peace liberates.**

By contrast, the fruit of the Spirit is love, joy, peace, patience, kindness, generosity, faithfulness, gentleness, and self-control. There is no law against such things.

—Galatians 5:22-23

Like all fruits of the Spirit, peace is free, and, just as important, it is free*ing*. It does not bind us to laws and rules, shoulds and shouldn'ts, oughts and can'ts. Instead, it liberates us to life in the Spirit.

Let's think about the liberating power of peace in the context of a significant relationship. When you and your friend or spouse have an argument, what rules tend to operate? Usually people have never thought about these rules, yet if they are somehow violated, an argument can quickly escalate. The rules might include: the other person *should* listen to me, *shouldn't* talk so much, *ought* to talk more, *can't* interrupt, *should* get to the point, *shouldn't* ask so many questions, *ought* to ask more questions, *can't* leave the room, *should* express feelings, *should* believe me, *shouldn't* talk down to me, and so on.

Sit down with your friend and talk about what rules come into play when you are in conflict. These are not the things that make for peace. You impose them on each other, perhaps without even thinking.

Now turn the conversation in a different direction. Talk with your friend about *guidelines* that you might follow when arguing in order to resolve your conflict in a peaceful way. These guidelines will not be the same as the rules you just brainstormed. In the first place, they will not operate in a hidden way, because you will write them down and keep the list in plain view. And second, these guidelines will not be imposed by one of you on the other. Either both of you will agree to follow a specific guideline, or it will not be used. For example, perhaps both of you will agree (1) not to begin big discussions after 9:00 P.M., (2) to deal with one issue at a time, (3) to call a time-out if your emotions start getting too intense, and (4) to have only one person speak at a time.

Let the peace of God liberate the two of you to work together in a spirit of *agape*.

Peace liberates.

Day 355   **Peace yields justice.**

And a harvest of righteousness is sown in peace for those who make peace.

—James 3:18

*D*uring Thanksgiving, some relatives from Texas traveled home to Ohio for the first time in many years. One morning Isabelle, the visiting great-aunt, was asked if she would please make a pie using the raspberries Grandma had set out on the kitchen counter. The handpicked berries had been stored in the freezer and were not quite thawed, but Isabelle went ahead, and before too long generous slices of the warm homemade pie were being doled out to eager taste-testers.

You can only imagine the looks on people's faces when they bit into Isabelle's pie and discovered that it had been filled not with raspberries, but beets!

What you end up with obviously says a lot about what you started out with.

We have said before that the *shalom* of God is a just peace. You might say that, in *shalom*, peace and justice are so intertwined as to be the same thing. So, if you have a peace that yields no justice, then you don't really have peace. And, if you have a justice that yields no peace, you don't really have justice.

Maybe you are beginning to understand that the justice that issues from God's peace is not "people getting what they deserve." God's justice is not punishment. It is not getting revenge. It is treating people fairly in the spirit of *agape*.

Think of a situation in which you may be wanting to "get even" with someone. Someone has injured you, and you would like to get back at this person. Ask yourself, "What *shalom* would come of my revenge? What *agape* would be expressed by it?"

Your answers to these questions will probably reveal that your continuing to want revenge in this situation would be contrary to God's desire for a just peace. So identify one thing that you can do instead to break this cycle of hurt and revenge. Forgive the person who has hurt you, in a spirit of love.

Peace yields justice.

Day 356   Peace returns.

"As you enter the house, greet it. If the house is worthy, let your peace come upon it; but if it is not worthy, let your peace return to you."

—Matthew 10:12-13

*Y*ou know, some people are terrified of real peace. They just don't want it. They are not comfortable with what they don't know—with what they are not in control of or controlled by. Rather than doing the things that make for peace, they would rather practice the arts of war: accumulating weapons, spying, strategizing, commanding, taking orders, doing battle, outmaneuvering opposing forces, retreating, shoring up fortifications for long sieges. Each of us, to some degree, has been a student of one or more of these "arts." But as the mind of Christ grows within us, we lay all these aside, and study war no more.

So what happens when we give up war but others don't want to make peace? Sometimes we can't do much of anything, except refuse to let their hardheartedness affect us. It is as if we are carrying a pouch of peace. We go to the one with whom we are at war, reach into our pouch, pull out some peace and offer it. If the peace is rejected, we place the peace back in our pouch. We do not, however, put into our pouch any of the other's hostility, hopelessness, or fear. Our pouch is meant to contain only the *shalom* of God.

You might find it helpful to memorize a word, phrase, or statement that you can repeat to yourself when, in the midst of a confrontation, you realize that your efforts at peace are being thwarted. This "catchword" can help you to remain calm and to resist an escalation of the conflict. Some people use the Serenity Prayer for this purpose. Then, there is the group of friends which has coined the word "IDMU" ("*It doesn't matter ultimately*"). Spoken quietly during a crisis, this word has the effect of diffusing anxiety. Whatever catchword you use, keep it simple enough to easily remember and powerful enough to be effective. Let your catchword be one of an increasing number of peaceful arts that you begin to practice.

Peace returns.

Day 357   I teach only peace.

Finally, beloved, whatever is true, whatever is honorable, whatever is just, whatever is pure, whatever is pleasing, whatever is commendable, if there is any excellence and if there is anything worthy of praise, think about these things. Keep on doing the things that you have learned and received and heard and seen in me, and the God of peace will be with you.

—Philippians 4:8-9

Peace. The word brings to mind different thoughts and feelings for each of us. Much has been "taught" about peace through the ages.

Below are a number of proverbs that teach different attitudes toward peace. Indicate how strongly you agree with each proverb by assigning each a number on a scale from 1 (strongly agree) to 5 (strongly disagree).

____ A bad peace is better than a good quarrel.
____ A disarmed peace is weak.

355

_____ One who would live at peace and rest must hear and see and say the best.

_____ If you desire peace, be ever prepared for war.

_____ You cannot live at peace unless your neighbor lets you.

_____ Nothing can bring you peace but yourself.

_____ Peace at any price.

_____ Peace feeds, war wastes; peace breeds, war consumes.

_____ Peace flourishes when reason rules.

_____ Peace is found only in the graveyard.

_____ Peace is goodwill in action.

_____ The sheep who talks peace with a wolf will soon be mutton.

Compare the proverbs with which you most strongly agreed and disagreed. What does this reveal to you about the kind of peace you teach? Are you teaching the world's peace or the peace of God?

Reread today's scripture text. Does the kind of peace that you teach sound close to what Paul asks the Philippians to focus on?

Conclude by creating your own proverb about peace. Be a willing teacher of God's *shalom*.

I teach only peace.

Day 358 Peace unites heaven and earth.

"Your kingdom come. Your will be done, on earth as it is in heaven."

—*Matthew 6:10*

This verse from the Lord's prayer is a couplet: it states the same truth in two different ways. God's kingdom comes whenever and wherever God's will is done, in heaven or on earth. The verse asks that the will of God be done now on earth, even as it is already being done in heaven. Whenever this happens, we are experiencing the kingdom of God.

Many of us are used to equating the kingdom of God with heaven. And heaven is "up there," in contrast to the earth, which is "down here." We think of the streets of gold being far away from our streets of concrete. But this verse from the Lord's prayer asks us to change our thinking. If heaven exists wherever and whenever the will of God is being done, the streets of gold and the streets of concrete can become one and the same.

Spend some time in meditation. Find your comfortable spot and relax. Close your eyes. Let go of anything that might distract you. When you are centered in the presence of God, visualize two pictures hanging on a wall. The first is a picture of a beautiful spot that you have visited. What is it? Get it clearly in mind. Then, beside it, visualize a picture of heaven. What does it look like? A burst of light? A display of colors? Many mansions? Let the picture create itself. When you have it firmly in mind, let it merge with the other picture into one larger one that incorporates the elements of each. Allow this larger picture to take whatever form it will. Be at peace as this merging happens. Know that your peaceful spirit allows heaven and earth to be united into one. Carry this image within you throughout the day.

Peace unites heaven and earth.

Day 359   **Miracles abound.**

The Lord replied, "If you had faith the size of a mustard seed, you could say to this mulberry tree, 'Be uprooted and planted in the sea,' and it would obey you."

—Luke 17:6

*F*red had no faith in God. He didn't believe in God. He was a scientist, and unless something could be put under the microscope and examined, it did not exist. He needed concrete proof before he could believe, and no one had been able to provide any. . . .

Until his wife gave birth to their first child. He was there for the delivery. When his daughter was placed in his arms, he stared at her in total amazement. He touched her little hands and unrolled her fingers. He traced the outline of her tiny ear with his index finger. He felt the rapid beating of her heart. How could he possibly explain such a wonder? He understood the facts of reproduction, but at the moment they seemed dull and irrelevant. How could this miracle have happened? One answer kept coming back to him. There must be a power in the universe greater than he had ever imagined. Surely this child was an act of God. In that moment of recognition, he felt a change coming over him. He felt the power of belief.

Two miracles took place that day: the birth of a child and the birth of faith.

Over the past year's journey, your faith has grown. Reflect on several ways that you have powerfully experienced the presence of God in your life. What miracles have made your faith grow? What miracles has your faith worked?

Celebrate what God has done, for you and through you!

Miracles abound.

Day 360 Miracles are natural.

Now the man who had been healed did not know who it was [who had healed him], for Jesus had disappeared in the crowd that was there.

—John 5:13

*J*esus did not stick around to be praised for healing the man in today's scripture. Interesting! Why would Jesus move on without first making sure that the man knew who had just performed the miracle? Why would Jesus take such a wonderful event so lightly?

Jesus understood that such miracles are a natural part of life. They are to be expected. On so many occasions when he healed someone, Jesus reminded the person that it was his or her faith or God's power that had made the healing possible. He consistently deflected attention from what he himself had done and tried to emphasize that miracles are simply the way God's world works.

What would life be like if we expected miracles to be an everyday occurrence? Would we treat one another differently if we understood that each of us is worthy of receiving a miracle? What would happen if each of our worship services began with the question, "What miracles have happened in our lives this week?" We might never get to the rest of the service!

Gather a group of trusted friends. Invite them to share stories of miracles that have happened to them. Share one of your own. Allow the conversation to flow from one experience to another as together you recount the ways in which God has been active in your lives. End the conversation by affirming that God has not only been active in the past, but will continue to act on your behalf in the future.

Miracles are natural.

I claim miracles.

Jesus stood still and said, "Call him here." And they called the blind man, saying to him, "Take heart; get up, he is calling you." So throwing off his cloak, he sprang up and came to Jesus. Then Jesus said to him, "What do you want me to do for you?" The blind man said to him, "My teacher, let me see again." Jesus said to him, "Go; your faith has made you well." Immediately he regained his sight and followed him on the way.

—*Mark 10:49-52*

*N*otice what happened when Jesus called this blind man to join him. The first thing the man did was throw off his cloak. The cloak was his means of protection against the heat of the day and the cold of the night. It was also something that could conceal him from other people. Before the miracle of healing happened in his life, he threw off his self-protective garment. In other words, he made himself vulnerable.

The second thing the blind man did was spring up. He did not wait around for something else to happen. He was ready and willing for a change—*now*. He literally jumped at the opportunity to be healed.

The third thing that the man did, in response to Jesus' question, was to clearly identify his wishes. He was certain about the outcome he desired. He wanted to be healed. He wanted to see again. So, he claimed his miracle.

Identify an area of your life that is troubling you. Is there any aspect of your life that you would like to improve? Is there a change that you would like to see happen? Write down the outcome that you would like to have; state what you want to happen. Now, shift gears. Think about your intentions in this area. What might you plan to do—what would you be willing to do—to change this part of your life? Write down your intentions, completing this sentence, "In this area of my life, I intend to _____." Finally, begin to take steps to follow through on your intentions, with God's help. Throw off your cloak! Spring up! Claim your miracle!

I claim miracles.

I receive miracles.

Well then, does God supply you with the Spirit and work miracles among you by your doing the works of the law, or by your believing what you heard?

—*Galatians 3:5*

$\mathcal{U}$pon finding out that she was being moved to a new parish, the young minister studied every book available on making smooth transitions. She even attended workshops offered by consultants on how to land in a new church with the least amount of stress. She mapped out every step that she would take. Once in the parish, she followed her plan to the letter. But it didn't work. She walked into a hornet's nest of controversy and conflict. Members of the congregation were so used to fighting among themselves and against their pastors that it seemed to be the only way they knew to behave.

Finally, in desperation, the minister laid her books and plans aside and turned the situation over to God. Convinced that God had called her to this place for a specific purpose, she continued to do what she believed was right, but she no longer forced the process. If this placement was going to be a success, it would have to be because God worked out the details.

And God did. Gradually things began to change. People who could not adjust to the new pastor found other places of worship that suited them better. Those who were tired of fighting—having long ago forgotten what the fights were about—became much more cooperative. And new people who wanted to work together toward common goals began to be attracted to the church. The minister found that letting go and letting God take over was the best plan of all.

This is the way miracles come about. When we try to make them happen, they do not seem to come our way. But when we open ourselves to believing in them and to receiving them, they begin to happen in our lives with increasing regularity. Our openness and trust in God seems to attract the miracles that we want. This is sort of like chasing after a butterfly. If you try to catch a butterfly bare-handed, you will find it nearly impossible to do. But if you sit quietly in a garden and remain open to the possibility that the butterfly will come to you, it is much more likely to happen. Create a miracle affirmation that you can use throughout the day. Some possibilities are "I believe in miracles," "I am ready to receive a miracle," and "God has a miracle for me." Choose or write one that fits you. Try to repeat your affirmation at least once an hour. Allow it to become a statement of fact. Watch with anticipation, and soon miracles will come on beautiful wings to light on your shoulder.

I receive miracles.

I do not doubt.

"Truly I tell you, if you say to this mountain, 'Be taken up and thrown into the sea,' and if you do not doubt in your heart, but believe that what you say will come to pass, it will be done for you. So I tell you, whatever you ask for in prayer, believe that you have received it, and it will be yours."

—Mark 11:23-24

A four-year-old boy had been "kicked out" of three preschools before the first month of the school year had ended. When his parents enrolled him in yet another preschool, they told the administrator about his past. They confessed that they didn't really expect him to stay very long in this new setting. But the administrator had no doubts about his potential for success in her program. She placed him with a veteran teacher, one who had taught for over twenty-five years and had earned a reputation for making each child feel very special.

After the first week, the parents checked in with the administrator. They couldn't understand why there had been no calls or notes to them complaining about their son's behavior. Despite the administrator's assurances that their son was doing well, they insisted on an immediate conference with his teacher. When they confronted her with their disbelief, she repeated that all was going well. But why, they wanted to know, had she been able to succeed where so many others had failed? She replied that, from the very beginning, she had simply treated their son as though he were no different from the other children. It had taken him a day or two to adjust, but he soon began to fit into the group.

What we believe, we will see. That's right. It is not that "seeing is believing." Rather, believing is seeing. First, we must hold in our minds the image of what we want. We must believe that it is already a reality, leaving no room for any doubt. Then, we will begin to see what we want right there in front of us.

Enter into meditative prayer. When you are comfortable and relaxed, identify a goal or hope that you have been holding in your heart. Picture it vividly in your mind, as though it were already a reality. See it in all its details. Now, in your imagination, move toward that reality. Gradually put yourself right in the middle of it. Experience it fully. Enjoy the accomplishment of your dream. Now, allow the scene to fade away. Realize that your dream is now behind you, having already come to pass. Rejoice in the fact that you have experienced your dream come true.

I do not doubt.

Day 364 My faith works miracles.

Now to him who by the power at work within us is able to accomplish abundantly far more than all we can ask or imagine, to him be glory in the church and in Christ Jesus to all generations, forever and ever. Amen.

—Ephesians 3:20-21

*Y*ou are coming to the end of a year's journey of spiritual growth. Your path has led you in new directions. You have gained new insights, had new experiences, made many new discoveries. You and God have together created new realities that you had not dreamed possible.

In short, you have been transformed. Your faith is stronger than it used to be. Your expressions of *agape* are freer than they used to be. Your commitment to forgiveness is deeper than it used to be. You now know that you are a healer, a peacemaker, a wonder-worker. You now know, more than ever before, that you are a radiant child of God.

The mind of Christ is growing stronger within you. You are seeing with spiritual rather than just physical eyes. Back when you saw only with physical eyes, you perceived a world filled with discord, pain, brokenness, divisions. But now, looking with spiritual eyes, you can perceive another reality. Beyond discord is peace. Beneath pain is strength. In the midst of brokenness, there is reconciliation. In the midst of division, there is unity.

See with faith! Keep the faith! Be the faith!

You have made great progress on your journey. But remember that your journey isn't over. The path continues on, for a lifetime. Choose today to continue to move ahead in your relationship with God, in your ability to think with the mind of Christ, and in your experience of the Spirit. As you move forward one step at a time, constantly remind yourself that your faith is working miracles of *agape* in your life and in the lives of others. To God be the glory!

My faith works miracles.

Day 365   **Each day my journey begins again.**

For I am convinced that neither death, nor life, nor angels, nor rulers, nor things present, nor things to come, nor powers, nor height, nor depth, nor anything else in all creation, will be able to separate us from the love of God in Christ Jesus our Lord.

—Romans 8:38-39

*W*hat does tomorrow hold for you? You have no way of knowing. But you do know that you will not face it alone. God has promised to be with you each step of the journey. Wherever your path may lead, you will always be accompanied by the One who created you and gives you life. Hold this thought in your mind. There is nothing else that you need to know. You have no reason to fear. Nothing can separate you from the love of God. Whatever hardships you encounter will only serve to strengthen your resolve. Whatever conflicts you endure will only be opportunities to offer *agape*. So, you will forgive. You will heal. You will create peace. By the power of God, you will live out your mission as a child of God. One precious day at a time.

Make a choice today to continue your journey of spiritual growth in a very intentional way. Here are some options that you might consider: Form a group whose members would assist one another on their journeys. Find one other person who would be willing to be a spiritual growth partner. Begin a formal process of education in matters of faith—say, in a sharing group or Sunday school class. Or, plan to carefully nurture one or more of the spiritual gifts that God has given you.

You might even want to return to the beginning of this book and start all over again. Know that if you do, you will not be repeating what you have just completed. You are a different person than you were a year ago. Your journey through the book will be familiar but ever new as you gain deeper insight into the mind of Christ. Each time you use the book you will perceive additional truths about yourself, your God, and your world. Invite a friend or a group to join you in your day-by-day walk through its pages.

Take time to celebrate what you have accomplished. Then write at least one letter of appreciation to someone who helped you grow in faith in the past year.

Finally, be open to whatever awaits you in the journey ahead. If on one day you stumble, cheerfully pick yourself up, and on the next day walk boldly once more. The journey is always beginning again. We offer you blessings for the road.

Each day my journey begins again.

We shall not cease from exploration
And the end of all our exploring
Will be to arrive where we started
And know the place for the first time.
— T. S. Eliot